ONLY IN AMERICA

Other books by Jack Newfield

A Prophetic Minority

Robert Kennedy: A Memoir

A Populist Manifesto
(with Jeff Greenfield)

Cruel and Unusual Justice

The Permanent Government
(with Paul DuBrul)

City for Sale
(with Wayne Barrett)

The Education of Jack Newfield

ONLY IN

AMERICA

THE LIFE AND CRIMES OF DON KING

JACK NEWFIELD

WILLIAM MORROW AND COMPANY, INC.
NEW YORK

To **J**anie, **R**ebecca, and **J**oey,
you're the best

William Morrow and Company, Inc., and its imprints and affiliates, been written, to print the books we efforts to that end.

Library of Congress Cataloging-in-Publication Data

Newfield, Jack.
    Only in America : the life and crimes of Don King / Jack Newfield.
   —1st ed.
       p.   cm.
    Includes index.
    ISBN 0-688-10123-2
    1. King, Don, 1931-   . 2. Matchmakers (Boxing)—United States—
Biography.   I. Title.
GV1132.K48N49   1995
796.8'3'092—dc20
[B]   95-16837
                                                                           CIP

Printed in the United States of America

2 3 4 5 6 7 8 9 10

BOOK DESIGN BY DEBORAH KERNER

Acknowledgments

I interviewed approximately 150 people for this book. But some helped me above and beyond the call of duty during the four years I worked on the project.

Former Cleveland detectives Carl DeLau and Bob Tonne retrieved and let me copy all the 1966 police reports on King's murder of Sam Garrett.

Tom Moran, Tim Witherspoon's manager, let me read and copy the complete financial records for all of Tim's fights that had become exhibits in his lawsuit against King.

Leon Gast allowed me to watch dozens of hours of film he shot in New York, Deer Lake, and Zaire, as part of his never-released documentary on the Ali-Foreman fight.

Sam Toporoff allowed me to read and quote from his unpublished manuscript with Larry Holmes.

Jeremiah Shabazz, Lloyd Price, Ernie Butler, Don Elbaum, Gene Kilroy, Hank Schwartz, Cedric Kushner, Alex Wallau, and

A c k n o w l e d g m e n t s

the late Harold Conrad were all helpful in filling in particular pieces of the story.

Tom Hauser was uncommonly generous in opening doors and sharing research. Jim Neff, who lives in Cleveland, was another who went out of his way to share tips, sources, documents, and ideas.

Steve Lott took the time to duplicate and give me tapes of all the fights I needed to describe.

Jose Torres and Joe Spinelli are close friends, and our hours of conversations and fight watching over the years enriched my understanding of the political economy of the cruelest sport, as well as its ring mechanics.

Photographers James Hamilton, Howard Bingham, and Arlene Schulman were kind enough to give me photos from their archives for the picture section.

Richard Emery, my lawyer/agent/friend, came up with the original idea that I should do a book on King and gave me encouragement at key moments.

Ken Chandler, New York *Post* editor, generously gave me blocks of time off to work on this book.

I wish to thank all the boxing writers who shared information with me over the last five years: Mike Katz, Larry Merchant, Mark Kriegel, Pat Putnam, Bert Sugar, and Wally Matthews.

Finally, I wish to thank all the fighters who talked to me, not just about King but about their feelings and their craft. They are: Muhammad Ali, Tim Witherspoon, Larry Holmes, Saoul Mamby, Mike Tyson, Michael Dokes, David Bey, Bobby Cassidy, Mark Breland, Jimmy Young, Earnie Shavers, Jeff Merritt, Eddie Gregg, Mitch Green, and Tony Ayala.

—JACK NEWFIELD

Contents

Contents

Introduction

This book is not intended to be a full-life biography of Don King. Its conception is to examine Don King in the context of the modern boxing system of unregulated, rapacious piracy. I have tried to write it as much from the point of view of the exploited, often voiceless, fighters as from the vantage point of King, who is doing the exploiting with consummate brilliance. The reader will soon discover just how much grudging respect I have for King's intelligence, single-mindedness, and pirate's boldness.

I have attempted to combine different genres of writing—investigative reporting, biography, memoir, and essay.

When I began my research in early 1990, I did not come to this project with a blank slate. I had already published two lengthy articles critical of King's financial practices for *The Village Voice*. King reacted to those in a bemused, forgiving way.

In May, June, and July of 1990 I wrote King three formal letters seeking his cooperation with this book, asking to tape-record interviews with him, and promising to incorporate his perspective and emotions wherever possible. He said maybe yes, maybe no, and we fenced about the proposition in several conversations. Our mutual friend, the late Harold Conrad, vouched for my fairness in several conversations with King.

In 1991, my relationship with King became more adversarial, in a very public way. I was assigned to be the correspondent and writer on a public television documentary about King that would eventually win an Emmy.

In the course of shooting the documentary, King lost his self-control and verbally attacked me one day in Las Vegas. Our camera was rolling and dozens of people were watching, including boxing writers from around the country. King called me a "scumbag" and other names, while I kept saying, "Answer the question." The confrontation became the dramatic centerpiece of our documentary, and the show was broadcast nationally at least three times by the PBS network.

Afterward, wherever I went, people remarked about the scene where King is screaming invective at me. That two minutes seemed to personalize the perception of our relationship, and therefore personalized this book to some degree. But it did not change my thinking about King. I had already been yelled at by experts—Senator Alfonse D'Amato, Ed Koch, landlords, judges, labor racketeers. This tantrum just happened to be on national TV a few times.

I regarded the scene with King as almost routine, as an attempt at intimidation, and felt that it was part of my job to resist it. But people who saw it on television seemed to remember it vividly, like it was Billy Martin and Reggie Jackson.

The image of King shouting insults, and me repeating the question—why did he accept money under the table in violation of the international boycott of apartheid—became a larger-than-life metaphor.

Before that scene, during the summer of 1990, King at least

pretended to give consideration to my written requests to get his point of view in a series of interviews. But when I pressed him for a definitive answer, he draped his arm over my shoulder and bellowed, "I've decided, no interviews for your book."

"Why?" I asked.

"Because the day your book comes out," King explained, "I want to be able to call a press conference and tell the whole world, that damn white boy didn't even have the decency to speak to this poor nigger."

With that, Don King laughed loudly and patted me on the back, like he had just put something over on me and wanted to gloat a little.

But I could see that his eyes were cold and dead.

Someday they're gonna write a blues song just for fighters. It will be for a slow guitar, soft trumpet, and a bell.

—Sonny Liston

It's like we're racehorses. They race us till we drop, and then they shoot us.

—Tim Witherspoon

Don, I'll pay you the money.

—The last words of Sam Garrett

One Last Vicious Kick

A loaded, unregistered .357 Magnum in his belt, $2,000 as usual in his pocket, Don King sauntered into the Manhattan Tap Room at 100th and Cedar in the Cleveland ghetto. His brand-new Cadillac convertible was parked outside. It was high noon on April 20, 1966.

With his imposing size and magnetic life-force, King had already risen to the top of the hustler's meritocracy. When he walked into the Manhattan Tap Room he was a celebrity. He was known as the biggest numbers banker in Cleveland.

King was a street Machiavelli, a ghetto Einstein. He dropped dimes on his competitors in the numbers business. He invented ways to cheat the system. He had influence with bad cops, judges, and politicians. He had survived two assassination attempts by his rivals. He was close to Italians in the traditional Mafia, who protected his operations for a price.

King dressed like a pimp, talked like an evangelical storefront preacher, and thought like a chess grand master. He believed his own life was destined to be an epic odyssey.

King was already a force of nature. He possessed the alchemy of a brilliant strategic mind, working-class ambition and anger— and no conscience. This is the combination that would propel analogous modern rogues—Mayor James Michael Curley of Boston, Teamster boss Jimmy Hoffa, and Morris Levy, the mob's music mogul.

Part of King's street stardom was his ownership of the popular hangout, the New Corner Tavern, at Seventy-eighth and Cedar. There musicians like Erroll Garner, B. B. King, Jonah Jones, and King's close friend Lloyd Price came to perform and mix with the elite of players. When King was in a particularly jovial mood, he would jump up on the bandstand and conduct the brass section.

In fact, Don King already displayed obvious similarities to the heroes of Price's two-million-selling songs. Like "Personality," King had "walk, talk, style." And like "Stagger Lee," he was a gambler who had already killed a man. (Years later I would ask Price whether King was more like "Personality" or "Stagger Lee," and Price replied, "Neither." He said King was really "more like Billy," the character in his song "Stagger Lee," who swore the dice read eight when Stagger Lee rolled a seven.)

In April 1966, "Donald the Kid," as he was known to the gamblers and grifters in the East Side ghetto, was the biggest of the five clearinghouse numbers bankers in Cleveland. He was grossing $15,000 every day on the poor people's lottery.

Each morning King left his comfortable home at 3451 Sutton Road in Shaker Heights with a wad of cash and a loaded gun. King carried the gun because he thought traveling with a bodyguard made him look like a gangster. And he desired respectability. Yearned for it.

Long before 1966, King had already killed a man with a gun. On December 2, 1954, three men from Detroit tried to rob one of King's gambling houses, on East 123rd Street. There was a gunfight with King firing a Russian revolver. When the shooting stopped, Hillary Brown lay dead on the ground. The county prosecutor, Bernard Conway, ruled King had fired in self-defense and the death of the stickup man was "justifiable homicide."

So Don King was already a star in his galaxy of outlaws when he sauntered into the Manhattan Tap Room for an early drink on April 20, 1966. The bartender knew him, some regulars at the bar knew him, and Sam Garrett, drinking early that day, also knew King.

Sam Garrett had been an employee of King's numbers organization. He had been King's friend. But now Garrett owed King $600 from a bet King had placed with him on number 743. King had hit the number but Garrett had not paid him yet.

King had placed this bet as part of a new system of betting, based on inside information and mathematical calculation, that he had invented. King called it "run downs" or "counts." It was a product of his mathematical talent and allowed him to make bets with the odds on his side, as well as take bets with the odds on his side.

King's insider trading in the numbers was based on a call he, or a subordinate, would place to New York about 2:00 P.M. each day. The winning number in Cleveland was three digits in the middle column of the final daily stock market quotation of stocks that gained, lost, or remained unchanged. There was also a separate winning number for the middle column of advances, declines, and unchanged in bond transactions.

At 2:00 P.M. King would get the stock quotations from a broker he knew in New York. If the advances were 217, the declines 307, and the unchanged 238, King then placed 35 or 40 bets in different combinations of the middle three digits of 103. He would bet 234, 194, 233, 143, 204, and so on. At $1 a number, for $35 King often hit the number himself, collecting at odds of 500 to 1, when he had actually lowered the odds of his winning to about 200 to 1 with the advantage of his creative cheating.

King used his own runners and pickup men to place the bets with rival policy bankers once he got the 2:00 P.M. information from New York and figured out the 35 or 40 most likely combinations close to that three-digit sequence.

So when King noticed Sam Garrett at the bar, he felt a jolt of anger at the man who had not paid off on his winning bet that was part of a method invented by King's own cynical ingenuity. Garrett was a sickly man, a drug abuser, a sufferer from tuberculosis in his left lung, and a man whose kidney had recently been removed in surgery.

King himself did not have the reputation for being a great fighter. While in high school he had had four amateur fights as an 108-pound flyweight. He won his first two by decision, lost his third by decision, and was knocked out in his fourth and last match. As an adult he was known to back down from physical confrontations with men his size. In high school King flunked physical education.

The two men argued at the bar for several minutes, King standing very close to Garrett, using his girth and size and loudness as a form of physical intimidation. Then the dispute spilled out onto crowded, sun-kissed Cedar Avenue. Suddenly King began to attack the smaller man. This was not a fight. It was a beating. King outweighed Garrett by one hundred pounds. And King had a gun, while Garrett was unarmed.

King knocked Garrett down either with a punch or, more likely, with the butt of his gun. Once Garrett was down on the sidewalk, King started kicking him in the head, without restraint. King's heavy shoes left footprints on Garrett's cheekbone.

Blood started to smear Garrett's swelling, mashed face. But King, swept up in the frenzy of the violence, kept on stomping, the revolver in his right hand glinting in the high-noon sun.

A crowd of fifteen or twenty people gathered to watch the beating, although no one intervened to stop the mismatch. They came out of the Tap Room, Rico's Confectionery, the 12 Counts Bar, a smoke shop, and a Laundromat. Others watched from the windows of the dingy apartments above the Cedar Avenue shops.

King kept stomping the smaller man. Most people would have stopped by now. Most people would have felt satisfaction, or remorse, or some cathartic release by now. But not King. Some bully demon deep inside him kept the violence going beyond reason.

Officers Bob Tonne and John Horvath were on routine patrol, in police car 962, driving west on Cedar at 12:30 P.M. Both were in plain clothes—suits and ties.

Detective Bob Tonne knew this violent turf along Cedar very well. He had joined the Cleveland police force in 1949, and in 1961 he had been jumped and pistol-whipped by a gang of men at Ninety-ninth and Cedar. He needed seventy-two stitches in his face to close the wounds.

The first thing Detective Tonne noticed from the radio car was a man's head bouncing off the asphalt pavement like a rubber ball. Then he saw a large man standing over him with a gun in his right hand, applying another kick to the head.

Tonne and Horvath jumped out of their radio car, drew their guns, and ordered the larger man to drop his weapon.

"Donald, don't kick him no more, he's hurt," a voice in the crowd said.

"Drop it!" Tonne said, with the urgent intensity of pumping adrenaline.

Don King turned slowly to place his weapon on the trunk of a parked car. As Tonne scooped the gun off the car, King got in one last vicious kick that Tonne would never forget.

Tonne handcuffed the man he did not recognize. But King recognized the police detective.

"Tonne," he said, "you don't have to cuff me. I'm Donald King."

Tonne thought King was suggesting he was too much of a celebrity to suffer the indignity of being cuffed. King's hands were so large that Tonne had trouble getting the handcuffs to fit around King's wrists.

Tonne then bent over Sam Garrett. Garrett's eyes were closed and blood was oozing out of his ears. There were bubbles of blood on his lips.

"Don, I'll pay you the money," Garrett moaned. Then he slipped into unconsciousness.

Tonne and Horvath drove King to the police precinct in their patrol car. They vouchered his gun—serial number 36222—because it had bloodstains on it and would be needed as evidence. They also confiscated King's shoes as evidence because they, too, had specks of blood.

Under questioning at the precinct, King gave Detective Tonne his version of the events leading up to the arrest. King claimed that it was self-defense, that Garrett had threatened him, and jumped him first, in a quarrel over the unpaid gambling debt.

King insisted that Garrett threw the first blow and that he knocked Garrett down only in retaliation. He swore that while Garrett was down on the sidewalk he "tried to pull something out of his pocket," and had tried to kick him in his testicles. King claimed that only then did he retrieve a gun out of his car to protect himself from whatever Garrett was trying to reach for in his pocket. But Garrett did not have a gun or a knife in his pocket.

When Tonne asked King what he was doing with the fully loaded gun, King swore that he was "on my way to get it registered," when the altercation occurred. A police check showed King's gun was unregistered.

King's arrest for aggravated assault was reported the next morning in the *Cleveland Plain Dealer* under the headline BARETS NAB NUMBERS OPERATOR IN BEATING. The story reported, "Witnesses told police they also saw Garrett beaten with a gun."

The story also said that Garrett was in poor condition after undergoing surgery at Lakeside Hospital. Garrett had a massive

Sir;

On April 20th, 1966, I was assigned to car 962 in company
with Rtl. Horvath.

At approximately 12:30PM we observed an assault take place
at the corner of East 100 and Cedar. A colored male was laying
on the northerly sidewalk and another colored was kicking him
in the face and head. We stopped the car immediately and as we
jumped out we saw the assailant had a gun in his right hand.
We ordered him to drop it and he threw it onto the trunk lid of
a parked vehicle, whereupon he again kicked the victim in the
face. At this time I grabbed him and handcuffed him and placed
the suspect into our vehicle.

We rendered what aid we could to the victim, he lost consciousness before the ambulance arrived. Car 503 arrived and conveyed him
to Lakeside Hospital.

We questioned the assailant and found him to be Donald King
of 3451 Sutton Rd. 34-C-M, DOB 8-20-31. He is a known numbers and
policy figure. He stated that the man owed him some money and refused to pay, the man threatened him and he had to defend himself.
He would give us no further information. We conveyed him to the
Detective Bureau and booked him for investigation in connection
with aggravated assault. We took all his outside clothing to be held
as evidence along with his shoes. We also confiscated a Trooper .357
Magnum, ser. no. 36222, which was fully loaded with six shells.
Donald King would give us no information about this revolver, a gun
confiscation report was made.

We learned from car 503 at Lakeside Hospital that the victims
name is Samuel Garrett 2176 East 76, 34-c-m. He had a punctured ear
drum, fractured jaw and a possible skull fracture.

We made statements at the Detective Bureau and turned all our
information over to the Homicide Unit.

Respectfully

Robert Tonne, Dt. 1521

---

*The original police report by Detective Bob Tonne on King's beating of
Sam Garrett, written before Garrett died. The report describes the gun in
King's hand, and the last kick to Garrett's head after Tonne ordered King
to drop the gun.*

clot of blood from a brain hemorrhage. Doctors privately informed the police that his chances of survival were "1 out of 500," and that if he lived, he would be a vegetable.

After five days in a coma, Garrett died at 11:15 A.M. on April 25. King now faced murder charges.

The autopsy report of the Cuyahoga County coroner detailed the cause of death. "The decedent came to his death as a result of: Multiple blunt impacts to head with basal skull fractures, subarachnoid hemorrhages, lacerations and contusions of brain, and confluent pontine hemorrhages. Homicide by assault."

In plain English, Garrett's brain had been broken like an egg and flooded with blood as a result of the kicks to his head and the crashing impact of his skull against the concrete sidewalk. The autopsy report showed that Garrett weighed 134 pounds. King weighed just over 240.

Two black detectives—Harry Davidson and Charles Reynolds—were placed in charge of the investigation into Garrett's murder. According to Lieutenant Carl DeLau, the chief of the homicide unit, the six-foot three-inch Davidson was the "smartest and toughest" of the twenty-eight detectives assigned to the homicide squad.

On April 21, 1966, Davidson and Reynolds submitted their first official report:

"Upon being informed of his constitutional rights, he [King] refused to make a statement or answer any questions pertaining to this crime." On April 26, after Garrett died and after King had surrendered to the police in the company of his lawyer, James Willis, the two detectives reported:

Statement was obtained from King in which he tells of having a fight with the victim after the victim had grabbed him from his auto. He further relates that the victim pursued him after he had tried to walk away from him. . . . King was asked for a sample of his blood but refused to give same.

King was clearly laying the foundation for the same self-defense excuse that got him off when he shot Hillary Brown to death in 1954.

Lieutenant DeLau had known King well for almost fifteen years. He had arrested King for illegal gambling in 1954. He had used him as an "informal informer" against other numbers operators. On a regular basis over the years, DeLau would pay a relaxed visit to the loquacious King, engage him in small talk, and invariably King would happen to mention specific locations where betting clips and adding machines might be found. Or King might casually drop the name of a new runner, or pickup man, for a rival who had recently defected from his employ. DeLau and King enjoyed a semi-friendly cat-and-mouse relationship.

By June, DeLau and his detectives had enough evidence, and King was indicted by a grand jury for second-degree murder—a charge that carried a maximum penalty of life in prison. At that point, Detectives Davidson and Reynolds had lined up four solid witnesses who had seen the one-sided beating King administered to Garrett.

After his arraignment, King was released on $2,500 bond and continued to manage his gambling operations, and indulge his lifestyle, in his routine fashion.

Now retired and silver-haired, DeLau says: "From the start, there was an awful lot of suspicious activity around the Don King murder case. Witnesses started to vanish and change their testimony. There were constant rumors that King was spreading money around on the street to reach witnesses. We heard witnesses were threatened. I know Officer Tonne was approached twice with bribe offers. The whole situation smelled bad."

Detective Tonne, now the elected mayor of the Cleveland suburb of Brooklyn Heights (population 1,400) told me in 1991 that two different intermediaries had offered him bribes to change his testimony about Don King. The first week of June, at the corner of East Forty-ninth Street and Central, Tonne was in his radio car when Herman Roberson, a bail bondsman of his acquaintance, waved him over and started to talk to him.

"Bob, I hear you're involved in the Donald King case," Roberson began.

"That's true, I arrested him," Tonne explained.

"You know, if you do right, Donald can do a lot for you," Roberson said. "Donald is a big man. He has lots of friends. You can make a lot of money. . . ."

Tonne shut off the conversation, feeling a rush of anger.

During the week of July 18, Tonne ran into a schlock criminal attorney named Milton Firestone in the hallway of the police court. Firestone was even more explicit than the bondsman in his overture.

"You can help Donald on the issue of self-defense," Firestone told Tonne. . . . "There's something in this for you if you change your testimony."

On August 2, 1966, Detective Tonne submitted an official confidential report about these two illicit approaches. One copy went to DeLau, and the other went to the Intelligence Unit of the Cleveland Police Department.

Sitting in the mayor's office in May 1991, next to an American flag, Tonne reflected and said: "I definitely think they were trying to bribe me and fix the case. After my conversation with Milton Firestone I heard through the grapevine that I would have made at least ten thousand dollars if I changed my testimony. They wanted me to testify it was self-defense. But it wasn't. It was a beating, not a fight. Just a vicious killing."

As Don King's trial date approached in February 1967, Assistant County Prosecutor Ralph Sperli, Tonne, and DeLau all felt confident they had an overwhelming case. They had a least four eyewitnesses who had given the police statements incriminating King the day after the arrest and had cooperated with prosecutors during the following weeks. But the day the trial opened, on February 21, all four had either changed their story or lost their memory or—in the case of the best witness of all—simply vanished from home.

The police were told by informants that all the witnesses had received threats from King's men in the rackets. Three of these reluctant witnesses were in the numbers business themselves and had arrest records for illegal gambling: Charles Johnson, Daniel Howell, and Jack Owens.

The most important of the eyewitnesses was fifty-three-year-old Rosa Wrines of 9907½ Cedar Avenue. She saw most of the beating and she was scheduled to testify early in the state's case. But the week before the trial, Rosa Wrines was not at her job. She was not at her home. And the police knew she had gotten threats.

At 3:30 A.M. on February 22, Detectives Joseph Fischbach and Clarance Jackman visited her apartment in a "night search" in a desperate effort to locate the missing witness on the night before her testimony was scheduled. A neighbor named Maude Mc-Queen was awakened by the heavy knocking on the door of Rosa Wrines's apartment. Ms. McQueen told the two detectives she had not seen her neighbor for the last few days.

A memo by Sergeant Mike Haney in the files of the Cleveland Police Department says that Wrines "had been run out of town by King and his men prior to the trial."

At 11:45 A.M. on February 22, as King's trial was in the second day, Sergeant Haney received a phone call at police headquarters from his friend and confidant Fred Mollenkoff, the city editor of the *Cleveland Plain Dealer*.

Mollenkoff had been a fine investigative reporter before he became city editor, and as a result of his experience in both jobs, he had developed a close working relationship with the police brass. Right after their conversation, Haney wrote the following confidential memorandum:

At about 11:45 A.M. this date received a telephone call from Fred Mollenkoff—City Editor of the *Cleveland Plain Dealer*—in which he informed me that he had a call from an anonymous caller who gave him information regarding the Second Degree murder trial of Donald King, which is currently being tried in Criminal Court, in Room #5. . . .

Fred Mollenkoff stated that the caller told him he had learned that Donald King was bragging in the street that he had spent $30,000 already to knock out the testimony of witnesses against him in the trial for the murder of Samuel Garrett, and that while in Houston, Texas for the Cassius Clay fights, that Donald King bet $5,000 that he would never serve a day in the penitentiary or jail for the above crime.

The informer stated he was nephew of slain man and that he did not want to see King get away with his murder; further he was thought to be a Negro from his voice. He also stated that the robbery report of Tracy Smith (Complaint #07781 dated 2-17-67) was a false report, and that Tracy Smith had been shot because he did not get a female witness against King to change her testimony. Tracy Smith is known to be connected with the numbers racket, and it is rumored that Donald King hangs around the shoe shine run by Tracy Smith at 1080 East 105 St.

The witness who Tracy Smith was supposed to get to change her testimony was Rosa Wrines c-f-53 9907 ½ Cedar Ave., Apt. #4, and the informant told Mr. Mollenkoff that she had been run out of town since the shooting of Tracy Smith by Donald King and his men, and would not be available for trial against King. . . . The caller stated that Tracy Smith was the only [person] who could exert any influence on Rosa Wrines in this particular case and was evidently shot because he did not influence her to testify for King.

The next day, the third and last day of King's trial, Haney wrote another memo for the files. It said:

[Ralph] Sperli stated that he had questioned Charles E. Johnson, Daniel Howell, and Jack Owens prior to putting them on the stand, and they testified other than what was in their statements, and even different than what they had said in their consultations prior to the time he put them on the stand. This ties in with information received from Fred Mollenkoff—city editor of the *Cleveland Plain Dealer*—on Feb. 22, 1967, that King had reputedly paid out $30,000 to knock out the testimony of witnesses against him.

Ralph Sperli further stated that Rosa Wrines c-f 9907 ½ Cedar Ave., Apt. #4, was missing and that she was a good witness for the state in this case; this also verified information received by this unit from Mollenkoff. Check with Lt. DeLau of the Homicide Unit reveals that Rosa Wrines is missing and that they have made night searches for her without success; which verifies information that she had been run out of town by King and his men prior to the trial.

Despite the threats, intimidation, money spent, and disappearing witnesses, the case against King was still compelling. Assistant County Prosecutor Ralph Sperli placed into evidence the .357 Magnum King held in his hand and pointed out Sam Garrett's blood on the weapon. Detectives Tonne and John Horvath both testified they saw King kick the defenseless and bleeding Garrett in the head. Tonne told the jury King had the gun with him in the bar and did not retrieve it for self-defense from his car.

At 4:30 P.M. on February 23, the jury of eight women and four men began their deliberations. It took them only four hours to return with a verdict of guilty of second-degree murder, punishable by life in prison. Judge Hugh Corrigan suspended execution of King's life sentence in the Ohio Penitentiary pending a motion for a new trial by King's attorney, James Willis.

Judge Corrigan did this in the privacy of his chambers. No one was present representing the prosecutor's office. No one was pres-

---

Sir;
    The following information was obtained from the Record Room and the
S.I.U.,of the Cleveland Police Depatrment,in regards to the arrest record
of Donald King.C.P.D. 98718.

10-30-51	Speeding violation
11-29-51	Stop Sign violation
11-30-51	Stop Sign violation
4-11-52	Speeding violation
4-13-55	Investigation
11-21-52	Stop Sign violation
8-3-53	Arrested for Policy
8-14-54	Scheme of chance
11-6-54	Speeding
12-2-54	Investigation
1-5-56	Policy
9-11-56	Policy
10-3-56	Scheme of chance
9-4-56	Policy
10-23-56	Policy
5-6-59	Invest C/W Drugs
8-7-59	Speeding
8-12-60	No Drivers License
8-12-60	Speeding
2-7-63	A.&B. (Nolleid)
6-11-63	Invest C/W Homocide
9-19-63	C.C.W.(Discharges)
5-6-64	Operating an auto without owners consent
6-8-61	Red Light
6-26-61	Speeding
8-21-61	Speeding
2-25-63	Scheme of change
7-11-63	Scheme of chance
8-20-63	C.C.W.
11-2-64	No drivers license
4-6-65	Wagering Tax
8-23-65	No drivers license
12-12-65	Wagering Tax
4-22-66	Aggravated assault (Nolle)
4-26-66	Manslaughter First Degree (Guilty,Life sentence at Ohio Pen.)

Respectfully

Ptl. James Colbert #185

Don King's arrest record in Cleveland between 1951 and 1966

ent representing the Cleveland Police Department. There was no court reporter or stenographer present. Only King's lawyer, Jim Willis, was present.

Twenty-four years later, Homicide Detective Carl DeLau told me: "This had to be a fix. This was a serious miscarriage of justice.

"I never saw anything like this in thirty years on the Cleveland police force," DeLau continued. "I know I wasn't there. Bob Tonne wasn't there. Ralph Sperli wasn't there. There never was a proceeding in open court. There was just a docket entry, just a signature of Judge Corrigan on a piece of paper. I'm ashamed to say that Hugh Corrigan is a former Cleveland police officer."

When *Cleveland Plain Dealer* reporter Terence Sheridan found out what Judge Corrigan had done in secret, he wrote a front-page story, making it clear the leniency was a scandal.

On July 24, 1967, the *Plain Dealer* ran a headline at the top of the front page: JUDGE CUTS HOOD'S MURDER PENALTY. Below this news was the headline: VIOLENCE GRIPS DETROIT; GUARD, TANKS SUMMONED.

Sheridan's story pointed out that Judge Corrigan himself had ruled during the trial that the charge of second-degree murder should be placed before the jury, when King's lawyer tried to exclude it from the jury's consideration.

Sheridan quoted from Prosecutor Ralph Sperli's four-page brief against reducing the murder two conviction to manslaughter:

> Moreover, since the question of whether or not the state established a *prima facie* case for the crime of second degree murder was answered by the trial court when the motion to remove the question of second degree murder from the consideration of the jury was overruled, and it now becomes a subject for the Court of Appeals, and not for a reconsideration of the trial court.

In 1976 Hugh Corrigan ran for the Court of Appeals and King arranged for Muhammad Ali to campaign for Corrigan. Nobody tried to conceal the fact that this was a contract, a favor for services rendered.

Ali recorded a commercial, played on black radio stations WABJ and WJMO, that said he was endorsing Corrigan because of what he did to help "my good friend Don King."

The *Plain Dealer* quoted Corrigan as saying, "As far as I know, I'm the only candidate in the country with Ali's endorsement. He usually doesn't do this kind of thing, King tells me."

In researching this book I discovered allegations that Judge Corrigan was corrupt and controlled by organized crime in the files of James Licavoli (Jack White), the late boss of the Cleveland Mafia. The document I received is dated June 1965, and is a "weekly summary airtel" to FBI Director J. Edgar Hoover from the Special Agent-in-Charge of the Cleveland field office. The airtel says:

> On 5/20/65 [informant's name redacted] advised that it appears that Judge HUGH CORRIGAN, Common Pleas Court, Cleveland, Ohio, received money for a favor. The amount involved was $6,000. . . .
>
> Another unknown male in conversation with JACK [WHITE] told him that "I've seen them give the [obscene] money to CORRIGAN [Judge HUGH CORRIGAN] and they didn't get no job from it." . . .
>
> The unknown male told JACK WHITE, "if he is going to do anybody a favor from CORRIGAN [Judge Hugh Corrigan, Common Pleas Court, Cleveland, Ohio], he was going to ask for SHONDOR [BIRNS]—anything he could get he was going to get for SHONDOR. He was not going to use the guy too much—he said he would get whatever he asked for him."
>
> The source was not clear as to the identity of the individual who has the contract with Judge CORRIGAN.
>
> The unknown male continues telling JACK WHITE that

SHONDOR will probably file "in front of CORRIGAN—CORRIGAN will probably grant him what ever he asks for. . . .

[Informant's name redacted] indicated that another unknown male, believed to be MONIQUE, told JACK [WHITE] on 5/20/65, that, "I've seen them give the guy the money—what more can they do than give CORRIGAN money." MONIQUE continues by indicating there was $6,000 involved.

At the time of this confidential report, Licavoli was a capo. He became the Cleveland boss in 1976 when John Scalish died. Licavoli himself died in prison in 1985, at the age of eighty-one, while serving seventeen years for the bombing death of a rival mobster.

At the time the FBI's confidential informant was reporting Judge Corrigan's fealty to the mob, both Licavoli and King were sharing the same attorney—James Willis.

Hugh Corrigan died in 1979. When I obtained his FBI file under a Freedom of Information request, the incriminating 1965 airtel to the director was absent from the documents. I had to obtain it from Cleveland author Jim Neff, who got it while preparing his book on Jackie Presser, *Mobbed Up*.

Judge Corrigan's sentence reduction was probably the turning point of Don King's life. If the murder two conviction had not been modified, King faced life in prison, with the first eligibility for parole coming after eight and a half years. Because of Judge Corrigan's decision, King would emerge from prison after serving three years and eleven months.

King listened to the first Ali-Frazier fight, in March 1971, on radio in prison. He co-promoted the last of the Ali-Frazier trilogy, on October 1, 1975. This would not have been possible without Judge Corrigan's ex parte kindness.

Detectives DeLau and Tonne both believe the judge was probably fixed. There is no question King did everything in his power to prevent a fair trial. DeLau told me in 1991, "We heard from good sources there was an exchange of funds; there was quite a transaction of money."

The key witness against King, Rosa Wrines, was terrorized into disappearing. Other witnesses vanished, were bought off, or changed their testimony. Two attempts were made to bribe Detective Tonne and get him to perjure himself by saying King was acting in self-defense. Judge Corrigan's ruling came in this context of external manipulation by King's friends, by lawyers, bondsmen, and thugs.

Over the years King has given his version of Sam Garrett's death in hundreds of interviews. In the retelling King makes himself the victim, not the executioner.

This is what he told *Playboy* in 1988:

"When I finally came up for trial, however, the judge reduced the charge against me to manslaughter."

"Why?"

"Because it had been an accident—there wasn't willful intent on my part. Witnesses to the fight had all seen that I'd been attacked without provocation. The primary reason, though, was when the guy attacked me, I had a .357 Magnum on the seat of my car and I didn't use it—and I could have gotten to it. I was getting into my car when he hit me from the back, and the gun was lying right there. But I left it sitting there on the seat."

It is easy for King to get away with fictionalizing his own past. Garrett is dead. All the clips from the trial seem to be missing from the library of both the *Plain Dealer* and the defunct *Cleveland Press*. The prosecutor, Ralph Sperli, is dead. DeLau is retired and nobody outside of Cleveland knows who Tonne is. Even if conscientious journalists wanted to get the other side, there was no place to go.

One evening late in the 1980s, Bob Tonne was watching television in his home in Brooklyn Heights, Ohio. He happened to switch to a channel that was showing King being interviewed by Sarah Purcell. And in his signature verbal style of rap opera filibuster, King once again was giving his account of how Sam Garrett died. King was blaming the Cleveland police for framing him, for targeting him because he was the czar of the numbers racket. He was saying it was just a fight in the ghetto that happened to end in tragedy.

Bob Tonne was enraged. He was watching history—and his own life—being falsified on national television. He still believed the death of Sam Garrett was "a vicious, cold-blooded killing." He still vividly remembered the disparity in size, the gun in King's hand, the last sadistic kick to Garrett's head, and Garrett's final words, "Don, I'll pay you the money."

Bob Tonne was so disturbed that for the first time in his life he wrote a letter to a television program, to set the record straight. He never received an answer. Don King kept getting the last word.

"Make me big"

When Don King emerged from Ohio's Marion Correctional Institution on September 30, 1971, three men befriended him and helped him begin his remarkable transformation from convict to millionaire celebrity.

One was the roguish, likable boxing matchmaker and promoter Don Elbaum, who had a network of small club operations in Pennsylvania and Ohio, and an eye for true talent.

The second was the legendary 1950s rock 'n' roll songwriter-performer Lloyd Price, who had known King since 1959, loved him unconditionally, and visited him on his first day out of prison.

The third was the Fighter of the Age, Muhammad Ali, with a twinkle in his eye and a fondness for all living things. His generosity gave King the keys to the kingdom of pugilism.

All three would play a critical role in launching King's career in boxing, opening doors, giving him credibility, introducing him to others with their imprimaturs, taking the stigma off "ex-con."

And over the course of the next decade, King would gradually betray all three benefactors, one by one.

King pulled off his first slick deal even before he got out of prison, when he knew he was coming up for parole in the spring of 1971. King managed to acquire a forty-acre farm in rural Ashtabula County, on Chub Road, for $1,000—a property with a market value of at least thirty times that in 1971.

The land was purchased on March 26, 1971, from a Cleveland city councilman named Charles Carr, who was also a lawyer with ties to Cleveland's numbers rackets. Carr had bought the same tract of land for $19,800 in 1967. So this sharp lawyer was taking an $18,800 loss to do this favor for a man still in prison for killing a constituent of Carr's. But this favor set King's family up for life.

The deed to the land was placed in the name of John Carl Renwick, King's fourteen-year-old stepson, later to become known as Carl King.

On May 17, 1973, the *Cleveland Press* published a lengthy muckraking story about the transaction, describing the teenaged John Carl Renwick as a "mystery figure unknown to local neighbors and local businessmen."

The story, by reporter Tony Tucci, read:

> Councilman Carr declined to shed any light on the identity of the man to whom he sold the farm.
>
> "I was just the trustee for the property," Carr said. "The man is my client. I can't discuss it. I can't be of any aid to you in this respect." [Carr died in 1987.]

John Carl Renwick's father was John Caldwell Renwick, a figure in the numbers racket, who died in 1961. He was an associate of Don King's and so was his wife, Henrietta, who lived at the farm and later married King.

The forty-acre farm, obtained almost for free, would expand over the years into the 188-acre luxury compound that would become King's trophy and sanctuary, with a $5 million thirty-room mansion, swimming pool, gym, cattle, and giant American flag.

Putting this jailhouse insider-trading aside, there is no question that King used his four years in prison to his advantage. As he repeatedly says, "I didn't serve time. I made time serve me."

King did read his way through the prison library, absorbing ideas from history's heavyweight thinkers, including Frederick Douglass, Adam Smith, Shakespeare, Voltaire, Sartre, Nietzsche, John Stuart Mill, Tolstoy, Saint Thomas Aquinas, the Reverend Martin Luther King, Jr., Marx, and Hitler.

In a 1988 *Playboy* interview, King recalled:

On my first day in prison, a guy gave me a book, *The Meditations of Marcus Aurelius,* and I lay there on my bed in a four-man cell, and I just went deep into this book. Reading about Rome gave me the appetite to read whatever I could get my hands on.

I then got a job in the kitchen making coffee for all the different shifts, and when I finished, I'd sit in a little room in the kitchen and read, and when I got off, I'd go to the library.

I tried to escape by reading other people's ideas and putting my ideas with theirs, and developing a sense of discipline.

Often when King quoted the great writers he read in prison he mangled their names, calling them "Kneeis itch" (Nietzche) and "Jean-Paul Shar-tay" and "Dis-aray-leee." Boxing writers would laugh about his malaprop pronunciations, or his verbose misquotations from Shakespeare. But King fully grasped the concepts, and how to integrate them into his agenda.

King used prison as a graduate school to supplement his diploma from the street. Prison helped him appreciate ideas and language. His values were not rehabilitated. But he came out of prison seeing a bigger horizon, with a richer imagination, with a more complex self-image.

The day after King was paroled from prison, Lloyd Price flew to Cleveland and came to see King at the house in Ashtabula County. It was an intense, emotional reunion for two black men of the same generation who had already been friends for almost fifteen years.

Price had been a smart businessman, one of the few creators of rock 'n' roll who owned the writing and performing royalty rights to his own material. He had discovered Little Richard, had a hit single at eighteen with "Lawdy Miss Clawdy," seen Elvis Presley and John Lennon record his songs.

Price had also seen his music-business partner Harold Logan murdered, perhaps by the mob. He had been a rebel himself within the music industry, fighting racism and organized crime to do things his way, which meant independence and quality.

Price also knew boxing at a sophisticated level. Growing up in New Orleans, he had listened to Joe Louis's fights on the radio. He knew Sugar Ray Robinson. He had met Muhammad Ali when Cassius Clay was a seventeen-year-old kid in Louisville, waiting outside a club to meet his idol, Lloyd Price, and hear Price sing his favorite song, "Stagger Lee."

Ali lived in Lloyd's Manhattan apartment when he was training for his first big fight, with Doug Jones at Madison Square Garden in 1963. And it was Price who took Ali to the hospital with neck pains after that difficult victory.

Price totally trusted King, thinking he was immune to the larceny in his friend's character. Price had ego and financial security, and his only motive was to help his friend get back on his feet.

He had first met King in 1959, when his band played King's tavern, and he returned every year, sometimes to play benefits, like when King had a fire, or when the black community was raising money for a charity or cause.

King liked jazz, and in those days Price's band included top jazzmen like trombonist Slide Hampton and trumpet player Kenny Dorham. When the band was really cooking, with a jazz and R&B fusion, King would leap up on the bandstand and conduct the music like he was Louis Armstrong, or Louie Jordan. King introduced Price to all the ghetto players, and Price can still name some of the numbers operators and Superfly pimps he hung with in King's circle of after-midnight friends.

The day after King got out of prison, he and Price had a long intimate conversation as they drove the sixty miles from the farmhouse to Cleveland. King was just forty, and the two men talked about what King might do with the rest of his life, with Price's assistance. The two old friends speculated about possible careers in music promotion, film production, show business, and boxing.

King knew how close Price and Muhammad Ali were because Price had already introduced King to Ali. The occasion had been the fifth birthday party for King's daughter, Debby. Price was there at King's house and he telephoned Ali, and put the champ on the phone to sing "Happy Birthday" to King's child.

So some of the conversation that day was about how King might use his contacts with Ali to break into boxing. Price remembers King saying, whenever they contemplated some joint venture, "Make me big, Lloyd."

At the close of the day, Don King, with his normal haircut and weighing a slim 180 pounds after his regime of prison food, hugged Lloyd Price, the big star and loyal friend.

"We're friends forever," King said. "Nothing will ever come between us. I love ya, partner."

By June 1972, Don King had an idea. He had read in the papers that a hospital with black doctors, that served mostly black patients, was in danger of going into bankruptcy. He decided to promote a benefit boxing show with Muhammad Ali to save Forest City Hospital.

King phoned Lloyd Price and asked him to convince Ali, who

had lost to Joe Frazier the previous March, to box a few rounds for charity on a card King would promote. All the money would go toward saving the hospital from the bankers, creditors, and regulators.

Price, the loyal, more famous friend, reached Ali and his manager, Herbert Muhammad, and pitched the idea, how it would be good for Cleveland, good for Ali, good for Don King, and good for poor, sick black people who needed decent care.

Ali knew King, but at that point in his life, offers and deals were coming to Ali every day, and someone like Price was necessary to certify this one and get Ali and Herbert to focus on it in a concrete way.

Once King got Ali on the phone, his unstoppable flow of words did the trick. Ali agreed to come to Cleveland and box ten exhibition rounds on August 28. The event would be the beginning of King's second career—boxing promoter.

Only King had never promoted a boxing match in his life. He didn't know how to get a ring, a license, referees, fighters, insurance, gloves. He knew boxing only as a fan, only as an amateur who got knocked out in a kid's tournament.

To guide him through his maiden promotion, King called Don Elbaum, the most knowledgeable local character who combined managing, promoting, booking fighters, and discovering young prospects before anybody else. Elbaum looked like Harvey Keitel and told stories like Damon Runyon.

Elbaum recalls that the first time he heard Don King's commanding voice he was in a motel room in Buffalo on a Friday evening. He was negotiating a deal for a match when the phone rang. It was Clarance Rogers, a prominent Cleveland attorney.

"I'm with a friend of mine named Don King," Rogers said. "I would like to put him on the line with you, he'd like to speak to you."

The next thing Elbaum heard was an earsplitting roar: "DON ELBAUM!"

He had to jerk the receiver away from his ear.

"Let me tell you something," the voice shouted. "There's a black hospital that's in a lot of trouble here, and you and I are going to be the heroes who save it.

"You *are* boxing in Cleveland, and I want you now. You have got to put it together for me. I got Ali, but now I need you."

King went on like a runaway horse for five minutes, nonstop. Finally Elbaum interrupted him to say, "Nice to meet you. And yes, I'll do whatever it is you're asking."

"I'm here in Rogers's office. How soon can you get here?" King asked.

"I just arrived in Buffalo a half hour ago," Elbaum explained. "I'm here closing a deal for a show."

King: "No! no! no! no! no! We gotta get with you tonight."

Elbaum: "I just can't do that. I have meetings here. I'll see you in Cleveland on Monday."

King: "No way. I will wait here in Clarance's office tonight until you get here. We got no time. By the way, what do you charge?"

Elbaum: "Five thousand, plus expenses."

King: "You got it. Now start driving. I need your expertise immediately."

So Elbaum checked out of the motel and drove three hours to Cleveland, arriving just before midnight to meet King for the first time and begin the Lord's work of rescuing what King kept calling "a black hospital."

"I was simply mesmerized," Elbaum now says of his first experience with King. "I thought he was the greatest promoter I ever saw. He just overwhelms you. He could talk you into anything. I believed in the guy immediately. I felt I could trust him and he would never screw me."

And Elbaum was no virgin in the boxing jungle. He had promoted club fights in Erie, Scranton, Akron, Cleveland, and other blue-collar towns. He had boxed a little himself as a pro. Boxing writers lived off his supply of anecdotes. He had promoted Sugar Ray Robinson's last fight. A few months earlier somebody blew up his car with a bomb. He had seen just about everything in the unregulated realm of the ring.

Elbaum remembers the first night they met, when King told him how he had graduated from Ohio State with a 3.9 grade average. When Elbaum found out a little later how far that was from the truth, he was just amused by the audacity.*

King and Elbaum set up shop in two adjacent suites in the downtown Sheraton hotel, opposite the old Cleveland Arena. From the start Elbaum saw evidence that King was still involved in the numbers game—envelopes, suitcases, guys with guns—but it didn't matter to him, and nothing explicit was said.

After a few days of watching King con reporters, preachers, politicians, and businessmen, Elbaum was telling him: "Don, you can take over all of boxing! You've got the personality! Do you realize all the black fighters are going to come running to you? Boxing needs a black promoter like you. We've got to go to New York right after this charity show."

While trying to sell blocks of tickets to the Forest City benefit, Elbaum watched King put on one of his vintage Reverend Ike style performances of evangelical huckstering.

A churchgoing elderly black couple of great dignity came to the suite at the Sheraton, and King was trying to sell their church a bunch of tickets out of civic duty and racial solidarity. Both Elbaum and boxing trainer Joey Fariello were in the suite, and both remember King's oration in call-and-response preacher cadences.

"We're blacks and we have nothing," King began, pacing and

---

*King has told many different stories about his education, including a version that he attended Kent State University. But his official record from John Adams High School indicates he was a problem student his senior year.

An entry dated March 31, 1949, says: "Donald King's mother came. Don will be 18 next year and will not be accepted back September because of truancy, tardiness and general bad behavior."

King's school record shows that he did get an 85 in economics and a 75 in speech, but he flunked Gym and Band while in Audubon Junior High School.

gesturing. "We don't have expensive suits, or big houses, or luxury vacations. We're poor. All we got is the word. Our only invention that belongs to us is a word. And that word is *motherfucker*!

"Nobody can take that away from us. That's our word. That's a black word. We should be proud of that word. It's our heritage."

Elbaum thought he was seeing embarrassment in the body language of the elderly couple. But he didn't know how to stop the bizarre sermon.

"Every black man and black woman," King continues, "should walk down Euclid Avenue with their head held high saying the word *motherfucker*. Because that's ours. They can't take it away from us. The whites can't steal that word from us. It's a beautiful word because it is owned by us black folk. We should be standing on the top of buildings, shouting our word—*motherfucker*!"

After a few minutes, King, the natural actor, stopped and asked his two sedate guests to shout the word with him. Elbaum couldn't look. Fariello thought the scene was surreal.

Finally, the elderly man said the word, "Motherfucker."

"Louder!" King demanded.

He said it louder.

"Beautiful, right on," exclaimed King.

Then the woman yelled, "Motherfucker!"

And Don King hugged them in racial pride and liberation.

"King could sell anything," Elbaum says in admiration. "Even the word *motherfucker* to God-fearing religious people who prayed every week."

Probably the best novel ever written about boxing is *The Harder They Fall,* by Budd Schulberg. In that book one astute character says, "Boxing is just show business with blood."

Don King understood this instinctively, from his first day as a promoter. Elbaum understood this, too, and this made them a fun, harmonious team for a while.

Elbaum was the matchmaker, pairing local Ohio fighters for the undercard of professional fights. King was the salesman and showman. He made drama, hype, excitement, celebrity, and style part of the event.

King marketed the show on radio, in churches, in union halls, in corporate boardrooms, in newspaper offices. He sold it with wit, bombast, originality, and attitude. In those days there was a light in his eyes.

King held a press conference with Jackie Presser, the president of the Teamsters Union, who bought up several rows of tickets for his members.

And Ali was the honey pot. King kept telling the local boxing writers Ali would return to Cleveland for a major fight if they gave his show free advance publicity, which would pump up the gate, which would actually get Ali to come back to Cleveland, which would give all of them better stories and more space in the paper.

With help from Lloyd Price in lining up performers, King added an R&B concert to the evening. Price and King convinced Marvin Gaye, Johnny Nash, Wilson Pickett, and Lou Rawls to sing before the boxing part of the program began.

The day before the benefit, Marvin Gaye was scheduled to arrive at the airport. He was then at the top of the charts with his politically pioneering Motown hit, "What's Going On?"

King asked Elbaum and Joey Fariello, who had a fighter on the card, to drive out to the airport with flash cameras and pretend to be photographers for the Cleveland dailies, to build up Gaye's ego with the prospect of front-page publicity.

Fariello told King, "Are you nuts?"

Elbaum was too busy to lend himself to the scam. But he did pay some gofers ten dollars each to impersonate photographers when Gaye got off the plane.

The night of the benefit the decrepit arena on Euclid Avenue was jammed with eighty-five hundred people. This was a remarkable promotional achievement in a city that hadn't had a big fight in years. However, Cleveland did have a rich boxing tradition as the birthplace of light heavyweight champ Joey Maxim and heavyweight contender Jimmy Bivins, and as the city where Ezzard Charles had many of his early bouts.

The gate was $81,000, the largest in history for a boxing exhibition, breaking the old record of $74,000 set by Jack Dempsey and King Lavinsky in Chicago in 1932.

Ali more than did his part. He never met a crowd he couldn't charm, and he put on an extravagant performance. He clowned for two rounds with Amos Johnson, a fighter who had beaten him as an amateur but was now broke and down on his luck. Ali playfully pretended that his old foe knocked him down during their two rounds of sparring.

Ali then boxed two more brisk rounds with his regular spar mate, Alonzo Johnson, bringing the crowd to its feet with the dazzling Ali shuffle and some fast-handed volleys.

Then the Greatest went four rounds with Terry Daniels, lifting the crowd with some pre-exile floating like a butterfly and stinging like a bee. Ali then tickled the crowd by boxing a round each with local radio personalities Rudy Greene and Gary Dee, even letting Dee put him on the canvas with a phantom punch.

The concert portion of the evening lasted so long that the three ten-round matches Elbaum had put together had to be cut to six rounds each to avoid overtime payments to the unionized staff of the arena, and to accommodate the portion of the crowd that took the early bus to work. King had no sense of time—or of leaving anything out—when he was the center of attention.

One of these six-rounders was a split-decision victory for Johnny Griffin over Sam McGill. Griffin's trainer was Joey Fariello, who vividly remembers what happened next in the dressing room after the fight.

"King tried to cheat my kid out of his pay, which was only twelve hundred dollars," Fariello says. "King told me there was a lien against the kid, but I knew that wasn't true. We eventually got the money, but we had to fight like hell for it. This was Don's absolutely first boxing show, and he began his career by trying to stiff my black fighter out of twelve hundred dollars on a charity card for a black hospital."

(In February 1975, I was in Scranton and witnessed a similar scene, where King cheated heavyweight Jimmy Young out of a measly $500. At the time Young was broke and King was on his way to the top. A lawyer was complaining to King that he had coerced Young to sign to different contracts within five hours with differing compensation listed for the fighter. King insisted on paying Young the lowest amount.)

The day after the benefit, the Cleveland papers declared the night a triumph and reported that the Forest City Hospital would "receive between $40,000 and $50,000 for its operating fund."

But what exactly happened to all that money remains in dispute even today.

Elbaum says, "Ali got ten thousand for expenses. I got paid one thousand instead of five thousand. The hospital got about fifteen hundred. And King pocketed the rest."

A month after the benefit Clarance Rogers announced he had given the hospital a check for $17,000 and that expenses ate up the rest of the gate receipts.

In 1992, I interviewed Rogers and Roger Saffold, the accountant for the benefit committee, and both of them were adamant that King didn't derive any money from the show, and that King had no control over the benefit committee's bank account into which the gate receipts were deposited.

Boxing Illustrated magazine reported in a 1993 article by Rick Hornung that King took $30,000 from the benefit and the hospital got $15,000.

In his 1988 *Playboy* interview, King boasted, "We raised enough money to save the hospital." But in fact, the 102-bed hospital had already been out of business for ten years when King gave the interview to *Playboy*. Forest City Hospital actually closed its doors to the public in February 1978. A February 2, 1978, story in the *Cleveland Press* on the closing described "steadily dropping admissions, heavy operating losses, and few doctors who admitted patients to the hospital."

The story, by Elizabeth Price, explained: "In 1975 the Ohio State Medical Board warned the hospital that eight unlicensed foreign doctors on its staff could not legally treat patients . . . patients began to go elsewhere for treatment, and the hospital revenue dropped. In late 1975, the hospital was losing about $30,000 a month."

After the Ali show, King and Elbaum kept their suites open at the Sheraton and began to draw even closer in comradeship and trust. They talked about collaborating on a film together based on a script by one of King's associates in the numbers business. The story line was how a group of black numbers operators band together and drive the dope-selling Mafia out of their community. It contained a lot of shooting and car chases. The script was heavily influenced by *Super Fly, Shaft,* and *Sweet Sweetback's Baadasssss Song,* which were all released during 1971 and started the trend in black exploitation films.

"I'll get you fifty thousand as the assistant producer," King told Elbaum, "But then you got to give me back twenty-five."

The project never materialized.

Elbaum recalls one conversation between him and King "that was as tender and eye-watering as you can get. Don put his arms around me and spoke from his heart."

King told Elbaum, "I want to become legitimate. I want to do something right in my life for my family. I don't want to be known as a numbers man anymore. I want boxing."

A few days later at the farm, King's wife told Elbaum, "You gotta get him out of the numbers business. If anyone can get him out, it's you." (Henrietta had been quite active herself in the business for years, getting arrested and once invoking the Fifth Amendment before a grand jury.)

One Saturday night King barged into Elbaum's room at the Sheraton and dropped off a briefcase and an overcoat.

"I got an emergency," King told his friend. "Whatever you do, don't leave this room. Just watch my briefcase and coat—I'll be back soon."

Elbaum sat up all night waiting for King. After midnight he started calling bars and after-hours clubs without success. He was worried about his friend's safety.

Finally at dawn King returned. He opened the suitcase and there were stacks of cash money inside. He reached into his overcoat pocket and pulled out wads of bills.

"Now I know I can trust you," King roared and hugged Elbaum.

Around Christmas of 1972 Elbaum introduced King to his heavyweight fighter, Earnie Shavers. Elbaum held the promotional rights to Shavers in partnership with affluent Youngstown asphalt and highway contractor Joseph "Blackie" Gennaro, and former playboy pitcher Dean Chance, the youngest player ever to win the Cy Young Award.

Shavers was a nuclear puncher and a lovely human being, but he had a problem with stamina and his chin was not the best. He had won thirty fights in a row, twenty-nine by knockouts, mostly over tomato-can opponents selected by Elbaum, in matches mounted in towns like Warren, Akron, Canton, and Youngstown, Ohio.

Elbaum trusted King so much he decided to bring him in as a partner with Gennaro and Chance, who were already fighting with each other and creating a tense climate around the fighter, who had an unusually sensitive temperament. Elbaum even escorted King to New York City and made an introduction to Hank Schwartz, then president of Video Techniques, the company that provided the satellite technology for most of the closed-circuit fights. Elbaum told Schwartz that if he had any brains he would hire King, because King was the future face of the sport. With a master's degree in engineering from MIT, Schwartz knew electronics, but not boxing or human nature as King did.

"Boxing needs a black promoter," Elbaum told Schwartz. "You've got to get away from Madison Square Garden. This is a man who could be a force. He's going to be able to control fighters because he is black, and all the good fighters are black. This man knows how to relate to them like nobody in the world."

With King sitting at the table, Elbaum told Schwartz, "Talk to this guy, hire this guy. Why don't you send him down to Jamaica for the Frazier-Foreman fight?"

About ten years later, when King was at the apex of his power and Elbaum was still scuffling and ducking last month's phone bill, the two men ran into each other at a fight.

"My man" was King's jovial greeting. "You took me into boxing, but you should have stayed with me, brother. You would have become a millionaire by now."

"I would also have gone to jail," Elbaum laughed.

Elbaum did go to jail for six months, on his own, in 1991 on tax-fraud charges.

Somehow King materialized in Kingston, Jamaica, before the January 22, 1973, heavyweight championship match between Joe Frazier and challenger George Foreman. It is not clear how he got there, what he was doing there, or who paid his passage.

Elbaum thinks King was already in the employ of Video Techniques. King says he went to Kingston on the invitation of Joe Frazier, although he would leave the stadium—and the island— in the company of George Foreman, in one of King's fastest shifts of loyalty. This was the first of many times he would step over the bloody face of yesterday's "main man" to seduce tomorrow's.

Hank Schwartz says, "King was at the first fight, and jumped into the ring with Foreman, but I don't think he was on our payroll yet. . . . We were hired by the government of Jamaica to do worldwide closed circuit and to help make the match. The government put up the money for the fighters and acted as the real promoter. We did the electronic feed via satellite."

Schwartz's memory is that his company hired King right after the fight because of his sudden influence with Foreman and his company's desire to promote Foreman's first title defense against Ken Norton. He says that Elbaum's introduction and advocacy were crucial, but so was King's performance in charging into the ring as part of Frazier's faction, and leaving the ring as part of Foreman's faction.

Schwartz says, "Signing Norton to a contract was easy. I flew to Los Angeles on a morning flight and conducted the negotiations in a conference room at the airport. I took the red-eye back to New York the same night with Norton's signature on a contract to fight Foreman in Caracas. . . .

"Foreman was a much more difficult personality. So we asked King, in his first assignment for our company, to arrange a meeting with Foreman through Dick Sadler, one of Foreman's many managers and advisers.

"But George required a cash payment to be delivered to him, and King helped with that. As I recall it, the deal was completed in a stall. After he finished counting the money, he signed the contract to box Norton, still in the men's room at the airport. King seemed quite familiar with that sort of transaction."

Even now, more than twenty years later, Schwartz will not say how much cash his company had to slip Foreman in the urinal to legally lock up the rights to the fight. But in boxing, cash under the table, or over the toilet, is routine.

During 1973, while still an employee of Video Techniques, King gained an interest in three top-of-the-line fighters: Earnie Shavers, Jeff Merritt, and Ray Anderson. In boxing there has never been a clear distinction between promoter, manager, booking agent, and silent partner, and King just followed in the footsteps of Mike Jacobs, Al Weill, and Jim Norris.

King quickly bought out Dean Chance's interest in Shavers in

March. Elbaum says he was present when King reached into a drawer in his home, counted off $8,000 in cash from a much larger stash, and handed the money to Chance. King began to make his own moves on the fighter, just as he had done with Foreman in Kingston, and soon there were turmoil and intrigue in the Shavers camp.

At one point there was supposed to be a big sit-down among all the partners in the back room of an Italian restaurant halfway between Cleveland and Youngstown. It was another one of King's rap operas. No one else got a word in. King started the meeting by punching the table with his fist for attention, and then gave a half-hour sermon of superlatives.

"We people in this room own something that is everybody's dream," King opened up. "We own the hardest-punching heavyweight in the history of boxing, the most awesome fighting machine who is going to dominate boxing for years to come.

"And what a magnificent team we have to do this! That gentleman over there, my friend Blackie Gennaro. That man has all the money to make things happen. His money can move mountains. And there is Don Elbaum. What a boxing mind he has! He's going to maneuver us into all the right matches, till we reach the championship.

"And here I am. I'm new to this business. But I'm going to start the greatest publicity campaign in human history for Earnie Shavers. Soon he will be more famous than Muhammad Ali."

King then turned to Gennaro and said, "I just paid Dean Chance eight thousand dollars to become part of this all-star team. I got the contract cleared up. Now I need you to reimburse me for the eight thousand I done gave him, and I need another eight thousand for expenses to get our publicity campaign started up. We gotta start making these things happen right away."

At the end of the meeting King left with two $8,000 checks in his pocket from Blackie Gennaro, a sweet man who had faith in Earnie Shavers.

For a while Shavers looked like the reincarnation of Joe Louis. On February 19, 1973, he knocked out Jimmy Young in the first round. On June 18 he came to Madison Square Garden and knocked out the well-respected Jimmy Ellis in the first round.

In the afterglow of the Ellis conquest, Gennaro, Elbaum, and King met to divide their share of the purse. But there was no money left for Elbaum and Gennaro because King had billed their partnership for hotel rooms and airfare to New York for all of his friends and family.

When Gennaro questioned this practice, King delivered another speech: "I need my people around me," he said. "They give me energy and inspiration. That's part of our expense. It will always be part of our expense. I can't be away from my people when I'm in New York."

Once again, by the end of a meeting Gennaro was opening his checkbook and writing some zeros. After a double-talk explanation of the ledger sheets and expense records, King somehow persuaded Gennaro that he was owed an additional $2,000 for reimbursed expenses, including entertaining boxing writers in New York.

The Shavers-Ellis main event was King's first exposure to the New York writers, and as a novelty he made an impression. As a new personality reinventing himself, throwing off great quotes, telling fantastic tales, dramatizing people and details, King was a beat reporter's dream. He made their job easy. And for years that aspect would help King get over with the media, long after the time his actions should have made him a public villain and a corporate pariah.

By the fall of 1973, King had managed to isolate Elbaum from Shavers and manipulate him out of the management team. King gave no pause to double-crossing the man who gave him his start in boxing, the man he trusted with his suitcase of cash, the man he'd apprenticed himself to ever since the Forest City benefit.

Elbaum says: "I was forced out. I had an agreement on paper, but I never enforced it. I just got very disgusted with the way Don was operating. I got demoralized. He turned Shavers against us, and that hurt me, and Blackie loved Earnie as a person. So I just said the hell with it and walked away. Don wants people to jump to his tune, and that's just not me. I go to my own jump."

On December 14 Shavers came back to Madison Square Garden to box Jerry Quarry—a white hope who could punch. Quarry took Shavers's best shot and stormed back to knock out Shavers in the first round. He hit Shavers on the chin and Shavers froze, standing up straight along the ropes.

Shavers says his mind was "one thousand miles away from the fight." He says he was depressed by all the infighting around him. He also says he never got paid by King after he lost the Quarry bout.

I interviewed Shavers for an hour during a bus ride with Muhammad Ali back to his training camp at Deer Lake. Shavers—now a minister, who says he was "saved" on April 24, 1986—spoke frankly of his past without rancor, self-pity, or defensiveness.

"Before the Quarry fight," Shavers explained in his oddly high-pitched voice, "King and Gennaro were fighting and trying to make me take sides. Don put a lot of pressure on me to take his side, but they both had been good to me.

"The main problem was that Don fired Archie Moore as my trainer just before the fight, and I had a lot of confidence in Archie. Don had made him the scapegoat when Jeff Merritt broke my jaw in the gym, but he must have had other reasons to want to get rid of a famous guy like Archie, who had been such a great champion.

"After Archie got fired, Don put a guy in my corner who was a friend of his from Cleveland. I can't even remember the man's name. But the whole scene killed my concentration and confidence. And after I got knocked out I didn't even get paid my money. Don had promised me seventy-five thousand, but he said there were expenses. But I blame myself. I was young and foolish and I let Don mistreat me."*

Listening to Shavers's story, I realized something that I would remember again in almost every interview with a former fighter who had been wronged financially: Boxing is the only jungle where the lions are afraid of the rats.

Whether it is Shavers, or Ali, or Saoul Mamby, or Tony Tucker, it has been my personal experience that gifted fighters, who know what their hands can do, tend to be unexpectedly gentle people, who try to avoid interpersonal conflicts and can be intimidated by promoters.

This was even true of Sonny Liston and champions from other eras, who had to deal with contemporary promoters and mobsters.

After Shavers lost, King lost interest in him. As always, the abandonment is swifter than the seduction.

In April 1974, Blackie Gennaro sued King for $500,000 in the Northern Ohio District Court. The suit accused King of not paying Gennaro his contracted share of the Quarry fight and included a copy of the March 1973 partnership contract that guaranteed King and Gennaro, as co-managers, would share any profits equally.

The suit also charged King with negligence in not consulting Gennaro on decisions, like the dismissal of Archie Moore, and argued this exclusion caused Shavers to lose the Quarry match. This would be the first of more than one hundred lawsuits filed against King over the next twenty years by fighters and managers he shafted.

In August 1974, the lawsuit was settled, with an agreement signed by King, Shavers, and Gennaro. King agreed to pay Gennaro $3,500 and Gennaro became Shavers's manager once again.

---

*Former FBI agent Joe Spinelli, who investigated boxing from 1980 to 1984, told me that Shavers was contracted to receive $75,000 for the Quarry fight and was actually paid $3,000.

King didn't want to have anything to do with Shavers after the loss, which King felt had made him look bad. The agreement contained a clause saying, "Shavers agrees he shall make no further attempts to contact King."

In the late 1970s, when Shavers's confidence and reputation were restored, he would fight for King the promoter in several major bouts, knocking out Ken Norton in one round, and knocking down Larry Holmes in a heavyweight title fight Shavers was one punch away from winning, before his old stamina-weakness betrayed his body.

On June 19, 1973, when he was in town for the Shavers-Ellis match, Don King appeared at the offices of the New York State Boxing Commission at 270 Broadway. The purpose of his visit was to register his name as the manager of a heavyweight named Jeff Merritt, who had considerable promise and considerable baggage.

One problem was that another man already had a valid contract on file with the commission as Merritt's manager—Norman King, who had an office at 375 Park Avenue. Norman King's contract did not expire until the following year.

A second problem was that Merritt had been arrested for burglary three months earlier by cops from the 20th Precinct on Manhattan's West Side. Merritt, in fact, had a criminal record almost as long as King's, with arrests for rape, robbery, and drugs. Merritt had been released from the Missouri State Prison on December 22, 1967, after serving two years for first-degree robbery.

Merritt had a great left and an addiction to heroin, and no one knew which would write his future. He was twenty-five, six five, 225 pounds, and had a professional record of eighteen wins, one loss, with fourteen knockouts.

On his license application, King was asked to state his experience and qualifications. He wrote, "I have been connected to boxing all my life. I love the game and want to contribute something meaningful to the sport."

He listed Cleveland Councilman Charles Carr as a reference and fully disclosed his manslaughter conviction, adding, "Also, I was in the numbers and arrested and fined for that activity."

Two days later, Deputy Boxing Commissioner Frank Morris wrote Merritt a letter in Kansas City, explaining he now had two managers and an outstanding burglary charge that must be disposed of before he could be licensed to box in New York.

Merritt got a release signed by Norman King and the burglary arrest was plea-bargained down to time served.

King quickly matched Merritt with used-up former champion Ernie Terrell in the Garden in September, in a live bout to precede the closed-circuit showing of the second Ali-Norton fight.

In the week leading up to Merritt's main-event debut, King the nonstop salesman was in town. He had a story line to sell, his exuberance was infectious, and his eyes danced with innocent hyperbole.

"I'm running a mission, not a gym," King told a group of boxing writers. "I consider myself a savior for guys like Jeff. I keep him out of the city until the day before the fight. Then I sit up with him till dawn to make sure he doesn't run off into the street. I've been to the joint, just like Jeff. I've seen the track marks on his arms. I can relate to him. And now we both want something better in life."

King instinctively knew how to market his fighter's story with narrative drama. King saw his own life as a modern epic, as a great drama of suffering and redemption, like Frederick Douglass's rise from slave to statesman. And King would always know how to dramatize and market the stories of his fighters. Sometimes it was a stretch. But with Merritt the drama and mystery of which way he would go was there.

Merritt, whose nickname was Candy Slim, overwhelmed Terrell in one round. It was such a mismatch it was hard to tell just how good Merritt could be.

In the dressing room afterward, King was shouting, "Remember the name Candy Slim. Champ next year. Don't bring us mortal men. We want to fight *giants*!"

But the next year, on March 4 in Oakland, Candy Slim was knocked out in the first round by an ordinary mortal named Henry Clark, and he never fought again. The loss annulled his self-esteem, and smack wrote the rest of his life. King walked away from him, and Candy Slim vanished into the night of drugs, pimps, nomadic travel, dumb crimes, and prisons.

When David Wolf interviewed King for his *True* magazine profile in 1974, he asked King why he had stopped calling the prospect he loved and nursed away from the needle.

"I still care, I'm just into bigger things now," King explained.

For years the fight crowd talked about Candy Slim like he had been a comet from another galaxy who burned bright and then suddenly disappeared.

In March 1991 I was in Las Vegas for the first Tyson-Ruddock fight when I noticed a tall, barefoot man in dirty clothes begging for money in the lobby of the Mirage Hotel. He was ranting about Don King, who was promoting the Tyson fight in the Mirage parking lot that week.

"Are you Jeff Merritt?" I asked.

"Yeah, I'm Candy Slim. Gimme a dollar."

Merritt said he was a crack addict and homeless. He had been in and out of prison for years. Even his mother had thrown him out.

When anyone who seemed to be in town for the fight came by—identified by a T-shirt or a press credential—Candy Slim whined, "Don't you know me, man? I'm Jeff Merritt. I was Don King's first fighter. Gimme some money, man."

CHAPTER 3

King

Makes His

Masterpiece

There was a power vacuum in boxing in the early 1970s. No promoter had a monopoly on heavyweight champion Joe Frazier the way Tex Richard had with Jack Dempsey and Mike Jacobs had with Joe Louis.

The March 1971 Ali-Frazier fight had been promoted by millionaire sportsman Jack Kent Cooke and his partner, Hollywood booking agent Jerry Perenchio. The fighters each got $2.5 million, but no percentage of the closed-circuit TV revenue around the world, which produced a $20 million gross. The promoters made a fortune.

But Cooke and Perenchio did not remain successful boxing promoters, or even partners. And Frazier and Ali both remained free agents.

In the early 1970s, with the exception of Jerry Quarry, all the top heavyweights were black—Frazier, Ali, Ken Norton, George Foreman, Earnie Shavers, Ron Lyle, Jimmy Young. And all the boxing promoters, led by Bob Arum and Madison Square Garden, were white.

According to singer Lloyd Price, he began to tell King on the day he emerged from prison in September 1971 that, being black, he was in a position to "take over boxing."

Black pride and consciousness were rising all over the planet. Gold-medal sprinters John Carlos and Tommy Smith had raised their fists in black power salutes on the victory stand at the Mexico City Olympics in 1968. (This helped make George Foreman seem patriotic and popular for waving a tiny American flag after defeating a Russian for the Olympic heavyweight gold medal.)

Muhammad Ali was a Muslim and preaching black pride, solidarity, and self-reliance wherever he went. His manager, Herbert Muhammad, was not only a Muslim but the son of the religion's leader, Elijah Muhammad.

Boxing was ready for, and in fact needed, a black entrepreneur. Don King would prove to be the wrong man at the right time.

In all that follows it should not be overlooked that Don King was a trailblazer—the first successful black promoter in boxing history. He did have to overcome racism in society at large, and in boxing history. We should remember that John L. Sullivan would never fight a black opponent, avoiding his Australian challenger Peter Jackson. Jack Dempsey also would never fight a black challenger, and he ducked both Harry Wills and the magnificent Sam Langford.

When Jack Johnson won the heavyweight title from Tommy Burns in 1908, it was the novelist Jack London who first popularized the campaign to find a "great white hope" to recapture the crown for the white race. After Johnson vanquished the former champion, James J. Jeffries, on July 4, 1910, there was rioting all over America, and nineteen blacks were killed and lynched.

Ever since Rocky Marciano retired undefeated in 1956 as the last white American heavyweight champion, there have been periodic revivals of the white hope campaigns. The box office success of the early *Rocky* films reflected this need and nostalgia for a white champion. Since Gerry Cooney couldn't beat Larry Holmes, there was a fantasy market for Rocky Balboa to beat Apollo Creed.

And King would eventually come around to catering to this white hope mentality. He would market Chuck Wepner and Gerry Cooney as representatives of their race. He would make an under-the-table deal in violation of the worldwide anti-apartheid boycott of South Africa because he controlled the promotional rights to white South African Gerrie Coetzee.

And in the fall of 1994, King would sign Boston's Peter McNeeley to an exclusive promotional contract. McNeeley was a white heavyweight who had built up a 32–1 record by beating a string of handpicked losers and retirees who had a combined record of 301 defeats in 424 fights.

McNeeley's opponents had been knocked out a total of 152 times before they were judged incompetent enough to be matched with McNeeley. But King staged a press conference with McNeeley in Manhattan, promised him a championship fight, and got him rated in the top ten, even though he did not deserve it.

Don King would exploit white racism and black racism with equal enthusiasm. But at the start he was a pioneer who opened doors.

Brooklyn-born Hank Schwartz, an electronics and satellite technology wizard, was the president of Video Techniques. He knew King at that point as a client and exhibitor from Cleveland who rented his equipment. His partner was Barry Burnstein, a sweet three-hundred-pounder, who was in charge of marketing. After what Schwartz saw in Kingston he would hire King as an employee, but Schwartz says, "King was in Kingston on his own. He had no official connection to the Frazier-Foreman promotion."

In Kingston before the fight, King demonstrated one of his basic gifts—talking to black fighters. He knew how to do it. He knew how to ingratiate, con, charm, brown-nose, befriend, impress, amuse, and seduce fighters. He knew their language, their weakness, their psychology. He knew how to give them a self-image, an idea of their role in history, how much money they could make if they only had "proper management."

Although King was in Kingston at Frazier's invitation, the chess master was thinking four moves ahead. He spent part of his time having fun with Frazier and his manager, Yank Durham, but he also spent considerable time flattering the challenger, who was then a remote, sullen, secretive personality, not the jolly, self-deprecating character he has become in his comeback reincarnation. Foreman had grown up trying to emulate the scowling menace of Sonny Liston, and he was deep into that intimidating persona leading up to the Frazier fight.

But King acted almost like a groupie, volunteering to pick up members of Foreman's family and extended entourage as they kept arriving at the airport. King, understanding the secret doubts and insecurities of all fighters, kept telling Foreman he was going to win, building up his confidence, and spinning out grand plans for making money after he was champion.

King roared and chanted the same ego-building phrases to Frazier in the hours leading up to their confrontation. Frazier now says he never liked or trusted King, and that King favored Ali against him. But on the night of his battle with Foreman, Don King rode to the stadium with Frazier in the same limo, behind a police motorcycle escort and blasting sirens clearing a path.

As the fight began, King was in his front-row seat in Frazier's corner. As Foreman knocked Frazier down again and again during the first round, Don King started edging closer and closer to Foreman's corner.

As Frazier went down again, was lifted into the air by an awesome uppercut, and started to totter in a daze, Don King started to climb up the steps toward the ring with Foreman's handlers.

As the referee stopped the fight and cradled the bleeding Frazier in his arms, King was in the ring, embracing the new champion as his lifelong brother.

"George, I told you, I told you so!" King shouted into Foreman's ear.

As Howard Cosell began to interview Foreman in the ring, King pushed himself next to the new champion, shouting, "I got him, he's my man," as Cosell tried to ask a question.

King insinuated himself into Foreman's exultant entourage as they left the ring and returned to his dressing room. When Foreman left the stadium to return to his hotel, King was in the limo next to him, laughing with Foreman over the sound of the police escort sirens.

Don King has told this story himself many times, seeing it as a tribute to his own political and business acumen. Each time he tells it, he ends with the same punch line: "I came with the champion, and I left with the champion."

Hank Schwartz remembers the audacious spectacle of King taking over in the ring with both irony and outrage.

"I was in the truck," Schwartz recalls, "producing the fight, looking at monitors, picking out replays for between rounds. Then I suddenly saw Don King, in the ring, on my cameras, on my monitors, at my fight. It was amazing chutzpah."

Although to this day King thinks the Kingston anecdote reflects favorably on his adroit maneuvering, it is, in fact, the symbolic act of opportunism that would sum up his whole career. Time and again over the next eighteen years, King would switch loyalties, abandon a loser he had called his son the day before, and insinuate himself into the life, dreams, and income of a new champion.

In January 1974 at Madison Square Garden, Muhammad Ali won a unanimous twelve-round decision from Joe Frazier in their second fight. This established Ali as the logical challenger to the invincible monster George Foreman then seemed to be.

Every promoter in boxing, and all the promoters who lusted to break into the sport, wanted to make the Ali-Foreman match. Teddy Brenner and Madison Square Garden wanted it. Bob Arum wanted it. Jerry Perenchio wanted it. And Don King wanted it.

Video Techniques promoted King to vice president, gave him a salary increase, and let him loose to make the Ali-Foreman match for them. Schwartz told King to line up Ali and he would sign Foreman.

This was the opportunity of a lifetime for Don King. He put everything into it—all his will, all his energy, all his showmanship, all his mastery of numbers, all his skill at preaching an evangelical paradise in the future to black brothers.

For two months Don King talked, traveled, and talked. A parolee, just two and a half years out of prison, he competed against boxing's incumbent power brokers in a marathon negotiation, with the most bizarre cast of characters in history, to stage the richest prizefight in history.

The stakes were high for King because his career as a manager was about to come to a crashing end. His top heavyweight prospect, Earnie Shavers, was knocked out in one round by Jerry Quarry in December 1973, and Jeff Merritt would be knocked out in forty-seven seconds by Henry Clark on March 4, 1974.

Ali had known King as a sportsman and player since before he went to prison, and he called King to offer condolences after Shavers lost. King immediately converted the call of empathy into an oration-lecture to Ali to let King promote his next fight if he believed his Muslim preachings about blacks helping blacks. Although King was Catholic, he knew the Nation of Islam rap well enough to use it in the art of seduction.

It was partly this failure as a manager that launched King's transition to a promoter, over a line so blurry no one in boxing paid any attention to it, although the two roles are in direct conflict when it comes to how much a boxer will get paid for his work.

The first thing King did was try to get Ali's commitment for the fight. This was no easy task, since Arum was Ali's lawyer on some matters and had promoted Ali's recent fights with Jimmy Ellis, Buster Mathis, George Chuvalo, and Frazier II. Arum now says he advised Herbert Muhammad to give King a verbal promise because he never believed King would come up with the $10 million he was promising the fighters.

In his first meeting with Ali and Herbert Muhammad, King played the race card, which probably had a lot of validity to it. He told the story of how Arum had deprived him of the closed-circuit rights in Ohio to the second Ali-Frazier match.

King had bid $75,000 for the Ohio rights, and says that Arum assured him he would get the contract. But he never did, and as King told Ali, "Arum gave it to a white man who never done boxing before."

At first Herbert Muhammad rejected the allegation that Arum was anti-black. But King rolled on, putting his loss of the Ohio contract into the historical context of slavery, segregation, and racism.

He even quoted Herbert's father, the Honorable Elijah Muhammad. "You gotta help the black man, that's what he teaches," King bellowed. "You find a black man who can do the job, you gotta let him do it before a white man, that what he teaches."

Ali, then thirty-three, feared Foreman wouldn't fight him till he was older. King assured Ali he would produce Foreman if Ali would agree first to the match. Herbert tried to suggest a co-promotion with King and Arum, but King, insulted by the closed-circuit rejection, insisted Arum be excluded from the promotion to make it an all-black event.

Over several weeks King wore down Ali and his manager, and they made an oral commitment to the fight—if King could produce $5 million for Ali and Foreman's name on a contract.

In February King found out that Arum and Teddy Brenner of Madison Square Garden were offering Ali $850,000 to fight Jerry Quarry in May. This would jeopardize the Ali-Foreman match planned for September. Ali could get injured or cut. He could lose. The interim match could discourage investors. Herbert's bonds with Arum could get reinforced.

According to an account by author and future manager David Wolf, in the September 1974 edition of *True* magazine, King hid in the bedroom of Herbert Muhammad's Manhattan apartment while Arum and Brenner tried to make the Quarry fight for the Garden.

Twice in the days prior to this meeting Ali had agreed to fight Quarry (whom he had already beaten twice) and then wavered under counter pressure from King, who talked a great game but still didn't have a dime of financing in place for the Foreman match.

King heard Arum tell Ali that Jerry Quarry "loved him," and that's why he deserved another chance and a big payday. Quarry, in fact, did like Ali and fought him in Ali's first comeback match after his unjust exile, despite considerable pressure to boycott the "black Muslim draft dodger." Arum and Brenner also kept telling Ali the Foreman match was a mirage, a fantasy not worth waiting for, when he was being offered a bird in the hand worth $850,000.

Ali then excused himself and slipped into the bedroom, where King made his pitch.

"It's bad business," King began. "You break your hand on his head and you'll be striking a leaf from the pages of history! . . . You are the greatest attraction, the greatest athlete the world has ever known! Here's an opportunity to regain what was *stolen*— your crown! If you fight Quarry, George will want another fight, too. Circumstances may never *again* be conducive to this meeting." Looking up to the heavens King added, "I feel we are just instruments in an overall plan."

Ali returned to the living room intending to veto the Quarry match. Arum's closing statement stressed Foreman's unpredictability and claimed Quarry was the victim of a black conspiracy, and that Ali was afraid of the fight.

According to Wolf's version, Ali shouted, "I ain't no coward," and returned to the bedroom.

King shouted, "The mere fact Arum tries to lead you down this path demonstrates his inability to relate to your blackness and the cause you've struggled for."

Putting his hand on Ali's shoulder, King reached a crescendo: "This isn't just another fight! Consider the *monumental magnitude,* the symbolic impact. Your regaining your title would do more for the cause of freedom and justice and equality than anything!"

King's appeal to history, liberation, empowerment, and personal redemption proved irresistible. Ali turned down the fight with Quarry.

As Teddy Brenner was leaving Herbert's apartment, he shouted out, "King, wherever you are hiding, you're full of shit. But if you can really pay him five million dollars, he would be a fool not to take it."

After several more lengthy meetings in Chicago, Ali agreed to the fight. Video Techniques paid him a $100,000 advance for signing, on February 15. Under a complicated agreement, Ali was guaranteed $100,000 more by February 25, with King then providing a $2.3 million letter of credit at Chicago's Guarantee Bank and Trust by March 15. A second letter of credit, for $2.5 million, was due ninety days before the actual fight. If any payment deadline was missed, Ali would keep all money already paid as "liquidated damages" and not be obligated to go through with the fight.

"I'm giving you your chance," Herbert told King. "But you must perform. If you fail, don't expect me to do anything different than I'd do with anyone else."

It is quite possible that, like Arum, Herbert Muhammad never really believed King could meet each deadline and come up with $10 million. He may have considered the agreement an easy way to make $2.3 or $5 million for Ali, without having to do any fighting.

King called Schwartz from Chicago as soon as Ali had agreed and asked if his boss had signed Foreman yet.

"We don't have Foreman," Schwartz had to admit. "I couldn't get to him."

Under the terms of the Ali agreement, Foreman had to be signed within a day or two, or the deal fell apart. King jumped on the next plane to California, where an angry Foreman was training to fight Ken Norton in Caracas in March.

In February 1974 George Foreman was a bitter man, surrounded by boxing's usual circle of leeches and hustlers. He was tied up in lawsuits and a messy divorce case that made it legally impossible for him to box inside the United States.

In the year since his crushing knockout of Frazier, Foreman's popularity had dimmed. His only title defense had been a one-round knockout of the inept Joe Roman, whom Foreman had hit while he was down. Despite Foreman's crown and unbeaten record, Ali now seemed more popular than Foreman was. Nobody roots for Goliath.

Even though Foreman had destroyed Frazier, and would soon demolish Norton, the two men who had beaten Ali, it was now the aging, heroic, comic, tragic, socially significant Ali whom the fans loved. As Ali acknowledged, he was "the people's champion."

This paradox made Foreman seethe in anger and envy.

Foreman was furious about his pending divorce settlement. His "business manager," Leroy Jackson, was trying to make deals for himself and shake down promoters and entertainment agents. Jackson continued to negotiate with Jerry Perenchio through the winter of 1974 for Foreman to fight Ali and Frazier on the same night. Jackson, an old ghetto classmate of Foreman's in the Houston Job Corps, paid himself a generous salary as the champ's deal-maker and gatekeeper. But the George Foreman Development Corporation, headed by Leroy Jackson, was $173,000 in debt.

All this swirling chaos was converging to make the champion an unpleasant, isolated man, as Don King arrived at his training site, facing a forty-eight-hour deadline to sign him to fight Ali.

Leroy Jackson, seeking to make his own deal with Perenchio, tried to keep King away from Foreman, confiscating messages and speaking ill of King.

King finally ambushed Foreman in an Oakland hotel parking lot after a sparring session and managed to convince Foreman to take a walk with him. The walk would last ninety minutes with King talking nonstop. King later told David Wolf, "My legs almost gave out, but I was spiritually motivated."

"George, I know people been screwin' you," King the salesman began. "But I'm bringing you something solid. You got an opportunity to make five million and—I tell you this as a man who cares about you—under no conditions should you let it slip through your hands."

"Ali don't want to fight me," Foreman interrupted.

"I can deliver him," King replied. "And this is a victory you must achieve. Otherwise people will never accept your greatness. But you must move *now*! Ali may not want this fight for long."

King played on Foreman's insecurity for a few minutes, on how liberating it would be for him to conquer the haunting ghost of Ali. Foreman asked about poster billing and getting a larger purse.

Then King stopped walking and pointed to the skin on his arm.

"You're two super athletes. Both black," he thundered. "You've got to forgo the pettiness. This event is bigger than both of you as individuals. It's *monumental*, not just in revenue but in the symbolic impact that will reverberate throughout the world— from a black perspective. This is MY promotion! And I'm BLACK! Here is an opportunity to give inspiration to the downtrodden, to show that black men, together, can succeed with proficiency and effectiveness!"

Foreman walked in silence for a few minutes, and then turned to King and said: "I'm gonna give you an agreement. This is with

ME! I've never done this before, but I'm giving you my trust. You got the fight."

Foreman recalls signing a blank contract that King would fill in later.

Hank Schwartz, who was in Oakland with King, recalls, "Foreman signed three blank pages. One of them he signed in the middle of the page, one he signed three quarters from the top, and one he signed at the bottom. Foreman instructed his attorney to go back with me to San Francisco and write the contract and use any of the three pages as the signature page, depending on where the language of the contract ended. His lawyer wrote the contract into those pages and we signed next to Foreman's name. I don't think Foreman saw the contract."

Schwartz says each fighter was told he was getting $5.5 million and the other was getting only $5 million. Foreman was assured that because he was the champion, he was getting a symbolic $500,000 more. Ali was told that because he was the fan and media attraction, he was getting $500,000 extra. In fact, each got the same amount, while feeling more wanted and superior to his rival.

On April 30, 1990, at a press conference in New York announcing a fight between Foreman, then at the start of his amazing comeback, and Adilson Rodrigues, King humorously thanked Foreman for giving him "the opportunity of my lifetime."

"George Foreman signed seven blank sheets of paper," King recalled, "and allowed me to put on a fight with him that became the Rumble in the Jungle."

Bob Arum, who was sitting next to King because the fight was a co-promotion, couldn't resist jabbing the needle: "George has learned. He won't sign any more blank contracts."

Although Schwartz and King had the signatures of the two fighters on pieces of paper, they did not have any financing in place. And they faced a series of deadlines to produce the funds that would make the fight a reality. And they did not have a venue for the match.

Schwartz flew to London in mid-February thinking—perhaps wistfully—he had a commitment for financing from British promoter Jack Solomons, who was then about eighty and well past his prime. Schwartz had spent about fifteen minutes with Solomon and his proposed investors—two brothers in the London film business—when he realized he was wasting his time.

It was all talk. Nobody had done any preparation. They didn't have any idea about a site. They had no knowledge of how many seats were in any American or European stadium. They had no business plan. And they didn't have any money, with the first deadline to pay binders to the fighters less than a week away.

Schwartz sank into a depression. He feared he would lose the deal. He called King, who was in New York, and told him they were in trouble. King was trying, without success, to get a backer, even appealing to Perenchio and Mike Burke at Madison Square Garden.

Schwartz started to walk around London in the rain feeling sorry for himself. Then he passed a townhouse with a plaque outside that read HEMDALE FILMS.

"I remembered that I had met the president of Hemdale several years before at the Pierre Hotel," says Schwartz. "I gave him some advice about video and pay-per-view systems in some hotels Hemdale was involved in. So I decided, why not? I might as well talk to somebody about this. And I made a cold turkey call to John Daly, the president of Hemdale.

"John was nice enough to see me without an appointment. I was dripping wet and he offered me tea. I told him I didn't know if he wanted me to stay long enough to have tea or take off my coat.

"I told him I had two great contracts from gladiators—Ali and Foreman. But we needed four hundred thousand in a couple of days. Daly was entranced by the idea. Also, I had not known this before, but Daly's father had been a fighter in his youth, and Daly had grown up around boxing. He had a good and close feel for it.

"Daly said, 'Take off your coat. Have tea. I'll call my partners in the United States.' He left the room, made some phone calls, and came back into the room and said, 'Okay. Let's work out the deal. Have you got the contracts?'

"Daly asked if he could copy the contracts. I told him he could see them, but 'you can only copy them if you give me a "hold harmless" letter that you will not reveal the terms of Foreman's contract, or the fact that we have a contract with Foreman, until he has completed his divorce proceedings.' "

For the next twelve hours a group of lawyers worked to draw up contracts that contained the basic structure of the deal. Because of a power shortage in London's business district, they worked by gaslight.

There were three entities to this original deal. One was a company chartered in Panama called Telemedia de Panama. This was Schwartz and a man named Alex Valdes, and the purpose of this company was to negotiate film rights and closed-circuit deals for the fight. The second party to the deal was Video Techniques. The third party was Hemdale Leisure Corporation. Hemdale immediately transferred $200,000 to each fighter from its American accounts.

The first deadline had been met. Schwartz flew back to New York.

A week later the deal almost fell apart.

Schwartz met with Daly's partners, who turned out to be the heads of the three biggest theater distribution chains.

According to Schwartz, "Their objective was to take over the promotion completely and to receive a larger percentage of the income derived from it because, in their mind, they were providing the money, and the closed-circuit venues. The negotiations broke down. I left the meeting upset that Daly's cash advances were exposed because I refused to sign a different contract than what we had agreed to in London."

At this point an international fixer named Fred Weymer entered the picture.

Weymer was an odious character, a vodka drunk, a former participant in the Nazi Bund in America who was banned from entering this country, a former investor with Bernie Cornfeld who was implicated in Cornfeld's financial scandals.

He was also the agent of Joseph Mobutu, the corrupt and homicidal dictator of Zaire. He managed Mobutu's Swiss bank accounts, which were numerous and ample.

He had the perfect credentials for boxing as it entered its internationalist age.

Weymer had been calling Schwartz for a few weeks. He had a proposition. His principal—Mobutu—wanted to stage an international extravaganza, like a heavyweight championship fight, to place Zaire on the map, to give him a status advantage over his rival, Idi Amin, in the imaginary contest for leader of the African continent. Zaire, with 70 percent of the world's diamonds and bauxite, wanted prestige and trade, not tourism.

Because Weymer was banned from the United States, a meeting was arranged in Paris. The agenda would be the impoverished and backward country of Zaire putting up $9.6 million to finance the Ali-Foreman fight. The attendees would be Schwartz, King, Weymer, Daly, and another memorable character named Modunga Bula, Mobutu's other "financial adviser," who lived in Brussels and could return to Zaire only by special permission of Mobutu.

It seemed Bula had been an ally of Patrice Lumumba, the original revolutionary leader of Zaire when it was the Belgian Congo, whom Mobutu had murdered, perhaps in complicity with the CIA. Bula was a possible rival to the paranoid Mobutu. But Bula also had a gift for moving and finding money. Mobutu was so concerned about plots against him that he compelled his whole cabinet to fly with him whenever he left the country. So he kept Bula permanently stationed in Belgium as a precaution.

Bula was accompanied to the meeting by attorney Raymond Nicolet, who had an office in Geneva and represented a secrecy-shrouded Swiss corporate entity named Risnelia Investment, Inc.

Risnelia, chartered in Panama, was a shell company that was sold three times in five years and then purchased by Mobutu. Risnelia was a front for Mobutu's offshore and Swiss "investments." It existed only as a folder in the office of Raymond Nicolet. It was not listed in the Geneva phone book. It had no employees. It was a conduit, a wash, for a dictator who commingled his dwindling national treasury and expanding personal fortune.

For several days this movie-set mélange of international financial fixers, merchants of menace, and dropouts from respectable society negotiated in Paris in search of honor among thieves.

Occasionally tossed into the middle of this volatile mix was the Paris branch manager of Barclay's Bank, who was a pathological racist, deeply uncomfortable having to deal with King and Bula as equals. At one point Bula actually knocked the obnoxious bank manager down during a meeting.

The negotiations produced an understanding that the fight would be staged in Kinshasa, Zaire, and that Risnelia (really Zaire and Mobutu) would provide two letters of credit, each for $4.8 million, one to Foreman, one to Ali.

Schwartz and King were told they could pick up the letters of credit at the main branch of Barclay's Bank, carry them back to the United States, and have them confirmed by a Barclay's branch in America, so that the funds would not be paid in Paris or Zaire for tax purposes.

This is how Schwartz recalls the final stage of the deal: "Each day Don and I would go down to Barclay's branch in Paris and find out that the letter of credit was still not there. The letter of credit was being sent from the Barclay's bank in Kinshasa under the guarantee of Mobutu himself and the government of Zaire. The letter of credit did not show up for two days because the manager of the Barclay's bank in Zaire was away for an extended weekend with his girlfriend. So Mobutu ordered the troops to Zaire to find and arrest the bank manager and separate him from his girlfriend and throw him in jail.

"So the president of the Barclay's banking system had to fly to Zaire to both get his branch manager out of jail and issue the two letters of credit, under the threat the government of Zaire would expel the Barclay's bank from the country.

"While this was going on, the white supremacist bank manager in Paris told Bula, and I quote, 'I don't have to take this rubbish in my country.' This is the same branch manager who had been kicked out of Zaire for mistreating his black employees.

"Bula went off the wall, reached across the desk, in Paris, in the Barclay's bank, and coldcocked the manager of the bank.

"Don King and I were absolutely astounded. The two of us had to jump onto Bula and the manager to stop them from killing each other over the fact the bank had not yet furnished the letter of credit.

"The next day the letter of credit arrived, and Don and I jumped on a plane. We got it confirmed and sent them off to the fighters, in time, thereby perfecting our fight contracts with Foreman and Ali."

According to the deal worked out in Paris, the profits from the fight would be divided several ways. Risnelia, having put up $9.6 million, would get the largest share of the "gross proceeds"—42 percent. Hemdale would get 28 percent on its early investment of $1.5 million. Most of the remainder would go to Telemedia de Panama, with Video Techniques receiving a fee for its technical services—cameras, satellite dish, computers, technology.

And what about Don King, whose labors produced the two fighters, without whom nothing would be possible? King was guaranteed 4.33 percent, which he immediately took in the form of Video Techniques stock and membership on its board.

Don King's name never appeared in the complex and volumi-
nous contracts for the Ali-Foreman match. You will see Risnelia,
Telemedia, Hemdale, Barclay's Bank, Video Techniques—even
the George Foreman Development Corporation and the Central
Bank of Oakland as Foreman's escrow agent. But not Don King,
although this fight would become his masterpiece, the showcase
of his vast talent to sell and promote when it was still pure and
inspired.

Being only an employee did not prevent King from dominating
the promotion from the moment it was formally announced,
through all the prefight publicity, through the weeks in Zaire leading up to the fight.

The fight was officially announced in Caracas, Venezuela, the
day after Foreman knocked out Ken Norton in the second round.

King, wearing a gold and white suit, walked into a conference
room where a press conference was about to start. Somebody
handed him a copy of the press release. As he read it, a shadow
of anger cross his expressive face. He crumbled the press release
into a ball, hurled it across the room, and stalked out.

Don King felt disrespected. The press release said what was
technically half true. The fight was being promoted by Hemdale
and Video Techniques. Risnelia was kept out of it. The fifteenth
line mentioned "in association with Don King Productions."

King screamed in his boom-box voice at Schwartz. Schwartz
felt contrite, and placated King by telling a group of reporters,
"Don King is mainly responsible for this fight. With the diverse
personalities of Foreman and Ali, he was the only one in the
world capable of bringing them together. He's a welcome addition
to our company."

Schwartz then added, with prophetic accuracy, "King will
probably have me riding in the back of the bus in a couple of
months."

CHAPTER 4

Survival

and Betrayal

in Africa

The Muhammad Ali–George Foreman fight in Zaire would be the turning point in Don King's life, his purest accomplishment and finest hour. He made the fight and he saved the fight.

This event would also firmly establish Survival and Betrayal as the recurring themes of King's career.

Over the seven months of prefight hype, King slowly emerged as the dominant public figure among the consortium of promoters, even though his signature was not on the contracts, and he was the most junior partner.

The magnetic force of his personality, his endless energy, and the unpredictable flow of events would propel King to the head of the table. The fight would also enable him to fashion the personal and business relationship with Ali necessary to displace all other rival promoters, including his patron, Hank Schwartz. When the fight was delayed for five weeks, King remained in Africa with the fighters while Schwartz spent most of that period in New York.

But at the birth of the promotion, in March and April, Schwartz, and his late partner Barry Burnstein, were running the show. They had the electronics expertise and international experience.

Schwartz flew into Kinshasa, Zaire, in March and walked into the first of many crises that would explode before the fight could take place. Zaire was mired in Third World poverty and had none of the facilities and infrastructure needed to accommodate the fight, the satellite technology, or the influx of two thousand media personnel.

"The country looked like a shithole," Schwartz recalls.

The first inadequacy Schwartz noticed was that the route to the May 20th Stadium was a dirt road. There was thick underbrush growing outside the 70,000-seat outdoor soccer stadium. There was no parking lot. The stadium seats were cracking and crumbling. There was human feces on the floor where the local athletes changed their clothes.

"The first time I walked into the stadium," Schwartz says, "I felt like I had made a terrible mistake. I went into a panic. It wasn't usable. There wasn't even a roof over the ring."

Schwartz, the MIT graduate and electronics whiz, also realized "there was no microwave interconnection to the satellite earth station.

"I got physically sick when I saw the conditions," Schwartz recalls. "I actually told the government people in Zaire that the fight could not possibly be staged in this stadium, that we couldn't go ahead with the contract.

"But their reaction was I couldn't even think such a thing. The government people just said to tell them whatever I wanted built or fixed, and they would do it in time for the fight, with money from the national treasury."

Zaire's monstrous dictator, Joseph Mobutu, promised Schwartz that the stadium would be the equal of the best in the world, whatever it took, whatever it cost. With Schwartz shuttling between New York and Kinshasa, Mobutu ordered his people to work around the clock to provide whatever modern necessities Schwartz specified.

The government built a new runway at the airport so jumbo jets could land. Lights were built on top of the stadium. An asphalt parking lot was constructed in the midst of the thick green foliage. A bar for the press was built out of one hundred different types of wood. Experts were imported from France to install one hundred simultaneous phone lines linking the stadium to the satellite station fifty miles away. The microwave system was refitted so the television signal could travel from the stadium to the uplink dish. A four-lane highway was built from the airport to the downtown hotels that would house the world's media. Mobutu also ordered the erection of huge billboards along the roadside to obscure the view of tin and straw shacks and squatter poverty.

One frequent sign Mobutu put up to conceal the squalid reality of his country read: BLACK POWER IS SOUGHT EVERYWHERE IN THE WORLD. BUT IT IS REALIZED HERE IN ZAIRE.

"It was an amazing transformation," Schwartz says. "Mobutu did everything he promised. He probably spent as much money on the modernization as he did for the fight itself. He converted a shithole into a first-class facility, a modern stadium that rivaled anything in a developed nation. And he did it in six months."

And it was all to impress tourists, journalists, and the two fighters; none of it benefited the nation's desperately poor and illiterate population.

This first stage, involving satellite technology and on-site construction, was Schwartz's main contribution. Once this stage was completed, Don King hijacked center stage, never relinquished it, and delivered a dominating virtuoso performance.

On September 10, the day Ali left for Africa, he held a press conference at the Waldorf Astoria Hotel, presided over by Don King. King announced there would be a three-day festival of black music in Kinshasa before "the greatest sporting event in the history of the world," and that James Brown, B. B. King, and Lloyd Price would be among the thirty performers. Then Ali took over, gave a twenty-minute stream-of-consciousness monologue, took off his jacket, and mimicked Foreman's rigid, robotic, roundhouse style.

"I'm going to dance all night," Ali said, as he danced and jabbed the air.

"I'm so fast I can turn out the light switch and jump into bed before it gets dark," he laughed. Then he challenged the room full of boxing reporters to make a public prediction right in front of him.

Ali, the 3-to-1 underdog in the early betting, asked, "How many fellows here picks George? Be men, tell the truth."

Foreman, remember, had just knocked out Joe Frazier and Ken Norton, and they had both defeated Ali, who was thirty-two. At that moment in time, Foreman looked like an unbeatable beast.

Most of the reporters raised their hands, indicating they were picking Foreman to win. Behind Ali, out of his view, King also raised his hand for Foreman, a prophecy recorded by the camera of Leon Gast, who was making a documentary film on the fight.

A few minutes later Ali turned to King and said, "I know you got him picked. I know George is your man. I saw you on TV predicting me to go down. I'm gonna show *you* how great I am."

At the close of the press conference, almost as an afterthought as the reporters were standing up, King said, "I want to introduce Hank Schwartz, who is doing the ancillary rights around the world, a dynamic young man."

Once the fighters settled into their camps in Zaire, King became the center of the promotion, and he never stopped promoting himself. He dealt with the government, the police, the army, the press, the hotels, the airlines, the musical performers, and the fighters. Especially George Foreman, who was sullen and petulant and constantly threatening to pull out of the fight if his changing demands for preference and attention were not met.

Foreman, for example, had demanded a first-class airplane ticket for his pet dog on his flights from San Francisco to Paris to Kinshasa. The president of American Airlines had to intercede personally before Foreman's dog was issued a first-class ticket in its own name.

As the fight got closer—especially after a five-week delay caused by a cut to Foreman's eyebrow—King had to spend hours cajoling, coddling, and confronting the champion, whose personality was very different from his present public image of a good-natured, self-deprecatory cheeseburger addict.

By this time King was rushing around Kinshasa, putting out fires and soothing egos, wearing colorful dashikis; his hair already had the modified, semi-electric standup look. King had short hair when he got out of prison and normal hair in early 1974.

Lloyd Price was present in Zaire, and present at the creation of King's hairstyle, an event Price places as sometime during mid-1974, probably while the two men were at Century Plaza in Los Angeles, working on the promotion.

"Don and I were talking one day," Price remembers, "and I was telling him he needed a distinctive look if he was going to become a star. He needed an image, a look, like Daddy Grace or Reverend Ike, who was his hero in those days. I told him all stars have some unique gimmick that fans can recognize them by—a hat, a uniform, a way of dressing.

"As I was saying that, Don was absentmindedly pulling on his hair, which was his habit when he was thinking. I stopped and said, 'That's it! That's the look right there!'

"So he started combing his hair straight up and it did look distinctive. I told Don he should have a crown to go with the name King, and his straight-up hair looked like his crown."

The look, which would become more extreme a few years later, was born out of this marketing and public-relations lecture by the singer who sold 42 million records. King, of course, would mythologize the hair gimmick whenever he was asked about it in later years. In his 1988 *Playboy* interview, King explained his trademark look this way:

"It's really an aura from God. Until ten years ago my hair was kinky and nappy and curly, like any other black's. But then one night, I went to bed with my wife, Henrietta, and she shook me because my head was rumbling and moving, and my hair was just popping up—*ping, ping, ping*. Each hair. All of them curls were straightening out and going up."

"Sounds strange to us," volunteered *Playboy*'s interviewer, Lawrence Linderman.

King responded, "It does sound a little unbelievable, but it happened. My hair is *au naturel*. I don't use any type of chemicals or mousse on it. It just grows straight up. No matter if it's when I go to bed, or get up in the morning, I can go straight to the mirror and my hair is in a pyramid, like there's 360 degrees of light."

Journalist Dick Schaap once quipped, "Don King's body did four years in prison, but his hair got the chair."

Boxing is the one sport where even the deepest expert can't always tell what is going on, who is winning a fight in progress, or who prepared best for the match. No one can really see from outside the ring how much a punch has hurt; no one can really tell how fatigued a fighter is; no one can know how much will to win a fighter has left.

In baseball, football, basketball, and hockey, the score is posted and always known to the crowd. In boxing, the running score is kept secret until it is announced. Boxing always has that element of surprise and drama. And that was never more true than in Zaire.

Boxing is based on deceit. Fighters are taught to lie—to conceal fatigue, mask pain, disguise intent with a feint, deny an injury, look one way and punch to another spot.

Most of those who watched Ali train at Deer Lake before he departed for Africa thought he had no chance to win. He was getting beaten up in the gym by a young lion named Larry Holmes and an old warhorse named Roy Williams. Ali seemed lethargic, passive, unmotivated, without offense.

No expert could tell this was by design. Ali had a plan forming in his mind. He was holding back, letting his sparring partners hit him. Holmes was not the better fighter: Ali wanted to practice how to endure punishment. He used the gym to make friends with pain.

Ali had self-knowledge. He knew he could not dance for fifteen rounds at his age, although he wanted Foreman to think he was going to dance. He let Holmes and Williams hit him every day to build up his body's resistance to pain, to let punches strike his liver, spleen, kidney, neck, lungs, heart.

Ali also believed he could hit and hurt Foreman, that Foreman lacked stamina, flexibility, balance, and defense. When he tired, his punches became looping. He believed if he found exactly the right distance to stand from Foreman, he could knock him out. After he took the pummeling in the gym, he watched tapes of Foreman in his cabin.

But the visitors saw only the pummeling, could not know what strategy was forming in Ali's protean mind. All they heard was Ali promise to dance all night. Ali was a great liar.

Ali's loyal friend and camp facilitator, Gene Kilroy, was with Ali as he packed his gear and prepared to leave Deer Lake for the Waldorf press conference and the flight to Africa. Kilroy says the last thing Ali did before closing the door to his cabin was to call boxing's self-exiled philosopher, Cus D'Amato, in Catskill, New York, and ask him what tactical plan he should employ to fight Foreman.

D'Amato told Ali, "I have only one piece of advice for you. You must hurt Foreman with your first punch. Foreman has the psychology of a bully. If you hurt him early, it will destroy his mind. Whatever you do, have bad intentions behind your first punch."

D'Amato then repeated his fistic Freudianism to Kilroy. But like everyone else in Ali's camp, Kilroy had a contrary opinion. They all thought Ali should jab, dance, and move for a few rounds, and not get too close to Foreman.

But Ali viewed Cus as a wise old owl, and the owl's advice coincided with what Ali was thinking, based on his studies of Foreman's tapes, and his self-knowledge of his own body, including his faith in his own punching power, which most experts derided as ordinary.

Ali believed that despite Foreman's unbeaten record, and his easy conquest of the two men who had beaten Ali, Foreman was not as mentally tough as he was. Some fighters have glass jaws; Ali's hypothesis was that Foreman had a glass mind.

At Deer Lake, in a moment of serenity, Ali predicted to Norman Mailer: "The fight will be easy. This man does not want to take a head whipping like Frazier just to beat you. He's not as tough as Frazier. He's soft and spoiled."

Part of what made Ali the champion of champions was his intelligence, his middle-classness.

The romantic conceit is that great fighters have to grow up in poverty, filled with anger from slum deprivation. This theory fits Dempsey, Liston, Duran, Tyson, and Graziano. The theory says that the memory of growing up hungry with no options gives a boxer the so-called "killer instinct," the unquenchable "will to win."

But the two great modern boxers—Ali and Sugar Ray Leonard—are both high school graduates who grew up in the suburbs, not the ghetto. They had education, travel, and middle-class values before they were eighteen.

Ali and Leonard were smart fighters, with psychological levels to their intelligence. They also both had fortunate faces that motivated them to become skilled at defense, so as not to have those pretty faces marked and disfigured.

One of the biggest factors—invisible to outsiders—working in Ali's favor in Zaire was the quality of his imagination.

Another invisible aspect to the fight was that Ali gained a spiritual lift just from being on the African continent, while Foreman never felt at home. Ali kept telling reporters, "This is my country. George is a stranger, an invader."

Ali loved hanging out with the musicians who came to perform, especially James Brown and Lloyd Price. Ali was mobbed by the local population, even in areas that had no television. Somehow his face was known. Ali relished the blackness of the country. He was nourished by the environment of Africa in an almost mystical way, partly because of his active historical imagination.

In contrast, Foreman avoided interviews, ducked press conferences, and sensed the country was rooting for Ali. He slipped into a surly seclusion with his sparring partners and his dog. Feeling isolated, in a hostile atmosphere, did not improve the champion's mental state.

Perhaps the deepest root of Ali's genius was that he was able to absorb energy and inspiration from external forces. He drew strength from being black, from being a Muslim, from Allah, from being a rebel who opposed the Vietnam War, from being loved by the poorest of the poor, from visiting children in hospitals, from seeing himself as a leader of his people, from believing he was a vessel of a grander destiny.

In the most desperate moments of his career—blinded by an ointment burning his eyes against Liston, feeling unable to continue against Frazier in Manila—Ali would summon something extra from some secret gas tank of spiritual fuel. He drew motivation from sources much deeper than sport.

Just before the fight in Zaire, Ali delivered a stunning speech for Leon Gast's camera and for posterity. The film has never been released, but this was Ali essence on the eve of battle:

"I'm fighting for God and my people. I'm not fighting for fame or money. I'm not fighting for me. I'm fighting for the black people on welfare, the black people who have no future, black people who are wineheads and dope addicts. I am a politician for Allah.

I wish Lumumba was here to see me. I want to win so I can lead my people."

On September 15, ten days before the fight, Foreman was sparring with Bill McMurray, a thirty-three-year-old journeyman who had lost almost half his seventy-five fights. McMurray raised his elbow to protect his face and George Foreman's right eyebrow accidentally collided with the bone of the elbow. A gash over the eye immediately began to drip blood and Foreman grabbed a towel, pressing it against the slice on his skin.

This freak accident caused the fight to be postponed, creating five days of uncertainty and intrigue.

Since Hank Schwartz was in New York at the hour of the cut, Don King in Kinshasa was thrust into the first series of bilingual meetings to decide what to do, what to tell reporters, when to reschedule, how to keep the army and police relaxed. King was masterful in this crisis, a fact not lost on Ali and Herbert Muhammad, his manager.

Foreman, the most paranoid of fighters, wanted out of the country he never felt comfortable in, a country where he kept thinking his water or food would be poisoned or drugged. He wanted the fight shifted back to the United States. When Mobutu was told this, he had his soldiers pick up Foreman's passport. The champion became a prisoner in Zaire, a condition that further preyed on his mind and mood.

For the first few hours Ali, too, said he wanted to switch the fight to the Los Angeles Coliseum or the Houston Astrodome, but he quickly realized staying in Zaire would place more psychological stress on Foreman, and he could wait five more weeks for the American pleasures of ice cream and miniskirts.

Hank Schwartz flew into Kinshasa the day after the cut and met with King and Mobutu to consider the options. At first Schwartz proposed switching the fight to America, where the live gate would be much bigger and the rainy season of torrential

waterfalls would not be a factor. The rainy season was due any-
time after October 21, and any new date in Zaire would be a risk.
Mobutu, having spent $20 million, said this was out of the ques-
tion. Next, Schwartz proposed moving the fight to a three-
thousand-seat indoor arena, but Mobutu ruled this out, too. The
dictator's only concession was a promise to build a much larger
roof over the ring to keep the television equipment and ringside
seats dry and covered during the fight.

Reluctantly, Schwartz agreed to October 30 as the new date,
in Zaire, placing the promotion right on the inside cusp of the
rainy season, which always arrived with thunder and a tropical
typhoon.

Would the African gods defer to Allah's fighter?

After days of rumors, and Foreman's being noncommunicative,
Don King and Bula, the money man for Mobutu, announced the
new date would be October 30, at 4:00 A.M. Zaire time, which
was October 29, 10:00 P.M. New York time. It was the earliest
possible compromise between the healing of Foreman's skin and
God's calendar of rain.

But at a confusing press conference an hour later, Foreman and
Dick Sadler refused to confirm what King had just announced as
official and definite. Foreman told a reporter, who pressed him
on the new date, to "shut up." Foreman and Sadler told the media
of the world they just weren't sure the eyebrow would be all
healed by October 30. They were actually still maneuvering to
get the fight out of the country, or get out of the fight.

But King backed Foreman down with one of his steamroller
filibusters in his hotel suite. And a few hours later, a contrite
heavyweight champion sat in King's suite and told the press he
had just been "kidding," and yes, the fight was definitely on for
October 30, and he was sorry for any misunderstanding.

Hank Schwartz, who still admires King to this day, gives King
all the credit for salvaging the fight. He says: "There is no doubt
that Don saved the fight. He held the deal together. He knew how

to talk to Foreman. He stopped Foreman from bolting. He was magnificent."

But Hank Schwartz spent most of the five-week delay in New York, dealing with exhibitors, arenas, foreign rights, television executives, and technology experts. This left King alone with the two fighters and gave King the time to work on the fighters, cement bonds of black unity, share his future dreams with them, promise them how much more money they could make with him as their promoter, how they owed it to history to give a black brother a chance. King understood that whoever controlled the heavyweight champion was on his way to controlling the business of boxing.

Don King, who over the next twenty years would outnegotiate Donald Trump, Ferdinand Marcos, Roone Arledge, HBO, Showtime, Caesars Palace, and Steve Wynn, had no trouble at all outmaneuvering an absent Hank Schwartz. He soon had both Foreman and Ali saying they would be doing their next match for Don King Productions, not Video Techniques, even before they stepped into the ring in Kinshasa.

A jailhouse Barnum, a vulgar Machiavelli, Don King was already five moves ahead of everyone else.

In the spring of 1974 King and Lloyd Price shared an office in Manhattan and saw each other every day as they planned the three-day music festival that would precede the big fight.

King liked music; he had top musicians like Jonah Jones play in his New Corner Tavern, and he had the best singers perform on his Forest City benefit card. It was logical for him to add such an event to the Rumble in the Jungle, a name for the fight that Ali coined and King adopted and popularized. King, as a promoter, learned a lot about his art by being around Ali in the prime of his verbal wit. And Ali says he learned his self-promotion style by watching the wrestler Gorgeous George.

In the course of planning the music festival, King and Price also talked a lot about other future projects, and developed a general plan to form an umbrella corporation that would produce records and films and use Ali's association to attract other black stars to the venture.

Since King and Price had pledged lifetime loyalty to each other in the emotion of King's first day of freedom, Price never considered bringing in a lawyer and putting anything down in contract form. He loved King the way Don Elbaum had at the beginning, and felt friendship was the real bond, not a piece of paper.

Price trusted King so completely that he put his own career on hold for a year. At that point Price was doing concerts and clubs about three nights a week, grossing about $200,000 a year in bookings. He decided to devote all his time to helping his compadre with the fight and taking the main responsibility for the concert, from booking the talent, to performing himself, to making travel arrangements, to building the stage, to setting up the sound system.

A corporation was formed called Festival in Zaire (FIZ). It had three partners—Price was the president, and King and Hank Schwartz each had a one-third interest.

Price's friend, the South African jazz musician Hugh Masekela, helped convince the government of Liberia to fund another entity called International Films and Records (IFR) that signed a contract with filmmaker Leon Gast to make a documentary about the festival with exclusive access. IFR was registered in the Bahamas.

The money for IFR came from a company called Mesarado Mining, which was really a front for the government of Liberia, just as Risnelia was a front for the government of Zaire, and the funder of the fight itself. Masekela, who then was living in Liberia, knew the nation's ruling family, especially the minister of finance, Steve Tolbert. Tolbert's brother, William, was the president of the country. (Steve Tolbert would die in a plane crash in 1979, and his brother would be executed in a bloody coup in 1980.)

Once the minister of finance got involved, he assigned a mysterious British accountant named Keith Bradshaw to monitor his nation's investment in the festival, which was about $2.6 million. Bradshaw was listed as the president of IFR and seemed to pop up everywhere in Zaire in the months before the fight.

And all of this money flow had to be kept secret from Zaire's Mobutu, who was underwriting the fight but was insanely competitive with the Tolberts, who managed their neighboring nation in an equally corrupt fashion.

At the same time, a letter of credit was negotiated with the Chemical Bank in New York, so that Price would get paid $250,000 when the concert took place. This money was supposed to come from the Liberian government, funneled through Mesarado.

Price spent the summer months traveling across the country trying to get black superstars to commit to performing at the festival, scheduled for September 21, 22, and 23, on the eve of the fight in the May 20th Stadium. He quickly lined up James Brown, B. B. King, Etta James, Bill Withers, and the Spinners. Masekela lined up his ex-wife, Miriam Makeba, the Pointer Sisters, and several Latin salsa bands. It was going to be a "black Woodstock," three days of soul music and good vibrations to celebrate two black men fighting for the championship for the first time in history on African land.

All the performers signed contracts with FIZ, and the company's assets became the performing rights to the artists and the exclusive rights to the film footage of the festival.

According to the Reverend Al Sharpton, who was present for some of the meetings as a buddy of James Brown, "Don King talked so fast that James told him, 'You must be with the Mafia.' Then James demanded King get him $100,000 in cash before he got on the plane for Kinshasa. This was after all the banks had closed on a Friday afternoon. When Don came back with the $100,000 in cash after two hours, James said, 'Now I know for sure you're in the Mafia.'

"James also told Stevie Wonder not to trust King. He told Stevie (who is blind and has a fear of flying) that Don would take him up in a plane, fly him to Hollywood, drop him in a hut on a movie set, and tell him he was in Africa."

All through 1974, Lloyd Price was only reimbursed for expenses by Bradshaw; he assumed the letter of credit would be cashed and he would be fully compensated after the fight.

"I first realized there might be a problem between me and Don," Price says, "during a meeting in Zaire that was between me, Don, Steve Tolbert, and Keith Bradshaw. The meeting was a day or two after Foreman's eye was cut.

"We were having a big problem that no tickets were being sold to the concerts. I mean none. Tolbert and Bradshaw couldn't see how they were going to get back any of their $2.6 million without any live gate. And they had expected to gross about $1.5 million over the three nights.

"King and Bradshaw weren't getting along at all. They were fighting about everything and calling each other names right in the meeting. So the minister of finance, trying to find a way to keep working together until the concerts, asked me if I could work cooperatively with Bradshaw. I said yes, I could get along with Keith Bradshaw for the sake of saving the project.

"But Don King was insulted by my answer. He jumped up and shouted, 'Are you going to betray me right here in the middle of this meeting? Then you can go work with this motherfucker yourself.'

"And Don just walked out of the meeting and pouted for a few days. I thought I was just giving an honest answer to a pragmatic question from the minister of finance, but Don took it in a personal way.

"We remained friends after the meeting, but from that day on, our relationship never had the same warmth and love."

The festival occurred on the scheduled dates, even though the fight had been postponed. The stadium was almost empty the first night, mostly because the tickets had been overpriced for a poor country, and most of the affluent Westerners had left when the fight was delayed. On the last night the government gave away all the tickets and the stadium was filled with freeloaders dancing in the aisles.

The music the last night was sensational, as recorded by Leon Gast's camera crews. James Brown outdid himself; the Pointers were in peak form; and Price did a set of six songs, including "Stagger Lee," which had Ali on his feet cheering for his friend and one of his favorite songs. Foreman did not attend.

Only after the concert was finished did Lloyd Price discover there was a loophole in the letter of credit and he would not get paid. The letter of credit was drafted in such a way that lawyers said it wasn't valid if the fight was not held on the original date. It was the completion of the fight on September 25 that triggered the release of the $250,000 to FIZ.

All the stars he had recruited got paid in advance, but Price did not get paid. He was never paid. All the documentary footage shot by Gast and his crew of forty-seven people got tied up in litigation for years (and has never been released).

David Sonnenberg, Gast's attorney, says, "Leon and Lloyd Price got one of the worst screwings I ever saw."

"I just got screwed," Price says without bitterness twenty years later. "I would say that Don King screwed me indirectly rather than directly. He just never lifted a finger to help me get paid. He never spoke to the minister of finance of Liberia to pay me, after the bank reneged.

"Don made money on the fight," Price says. "I had helped him get Ali to do the fight. I had introduced him to Muhammad. Don made four percent of the profits. He told me we were partners for life. But he never offered me a dollar of his share after I got screwed. . . .

"In retrospect, I must have been naive. I think Don resented all the times that people came up to us in hotels, in airports, at fights, in restaurants, and asked me for my autograph and not his. In those days I was more famous than he was. But I always told the person to get Don's signature, too, because he was going to be famous.

"I still like Don in a way. But he has screwed everybody who ever loved him."

Don King also used the five-week delay to display his showmanship for the world's press corps, waiting in Kinshasa as a captive audience with idle time.

This revolving group not only included the premiere American sports columnists like Jim Murray, Dave Anderson, Jerry Izenberg, Larry Merchant, and Dick Young. It also included writers bigger than boxing, literary heavyweights like Norman Mailer, Budd Schulberg (who wrote the film *On the Waterfront* and the classic boxing novel *The Harder They Fall*), the aristocratic George Plimpton, and the gonzo Hunter Thompson, who added to his legend by missing the fight.

King tried to flatter and impress all of them. When he first encountered Mailer, King greeted him with: "You are a genius in tune with the higher consciousness, yet an instinctive exponent of the untiring search for aspiration in the warm earth embracing potential of exploited peoples."

Mailer quoted this avalanche of words in his book *The Fight*, which is a small overlooked gem. After quoting King's mouthful, Mailer observed, "King was letting you in on King's view of himself—a genius in tune with the higher consciousness . . . it would be hard to prove King was not a genius."

Mailer's description of King in Kinshasa began: "A hustler of dimensions is a financier. How King could talk. . . . He was kuntu in full dialogue, and no verbal situation could be foreign to him."

In one of his intoxications of rhetoric, King even informed the novelist with a bent toward the existential, "Ali even motivates the dead." King then began to talk to Mailer about his years in prison.

"I had to learn how to meditate in a room full of violent men,"

King said. "It was sheer hell to go to the hole. You could wake up in the middle of the night and have to take a leak. What a sight in the urinals. Prisoners sucking guards. . . . Guards going down on prisoners. One man taking another's ass. Hell, man, you got to get your head in order."

As this rap subsided, Mailer heard Hunter Thompson whisper, "Bad Genet." King continued to perform for Mailer.

"I read Karl Marx, a cold motherfucker," he said. "I learned a lot from him. Hitler and Marx—I think of them in relation to some of the things they're doing here, you know, the country is the family, concentrate on the young."

At the next table Mailer overheard Thompson refine his opinion to "*Very* bad Genet."

King also told the writer with an interest in manhood and violence another anecdote from his past. Mailer described it this way: "Once when one of his lesser known fighters hinted that a contract was unsatisfactory, and King could get hurt, Don leaned forward—fond was he of telling this story—and said, 'Let's not bullshit each other. You can leave here, make a call, and have me killed in a half hour. I can pick up the phone as you leave and have you offed in five minutes.' That was expression appropriate to the point."

At a lavish cocktail party, George Plimpton, who was covering the fight for *Sports Illustrated,* had an exchange with King that was captured by one of Leon Gast's camera crews. Plimpton seemed to surprise King by asking why he didn't donate a small portion of the profits from the fight to assist poor black people in the United States.

King replied, "I need white counterparts to do this here. I have to put money in the sun, so it can germinate, blossom, and grow."

Plimpton looked perplexed by the words without meaning, and King changed the subject away from social responsibility.

*   *   *

The outdoor weigh-in for the fight was a Mobutu–Don King extravaganza that became a parody of Western decadence coming to enlighten Africa. The event became an absurdist ritual, staged for American television at midnight in the outdoor stadium, with twenty thousand Africans who had never seen a weigh-in before let in for free.

First Foreman ran out onto the stadium floor like an African imposter in a tribal robe. He was waving to the crowd, which was chanting, "*Ali, bomaye,*" which meant Ali should kill Foreman.

Ali then came out leading a parade of about five hundred supporters, who all seemed to be fighting to be the seventh in line, behind his brother Rachman, Bundini (Drew Brown), Angelo Dundee, Gene Kilroy, Walter Youngblood, and Ferdie Pacheco. There was pushing and scuffles as the column snaked toward the scales and television cameras, looking like a moving mosh pit.

Foreman had his beloved dog with him, and while the champion was slipping out of his tribal robe, preparing to step on the scale, some prankster in Ali's faction tried to steal the dog. This made Foreman go berserk.

The undefeated champion of the world was screaming like a little child, "Where's my dog? Where's my dog?"

King was also in an African robe (the money men like Bradshaw and Bula were wearing Western suits), and he seemed immune to the absurdity of the scene around him. King was just smiling for the cameras, making sure the ABC-TV crew would get its interview because the interviews would help sell tickets to the hundreds of closed-circuit locations in the United States.

The whole event became even more absurd when the television feed from the satellite went dead for a few minutes, delaying everything in the stadium, while Howard Cosell filled time on live television.

When the satellite feed was restored, Ali told the American

audience, "Don King is the world's greatest promoter, and if it wasn't for him we wouldn't be fighting here in Africa." The challenger also apologized for what sounded like a bad sore throat, explaining, "I've been debatin' all day."

Before he gave this interview, Ali had gone into the ring and carefully measured it, counting off the steps between the ropes, to get the sense of distance imprinted on his mind. Boxing is geometry. Everything depends on distances and angles. And Ali, the Einstein of the Sweet Science, wanted to know exactly how many steps he and Foreman had to take to reach the ropes.

For months Ali had set the trap, telling every reporter he was going to dance all night. That was his feint. By now Ali knew he would have to hurt Foreman in the first round, and that the question was what distance from Foreman to position himself, to be close enough to strike a damaging punch. His "dance, dance, dance" mantra was a ploy to mislead the robotic Foreman.

When it was Foreman's turn to be interviewed on American television, with King hovering next to him, the champion lied like a politician.

"I love Zaire," he said. "It's the cradle of democracy. I'm enjoying this country."

The fight itself was an epic, a miracle, a revolution. It became one of those sporting events that grows bigger with the passage of time, like Joe DiMaggio's fifty-six-game hitting streak, or Ted Williams hitting .406 in 1941, or the Jets upset of the Colts in 1969.

It was a miracle because of the way Ali won, and because nobody expected him to prevail. It was a revolution because it made Don King the king of boxing.

Dr. Ferdie Pacheco, Ali's personal doctor who worked in his corner, didn't merely expect his own fighter to lose. He feared so strongly for Ali's life that he had quietly made advance arrangements for a plane to be waiting to fly Ali to Lisbon, in case he needed brain surgery from Foreman's blows.

Gene Kilroy was in Foreman's dressing room before the fight to watch his hands get wrapped. He heard Foreman say, "I'm going to kill him," and his trainer, Archie Moore, say, "I feel death is in the air." Moore later disclosed that he said a silent prayer "that Ali not die in the fight."

There was a sense of dread in Ali's dressing room, although he was serene and playful. Sensing this defeatist mood at a moment when his ego should be getting maximum reinforcement, Ali told Norman Mailer, who was allowed into the room: "Nothing to be scared about. It's just another day in the dramatic life of Muhammad Ali. Just one more workout in the gym to me. I'm afraid of horror films and thunderstorms. Jet planes shake me up. But there is no need to be afraid of anything you can control with your skill."

Then Ali retreated into the bathroom to pray to Allah with Herbert Muhammad.

The final thing Ali did before departing for his destiny was to play one last mind game with Doc Broadus, Foreman's observer in his dressing room.

"We're going to dance," Ali said. "You tell him to get ready." Then he added, "Tell him to hit me in the belly," an Ali attempt to double-think or triple-think Foreman, who might do the opposite, or might not, but would think about what the message meant.

Zaire's dictator, Mobutu, who had depleted his nation's treasury of $20 million to get the fight, didn't even come to the stadium to watch it. Although he ordered a forty-foot portrait of himself hung over the grandstand, Mobutu was so paranoid about being in the open air with seventy thousand of his countrymen that he watched the fight in his mansion, on closed circuit, with Idi Amin, the mad tyrant of Uganda, as his guest.

The fight would become known for Ali's use of the "rope-a-dope" defense, a tactic he later said he first learned from watching

Archie Moore, Foreman's trainer. But there was much more to the miracle of the African night than just Ali lying on the ropes. There was a greater psychological dimension to this fight than any other I have ever seen.

It began as the referee, Zack Clayton, gave the two fighters their final instructions in center ring. Ali, his mouth inches from Foreman's ear, talked over the referee's words. He told Foreman: "You have heard of me since you were young. You've been following me since you were a little boy. Now, you must meet me, your master."

At the opening bell, Ali followed the counsel of Cus D'Amato. He circled, he did not retreat. He stayed within Foreman's hitting range, his eyes searching for an opening.

One minute into the fight Ali hit Foreman with a fast, straight right to the head. The look in Foreman's eyes made Cus a prophet.

A minute later Ali hit the bully with a second right, straight as an arrow, to a head that did not move. It had bad intentions, and it had to make Foreman think, which was not healthy for Foreman.

In the second round Ali retreated to the ropes and Foreman started to bomb away, missing some but landing enough to make many fans think they were watching Ali in the process of losing.

Even Dundee, Bundini, and Pacheco in Ali's own corner did not immediately recognize they were seeing Ali winning, not losing.

"Dance, champ, dance," Bundini screamed in his hoarse, soulful, musical voice.

At the end of the round Dundee told Ali to get off the ropes, and Ali told him, "Shut up, I know what I'm doing."

An ingredient of Ali's genius was improvisation, his ability to invent tactics spontaneously, from his soul, like the best jazzmen. Ali was like Louis Armstrong, Charlie Parker, Miles Davis, and John Coltrane. He made daring, thinking, and surprise part of his art.

He alone could bend time to his imagination. He alone could sense during the fight what creativity was needed to defeat Foreman. Although he had trained to endure pain, his minute-to-minute, round-to-round movements were like a long jazz solo. They were composed by instinct, mood, spirit, and the rhythm inside his mind. Ali had had to improvise when to change the speed of his punches, when to lie on the ropes, when to go for the kill. Like a jazzman, the spontaneous performance was everything, with no margin for error.

Ali may have invented the modern tradition of trash-talking during this fight, thinking up new psychological jabs and taunts each round. Ali had to imagine a structure to the fight in his mind, a tempo, a harmony, a coda. Ali had to feel all this in the moment, in the ring.

Zaire would be Ali's Birdland, and this fight would have to be his existential solo.

In the third and fourth rounds Ali kept talking to Foreman, playing Ping-Pong with his mind, telling him his best punches were nothing. Couldn't he hit any harder than this? Why was he swinging like a girl?

Soon Foreman began to doubt his own power. Ali, who did feel severe pain, was conning the champion. His taunting disdain was breaking down Foreman's will.

This was the miracle—geometry was melting brute force; the human imagination was making power and confidence doubt itself; mind games were snapping a champion's mind. Ali's ability to survive pain was subverting Foreman's durability to deliver pain.

After a savage fifth round, in which both were hurt, Foreman fell apart. His punches became looping and slow-motion. Ali, the geometrist, stayed exactly the right distance and pumped in accurate rights between Foreman's gloves, puffing his face, glazing his eyes till he looked drunk. Ali's timing and mastery of distance made his punches seem guided by radar.

In the eighth round Ali hit Foreman with seven devastating

head punches in a row, and Foreman lost his equilibrium, spun around, and went down for the count. It was 4:00 A.M. in Africa, the hour of witch doctors and voodoo magic.

The rainy season finally arrived about an hour after the fight ended, with roaring thunder and blinding sheets of tropical rain. If it had come during the fight, with Ali's fear of thunder, who knows what might have happened?

The torrential rainstorm knocked out all the satellite communications between Kinshasa and the outside world. The city of joy was isolated. The rain stopped after an hour, and Ali arrived at his villa on the banks of the Congo River. Jerry Izenberg and a few writers were waiting there and glimpsed paradise in his eyes.

"You will never know what this night has meant to me," Ali told Izenberg.

Twenty years later I would ask Ali what the biggest thrill of his career had been.

"Zaire," he answered in his Parkinson's whisper, his hand trembling but his mind as sharp as ever. "Foreman. Got my title back. In *Africa*," he said.

The fight between Muhammad Ali and George Foreman will always endure as a boxing landmark. As Ali said, it would never have happened if it wasn't for Don King. King will always have this honor associated with his name.

The great tragedy is that if Don King had gone straight after this fight, he could have become one of the great black role models in contemporary history. He could have been the black Horatio Alger hero.

King could have become a universal inspiration, a black man given a second chance, who rose from prison to the pinnacle of entrepreneurship by hard work, desperado bravado, grand ambition, evangelical salesmanship, and by the mean standards of boxing—merit.

CHAPTER 5

"So he went to see some mob guys in Cleveland"

It was December 1974 and Muhammad Ali was starting to think about his first title defense. Don King was certainly in the picture, but he had to compete against Madison Square Garden, Bob Arum, and several countries that wanted the honor of hosting Ali's first fight after his Zaire triumph.

Don King, three years out of prison, was not an institution like the Garden. He was not a big corporation with a line of credit at a major bank, although he always could produce cash. King did not have resources, or partners, or an organization with assistants and specialists. All he had in this competition, as he would say many times, was "wit, grit, and bullshit."

Boxing is not just unregulated, it is unstructured. There are no leagues with schedules enforced by a commissioner. Boxing has always been closer to eighteenth-century piracy than to an organized sport. In football, the playing field is one hundred yards, but in boxing the size of the ring can be negotiated. In baseball, the

Los Angeles Dodgers have to play the San Francisco Giants. In basketball, the Bulls have to play the Knicks. In football, the Cowboys have to play the Redskins.

But in boxing no champion ever has to fight a particular contender unless an ad hoc deal is made. Every fight is a free-lance negotiation. There is no schedule that says Ali had to fight the Number 1 or 2 contender. He could fight whomever he and a promoter wanted.

Ali always remained a free agent. He never signed an exclusive long-term contract with any promoter. He never signed option contracts with any promoter. This is how Herbert Muhammad always got the best price for all of Ali's fights—each one was put up for bid to the highest bidder. And after the Foreman fight, Ali was at the peak of his marketability.

In December 1974 Herbert Muhammad began negotiating with Mike Burke, the president of Madison Square Garden, and matchmaker Teddy Brenner, for Ali to defend his title in the Garden against the Number 3 contender, Ron Lyle. Lyle had lost only one of thirty-two fights and was a heavy puncher.

The Garden had also brought into the deal John Daly of the British Hemdale Leisure Corporation as a partner. Daly had put up the front money for the Zaire match, and he had useful ties to the byzantine camp of the champion.

The negotiations between the Garden and Ali reached the stage where contracts were being drawn up and terms and conditions had been orally agreed to. News of the match began to appear in the New York and London papers.

That's when Don King, who never sleeps, began to pick Madison Square Garden's pocket. In a one-week period, King flew to London, Cleveland, Chicago, and Kingston, Jamaica.

Mostly King was searching for "OPM"—other people's money—to underwrite the Ali defense. The contender King had in mind was a thirty-five-year-old bouncer and liquor salesman named Chuck Wepner, who had lost nine fights and was not among the top seven legitimate contenders (Foreman, Frazier, Lyle, Jerry Quarry, Ken Norton, Oscar Bonavena, and Earnie Shavers). Wepner had already been knocked out by Joe Bugner and Jerry Judge, as well as Liston and Foreman. He was so famous for the scar tissue around his eyes, he was nicknamed The Bayonne Bleeder. He already had over three hundred stitches in his eyebrows.

In London, King tried to meet with John Daly, to win his former partner and his money over to his side. King believed he had an appointment and went to Daly's office and waited several hours. Daly finally stuck his head out and said he would see King at his hotel for cocktails at 7:00 P.M. Daly never showed and King left London in a fury over being snubbed.

"Daly treated me like scum," King told reporters in New York.

In Chicago, King made his appeal directly to Herbert Muhammad, once again quoting Herbert's father to him about the obligation to give the struggling brother an extra chance. Herbert, a religious and private person, was put off by King's loud style of heavy gold jewelry, hyperbole, and vulgarity, but he also respected King's understanding of economics and gifts as a salesman and deal-maker.

King also flew, with Ali, to Jamaica to try to persuade the government there to put up its own money to underwrite the fight.

Through all of this, Teddy Brenner, the Garden matchmaker, still believed he would get the Ali-Lyle fight for March 24. He had actually arranged a meeting for January 6, 1975, where all the contracts were supposed to be signed. But John Daly had to fly back to London with the unsigned contracts still in his briefcase. Herbert Muhammad had stood up Daly, just as Daly had stood up King.

The appeal of King's offer was that he was talking the most money for the least risk. He was offering Ali $1.5 million to fight someone who was not a competitive threat, a club fighter with little professional skill.

The mystery was that the fight at that price did not make any sense in the context of boxing economics. Ali should be getting only about $500,000 for meeting a challenger of Wepner's caliber. Only hard-core Ali fans would pay to see what amounted to a glorified gym workout. Why would anyone invest $1.5 million in a fight that seemed unlikely to gross $750,000? Where would King find a mark, or a sucker, or a friend, to underwrite his game?

Carl Lombardo agreed to put up the money for the fight.

Lombardo was a thirty-five-year-old Cleveland millionaire who owned the Lombardo Brothers Construction Company, a dog track in Daytona Beach, five auto raceways in Ohio, and a Thoroughbred racetrack near New Orleans. Others said he owned porno locations in Cleveland, but this was never proven. He told reporters, "I'm in the pari-mutuel industry. I expect to make a profit on the fight. That's the only reason I'm putting up $1.3 million."

From the beginning, it was an open secret in boxing circles that the mob put up the money to finance the fight. Members of the Ali camp, the Cleveland police, and most boxing writers believed that was the case. Even Bobby Cassidy, who fought in the semifinal, heard that mob money was behind the promotion.

In 1988, Bob Arum told me, "Mob money for the Wepner fight was the key to King's emergence in boxing."

In 1989, Teddy Brenner told me that not only did organized crime underwrite the Wepner fight, but King owed them money for years and was nearly killed over the debt in the early 1980s. "King went to a friend of mine," Brenner told me, "and begged him to cancel a contract put out on his life by the Cleveland mob. There was a hit man coming after King in New York because he hadn't paid back the debt for the Wepner fight."

Finally, both Bob Arum and Don Elbaum went on the record with the story and both allowed themselves to be quoted in Tom Hauser's authorized biography of Ali, published in 1991. King never sued Hauser, Arum, or Elbaum. He didn't even write a letter to the publisher.

This is how Arum described the deal: "King wanted to stay in the heavyweight picture. If possible, he wanted to control Ali. So he went to some mob guys in Cleveland, and got financing from the mob. That enabled him to offer more for the fight than anyone else could afford. . . .

"I know for a fact, because some FBI people told me, that the interest he owed on the loan from the mob kept building and building, and King wasn't able to pay it off until after Holmes-Cooney in 1982. That's how long it took him to get clear again."

Some of Arum's knowledge may have come from Brenner, who was working for Arum at the time Hauser interviewed Arum.

Hauser quoted Elbaum, who knows Cleveland, as saying: "King financed the Wepner fight with mob money. I've heard that since he put the fight together, and while I can't prove it, I believe it to be true. I heard he borrowed a million and a half from the mob in Cleveland, and then he had trouble paying it back.

"In fact, I heard that part of how he paid it off was by giving them his numbers business. And by 'them' I mean the people he borrowed the money from. He had the numbers business going after he got out of prison. There's no question about that. I know that."

In 1982, when FBI agent Joe Spinelli tried to interview Lombardo about the financing of the Wepner fight, Lombardo declined to be interviewed. There is no evidence actually linking Lombardo to organized crime, and it is possible that he was simply an innocent dupe of Don King's.

Bahar Muhammad, who was part of Ali's camp in 1975, also told me that he knew at the time the Cleveland mob was lending King the money to promote the Wepner fight. Bahar told me in 1990, "Don kept his influence up with Ali by paying guys around Ali. I saw it myself. I used to see Don come up to Deer Lake and give guys cash to spy for him and tell Ali positive things about King, to let King become his promoter and not other guys. There was always factions around Ali, and King was smart enough to buy people's loyalty with cash. I think this was another reason why he got the Wepner fight."

On February 9, with Ali and Wepner at his side in New York, King officially announced the fight for Cleveland on March 24. King said Ali would get $1.5 million, plus $200,000 in training expenses. Wepner would get $100,000.

Later King would add a semifinal in the Garden between Ken Norton and Jerry Quarry to boost the closed-circuit sales, and this would cost his investors $400,000 more. With travel, "finder's fees," and publicity expenses, the fight would cost more than $2.5 million to put on.

But to King it was more than worth it. He was not risking his own money. It looked to the world like he was in control of Ali's destiny. He seemed to have the inside track for Ali's coming megamatches with Frazier and Foreman. And King had outfoxed Madison Square Garden and gotten even with John Daly for the London snub.

At the opening press conference King started to market Wepner as a white hope, calling himself "an equal opportunity promoter who wants to give the white race a chance, a chance to reclaim the heavyweight crown."

Ali, however, began to call Wepner "a white with no hope."

For the fight King hired his former boss, Hank Schwartz, to handle all the closed-circuit rights with exhibitors. As Schwartz had predicted in Caracas, he was now riding in the back of the bus and King in the front of the bus.

As in the record business and horse racing, almost everyone in boxing seems like a character. That's why writers and filmmakers are drawn to it. Almost everyone in boxing is a colorful storyteller with a touch of lunacy or larceny. Chuck Wepner was one of those characters. So was his manager, Al Braverman, and his trainer, Paddy Flood. One of Flood's former fighters once told me, "I loved Paddy. I just didn't trust him."

Don King was shrewd enough to try to market his mismatch

by letting Wepner be Wepner. He didn't try to sanitize him for the media. Wepner was himself—a boisterous, funny, crude, average fighter with a dream. He was an Everyman with whom the public could identify—a hard-drinking, limited journeyman with a big heart, being given the chance we all dream about—get even in one night, land a lucky punch, hit the lottery number, and change your low-rent life forever.

Wepner made such an impression as the underdog, blue-collar, fearless tavern gladiator that Sylvester Stallone, who watched the fight in a theater, used him as the inspiration for Rocky Balboa in the series of five *Rocky* movies that grossed millions.

When a reporter asked Wepner what his best punch was, he replied, "My three best punches are the rabbit punch, the choke hold, and a head butt."

Wepner lived in the bar, disco, and fringe mob culture of white ethnic Bayonne, New Jersey. He usually trained by drinking at Johnny Di's Lounge and playing pool until the other guy let him win.

The fighter told Vic Ziegel, who wrote dozens of raffish columns about him, "I'm good for a quart of vodka on a given night. I just get a little silly."

Of his daily routine, he told Ziegel, "We don't think nothing of jumping on a plane and going down to Puerto Rico for a weekend, calling our wives from Puerto Rico and saying, 'Hey, guess where we are?' We aren't henpecked. We like to party."

Wepner told one local television reporter—female—who had done a story on his wife, "We raffled your body off at the bar. Three guys won. They'll see you after the fight."

Wepner's manager was Al Braverman, a former boxer, a twice-convicted former bookmaker in New York City, who got into managing local club fights like Rinzy Nocero and Bill Bossio.

In June 1970, Wepner fought Sonny Liston at the Jersey City Armory, in what turned out to be Liston's last fight before his death, a bout I covered for *The Village Voice*.

Liston was then over forty, but he could still hit, and he gave

Wepner, who acted like moving his head was a crime, a brutal beating. Wepner's nose was broken, his mouth and both his eyes badly cut. His trunks looked like a butcher's apron, and the canvas looked like a work in progress by an artist who used only red paint. The referee mercifully stopped the butchery in the tenth round. Afterward, Wepner needed seventy stitches in his face.

In the winner's dressing room a younger reporter asked, "Mr. Liston, is Chuck the bravest man you ever saw?"

"Shit, no," Liston growled.

"Well, who is the bravest?" the reporter persisted.

"Wepner's manager," Liston answered, breaking up the room full of reporters who all knew Braverman.

Despite a lot of free publicity, the fight wasn't selling many tickets at the Cleveland Coliseum, or at 135 theater TV locations around the country. It just wasn't a fight with any doubt about the outcome. It was a curiosity, more like the pilot for a sitcom than a competitive sporting event.

Ali trained minimally for the fight, weighing in at 223½, compared to 216 at Zaire. The day before the fight he just hung out with comedian Redd Foxx, singer Billy Eckstine, and James Brown, who would sing the national anthem.

"Wepner's chances are slim and none," Ali was saying to a few reporters.

"And Slim left on the eight o'clock train," Eckstine cracked.

Redd Foxx started to tell Ali one of his very dirty jokes, and Ali broke in, saying, "Louder, let the reporters hear it, too."

"Not at these prices," Foxx replied, and everyone broke up laughing.

When Ali was asked if he considered Wepner as "representing White America," Ali rolled his eyes like an actor and said, "White America would never pick hiiiiim."

Ali then playfully mused to the writers that he might handicap himself by giving away the first five rounds, or by trying not to hit Wepner near his eyes. He seemed to be looking for a way to make the contest equal, like a father who gets down on his knees so his six-year-old son can reach his chin.

The day before the fight, Braverman, a low-rent Barnum in his own right, told a few reporters that he had a secret, magic elixir that would prevent any cuts to Wepner's eyes and face.

"I got the last batch of this miracle gook," Braverman said with gruff sincerity. "I got the secret formula from Doc Kearns, who got the recipe from an old Indian in the desert. It has Indian herbs in it and some kind of smelly stuff. I rub it in an hour before the fight and Chuck won't bleed." (Doc Kearns was the manager of Jack Dempsey, a con man the equal of King, who ripped off Shelby, Montana, in the same way King ripped off Zaire.)

To boost the lagging ticket sales, King announced the day before the fight that he would donate half the profits to charity—secure in the private knowledge there would be no profits.

On the day of the fight, Carl Lombardo was quoted in the New York *Daily News* as saying, "The live gate is doing very well, and the closed circuit should be a pleasant surprise."

When the fighters entered the ring, Wepner's chances were so remote, there was no betting line. But Wepner's heart made it an interesting night. He had no fear of Ali, no stage fright. He kept swinging and missing, and coming forward. Wepner also fought barroom style as usual, starting to foul Ali in the first round with his hard rabbit punches, and attempting other illegal tactics, including low blows, all through the fight.

Ali loafed, clowned, talked, mimicked, and hit Wepner whenever he felt like it.

In the ninth round Wepner stepped on Ali's foot, jabbed him in the chest, and Ali went down. The referee, Tony Perez, ruled it as an official knockdown, but as I look at replays, and at the film over many years, it seems more like a trip, or a slip.

But it fed into the coming Rocky myth that anything can happen, and gave the fight the drama of the old loser with no hope knocking down the great Ali. It created the illusion of a potential miracle. Everyman, down on his luck, a lottery ticket in his glove, was getting cheered by the crowd.

In the ring Ali was actually winning almost every round, and Wepner was bleeding as usual, despite Braverman's magic gook. Ali was also getting deeply angry from the constant fouling and the embarrassment of being ruled an official victim of a knock-down.

The dramatic tension of the fight was becoming: Can the old guy with guts go the distance? Will Wepner be able to get free drinks for the rest of life by boasting the great Ali couldn't stop him? Can a bum gain glory and dignity by refusing to give up?

In the last round Ali went for the kill in a way he had never done before with an inferior fighter. Ali had gone easy on Jerry Quarry. He didn't want to hurt Blue Lewis or Buster Mathis. He played with Joe Bugner and Rudi Lubbers. He took pity on Mac Foster and let him last fifteen in Tokyo.

But now he wanted to deny Wepner the honor of going the distance. The drama built as Wepner struggled to hang on and the fight dwindled down to the last sixty seconds.

Wepner was valiant, but Ali was too quick and too emotional. Left, right, left, right. Then one last tremendous right to the jaw. Exhausted, his legs spaghetti, Wepner sagged down along the ropes. The moment looked like a live replica of Bellows's famous boxing painting, *Stag at Sharkey's,* a beaten fighter draped on the ropes.

Wepner pulled himself back up at the count of nine, but referee Tony Perez stopped the fight. There were nineteen seconds left. Everyman would not go the distance this night. The ending made a farce look like tragedy.

Paddy Flood stormed into the ring, screaming curses at Perez. He threw all the blood and dirty water on his sponge all over Perez, and then he cradled the badly hurt Wepner in his arms.

Later Perez said he thought Ali was one punch away from killing Wepner. Ali said, "Usually I back off, but I tried to annihilate him. I had no mercy."

Wepner got back from the hospital at 6:00 A.M., after they put twenty-three stitches in his eyebrows and repaired his broken nose.

"I told the doctor not to worry about my nose," Wepner told Braverman in their hotel suite. "This is the fifth time. It's Silly Putty now."

Paddy Flood told a reporter, "We love that bum," gesturing toward Wepner as he lay on the bed, stitched, swollen, and spent.

The next morning Larry Merchant's column in the *New York Post* was called "A Great Bum." It was a song to Wepner's courage.

In June 1991 I was with Ali at a ceremony honoring him at Gracie Mansion, the residence of New York's mayor, then David Dinkins. There was a crowd of about two hundred, and out of the corner of his eye, Ali noticed Chuck Wepner. Wepner had just gotten out of prison after serving seventeen months for selling cocaine.

Very slowly, afflicted by his Parkinson's, Ali inched his way over to Wepner and tried to trip him by stepping on his right foot, and the two old foes hugged each other. Ali's memory was fine.

"You stepped on my toe," Ali said. "You must have ate a lot of carrots when you was little, because you had a helluva rabbit punch."

The Ali-Wepner fight lost money, just as everyone predicted. The live crowd at the 22,000-seat Coliseum was announced at 14,900, but much of this was papered.

The day after the fight Hank Schwartz told reporters he estimated that 50 percent of the closed-circuit television seats had been sold, putting the promotion near the break-even mark. Three weeks later Schwartz admitted the percentage of seats sold was closer to 35 percent. He conceded the losses would be about

$1 million. Vic Ziegel, in the *New York Post,* estimated Carl Lombardo's personal loss at "close to a million dollars." Two years later, the *Cleveland Plain Dealer* reported Lombardo lost $750,000 on his investment.

Hank Schwartz told Ziegel: "We got ourselves emotionally involved in the fight. We won't let it happen again. I'm a businessman, while Don operates in an entirely different framework. . . . He's capable of carrying you along like a swift current, and we have to put the paddle in the water to stem the flow a little bit."

On October 1, 1975, King and Bob Arum co-promoted the Thriller in Manila, the last act in the Ali-Frazier trilogy, won by Ali, in a war that ruined both men, both of whom would have been wise to retire that night, in the ring, at the apex of their glory.

The uneasy alliance between the two rivals had been brokered over a lunch at the Friars Club in Manhattan, arranged by public relations legend Harold Conrad, whom King admired because he had once worked for a Florida casino owned by Meyer Lansky. They agreed King would be the main promoter of the fight, but Arum would handle the closed-circuit because King had a bitter falling-out with Hank Schwartz. Arum was also supposed to get a percentage of the gross, plus a guaranteed fee of $300,000.

But weeks before the fight Arum was already accusing King of skimming, finagling with a letter of credit, and scheming to underreport the gross receipts to cheat Arum on the percentage.

Arum says, "By the end I let King buy out my interest, I was so disgusted. I was terrified Don was doing things that would get us all arrested. Ferdinand Marcos [the one-man ruler of the Philippines] was putting up all the money for the fight, and I was in his country, and Don was fooling around with his money. That's why I pulled back at the end. Don wanted me to sign some documents and I just refused. I was scared."

By the close of 1975 King had badly overplayed his hand. He tried to drive a wedge between Ali and Herbert Muhammad and take over Ali's career. King was not satisfied being Ali's preferred promoter. He wanted to be his only promoter, total control, monopoly, the way Mike Jacobs had been with Joe Louis.

This direct move for control ruptured King's relationship with Ali and Herbert. It was a violation of trust, friendship, and Muslim etiquette.

King had a great thing going. He had co-promoted the third Ali-Frazier fight after listening to the first one in prison. He was becoming rich and powerful. But the street hustler demon inside of him couldn't be contained.

Bahar Muhammad recalls, "Don tried a hostile takeover of Muhammad Ali and it failed. He was relying on the flunkies he was paying off. He underestimated the bond between Ali and Herbert, the religious piece. That's why, to this day, orthodox Muslims don't like Don King. He tried to cheat the messenger's son."

Herbert Muhammad candidly told the whole story to Tom Hauser for his authorized biography of Ali:

I know he [King] paid people in the camp. I know he tried to talk to Ali behind my back.

Ali was hearing from certain people, "Herbert is taking one-third and he's not even here. Maybe we should get rid of Herbert."

But I never confronted Don about it, because I had confidence in my closeness to Ali. I knew Don would never be able to come between us. And Don resented that. To this day he doesn't like me. He hates my guts, really.

Herbert also told Hauser:

I was never able to travel all the time with Ali because my religious obligations came first. And in 1975, when my father passed, I felt an obligation to keep the community strong, and help my brother, Wallace D. Muhammad. So then especially, I wasn't in camp every day.

And what happened was, certain people took that as a sign that maybe they should seize the opportunity to get to Ali.

Now Don King, it seems he tried to destroy the image of managers. Don wants to make any fighter feel he doesn't need a manager. . . . Believe me, if you're a fighter you don't want to deal with Don King without a manager.

As a result of King's desperado move to displace Herbert and monopolize Ali, Ali cut King off after the Frazier fight in Manila.

Arum hired Butch Lewis (who is black), and Herbert gave Lewis and Arum Ali's title defense against Richard Dunn in Germany. King retaliated by calling Lewis an "Uncle Tom" to Ali.

Then Herbert let Arum promote Ali's moneymaking rematch with Ken Norton in Yankee Stadium in September 1976. And King had no role in Ali's later title fight with Earnie Shavers in Madison Square Garden or his two matches with Leon Spinks in 1978.

King was now on the outside. He needed to find some new supply of OPM to replace Mobutu, Marcos, and Carl Lombardo. That's when he approached the ABC television network, a mark with a corporate logo and more financial reserves than a Third World country.

CHAPTER 6

"Dung King and Johnny Bought"

It was the spring of 1976 and it was the first time anyone could remember seeing Don King even a little bit depressed. This most resilient and extroverted and goal-oriented of promoters was subdued for long stretches of time, spending hours alone, behind the closed door of the sixty-seventh-floor penthouse in the RCA Building, behind his big desk, brooding, and planning his next move.

King was distressed over losing his hold over Muhammad Ali. He had worked four years to get Ali, and now he had lost him. His gargantuan ego could not handle rejection. King even took down the beautiful, life-size oil portrait of Ali that had dominated his suite. He replaced it with two huge blowups—himself with Jimmy Carter, and himself with George Foreman, the fighter he was now promoting.

By now King had taken in Wepner's rowdy team of Al Braverman and Paddy Flood as "consultants," and they had offices in the penthouse suite that looked down on most of the Manhattan skyline. Braverman, however, had said, "Just gimme a pay phone in a candy store. All the rest is garbage."

During the summer of 1976, King, an instinctive reader of trends, noticed the national enthusiasm for America's boxing team at the Montreal Olympics. King sensed the upsurge of nationalism and patriotism as five Americans won gold medals for the first time, including Sugar Ray Leonard and the Spinks brothers, Leon and Michael.

The notion of organizing a tournament to crown "American champions" in each boxing weight classification was in the air that summer of televised gold. Hank Schwartz says he had the idea. Teddy Brenner says he had the idea. Paddy Flood said he had the idea. But Don King ran with it and sold it.

It was a resourceful and timely concept. Other than Ali, all of the dominant boxing champions of 1976 were from South or Central America, not the United States. Light heavyweight champion Victor Galindez was from Argentina; middleweight champion Carlos Monzon was from Argentina; lightweight champion Roberto Duran was from Panama; and featherweight champion Alexis Arguello was from Nicaragua.

Seeing the pride in America generated by the Olympics, and the dearth of Americans holding world titles, King identified an opening. He decided to approach the ABC television network with the concept of staging an elimination tournament of the best young American fighters, to crown "true-blue, loyal American champions."

Flood and Braverman would be his matchmakers and talent scouts, the way Elbaum had been at the beginning. They did know boxing, and King's real knowledge about fighters was quite superficial. When King was still in prison, he bet all his cigarettes on Buster Mathis to beat Joe Frazier, but Frazier easily stopped Mathis in eleven rounds in 1968.

King wanted *Ring* magazine, known as "the bible of boxing," to give his tournament instant credibility and to use the publication's ratings as the gateway into the tournament.

In April 1976, before any meetings were held with ABC executives, King gave Johnny Ort, a writer for *Ring* and a man who controlled the ratings, $2,000 in cash. Later in the year he would give Ort $3,000 more in cash.

King also approached James Farley, the chairman of the New York boxing commission (and the son of FDR's postmaster general), and won his agreement to be the supervisor of the tournament in exchange for expenses and travel reimbursements. This was a curious choice, since none of the fights would be held in New York, the only place where Farley had any legitimate regulatory jurisdiction.

The first two fight cards, in fact, would be held at "patriotic" venues—the deck of the battleship U.S.S. *Lexington* in Florida, and the U.S. Naval Academy in Annapolis—federal property, where no local boxing commission could supervise the selection of officials. The third card, in a masterstroke of gimmickry, would be held at King's alma mater, Marion Prison.

In June and July 1976, King held a series of negotiating meetings with executives of ABC Sports, pitching his tournament idea. He was brilliant, farsighted, funny, charming as ever, in the seduction phase of a project. King promised to provide a reliable, steady stream of low-cost fights to ABC, at a time when boxing was enjoying a resurgence of popularity. Like all great grifters, he dangled the honey pot of futures—if ABC did this deal, then it would get all the big heavyweight fights involving Foreman. King also invoked *Ring* and Farley as guarantors that the tournament would be above reproach.

During this period, King met mostly with Jim Spence, the vice president for program planning for ABC Sports, who was not particularly sophisticated about boxing and seemed eager to have a character like King able to deliver fighters no one at ABC knew how to talk to. Years later, John Martin, the vice president of

ABC Sports, would tell me, "King played Spence like a Stradi-varius."

By the end of July, ABC was sold on the project, and draft copies of contracts began to be exchanged between Spence and King. The basic deal was that ABC would pay Don King $1.5 million (later increased to $2 million) to provide forty-eight fights, twenty-three hours of boxing programming, leading up to the crowning of American champions after an elimination tourna-ment. King would get a $250,000 fee as a promoter, and another $200,000 fee would be paid to the matchmakers, presumably Flood and Braverman.

On July 30, King sent *Ring* magazine a $10,000 check "to alleviate expenses incurred in preparing the ratings of the many fighters that will be participants" in the tournament.

Almost from Day One the tournament was a scam, a good idea corrupted in its cradle.

Only fighters allied with Flood, Braverman, Ort, or their friends were allowed into the tournament, which meant good pay-days and television exposure. Ort began to manipulate the *Ring* magazine ratings to justify the entry of some fighters, or to justify the exclusion of others. Some boxers who wanted admission were told they had to kick back a portion of their purses, or they had to get rid of their present managers and turn their careers over to King.

Boxing is a small community with an active grapevine, and this kind of chicanery was not a secret for long. A phone call to Texas, or a conversation in a Detroit gym, can quickly become known to a few hundred managers, trainers, matchmakers, and fighters who live the sport twenty-four hours a day, eking out an existence on the margin.

In September 1976, John Martin of ABC Sports met with Hank Schwartz, who was trying to organize a competing tournament in partnership with Don Elbaum. Martin says that Schwartz told him exactly how ABC's venture was being tainted.

Schwartz warned Martin that only "house fighters" owned or controlled by King, Flood, and Braverman were being allowed into the tournament. Around the same time, Teddy Brenner of Madison Square Garden wrote a letter directly to Roone Arledge, the president of ABC Sports, alerting him to King's methods and offering to provide higher-quality fighters and more competitive matches.

On September 22, King held a press conference at the '21' Club, announcing the tournament, although he had not yet provided ABC with a list of any of the fighters who would be participating. At the press conference King did not announce any of the first-round pairings but declared, "This is a monumental, historic moment." He also promised to promote some of the fights in New York, which never happened.

James Farley, the quality-control supervisor, declared, "I'm proud to be part of it."

To spice up his press conference, King had ex-champs Rocky Graziano and Jersey Joe Walcott there, talking up the tournament and schmoozing with the press. Despite the absence of hard news, the press conference got a three-column headline in *The New York Times,* a two-column headline in *Variety,* and good space all across the country.

King was out of his glum period. He had a deal, he had OPM, and he had a project to sell. He started taking reporters out to dinner, picking up tabs, being accessible, slapping reporters on the back and pleading, "Make me big," and promising to stage fights "like Zale and Graziano" and to discover "the next Ali, who just needs a break."

Ike Fluellen was not exactly the next Ali. He was a cop in a Houston suburb and a former fighter who had not been in the ring in over a year. In late September, he got a call from manager Chris Cline, a Johnny Ort friend, who told Fluellen he could get him into Don King's television tournament. He also told the police officer he could get him rated in the top ten by *Ring* magazine—if Fluellen agreed to hire Cline as his manager. He told Fluellen getting into the tournament "meant big money."

Fluellen was a good cop but not much of a fighter. He had no fights during all of 1976, had lost his last fight in mid-1975, and had never defeated a rated boxer in his life. He was basically retired. But he agreed to pay Cline a booking fee, and was told he was in the tournament. Fluellen started out to the gym and training again.

About ten weeks later, Fluellen brought the January 1977 issue of *Ring* magazine and was pleasantly surprised to see that he was suddenly rated the Number 10 junior middleweight in all of the United States. Fluellen then called Johnny Ort at *Ring* and told him that he hadn't had a fight in well over a year. Ort just told him that he had a helluva manager in Chris Cline, whom he could trust because he was honest.

Meanwhile, some of the most talented young fighters in America—all black and Latin—were being excluded from the tournament. Among this group were Eddie Gregory, Mike Ayala, Marvin Johnson, Matthew Franklin, and Ronnie Harris.

The best was Marvin Hagler, already the most feared middleweight in America, the uncrowned people's champion, ducked by the top contenders, broke and in need of a break, in need of a fight on television to show the world how good this lefty from Brockton, Massachusetts, really was. Hagler's co-manager, Goody Petronelli, desperately wanted to get his fighter into the tournament, and he wrote to King, *Ring,* and ABC to make his case. But he was told he would have to pay a kickback to Flood.

"King and his people wanted to take over Marvin's career," Petronelli told me years later. "They insisted me and my brother surrender all our rights to Marvin, if they let him into the tournament. King would have become his new manager if he won. We don't do business that way. Marvin won the world title in 1980, and we never did a single title defense promoted by King the rest of Marvin's career."

To add insult to Hagler's injury, King put Johnny Baldwin in the tournament, a boxer Hagler had defeated on December 20, 1975, who had not fought since that punishing one-sided beating.

King also put middleweights Bobby Watts and Willie Monroe in the tournament, both of whom were qualified. But Hagler would later beat both of them, knocking out Monroe in February 1977, and knocking out Watts in April 1980.

The record shows that Petronelli wrote directly to Roone Arledge on February 22, 1977, protesting Hagler's exclusion from the tournament and saying the price of admission had been King's future control of Hagler.

Some of the fighters who got in were openly managed by Braverman and Flood, and others were semi-openly managed by King himself. The top heavyweight who got an invitation was Larry Holmes, whom King had already stolen from his first manager, Ernie Butler of Easton, Pennsylvania. Holmes's official manager in 1976 was Sportsville, Inc., a company whose president was King's stepson Carl.

Two parallel trains were now on the track. King, ABC, and $2 million were on an Express, getting favorable publicity, laying the groundwork for a future monopoly, based on King's inventory and ABC's corporate wealth.

The handful of powerless critics were boarding another train, a Local still in the station, collecting anecdotal evidence, warning anyone who would listen that the Express would eventually go over a cliff. But no one was taking the critics seriously yet; subsidized hype always has a big head start on truth that has no institutional base.

In mid-October, ABC's John Martin met Schwartz and Don Elbaum for drinks in Manhattan, at the Gattopardo Restaurant. Martin was not a boxing expert and had no direct role in the tournament, but he was already becoming uneasy about King's practices and was willing to listen to the two insiders who'd known King longer than anyone else.

Schwartz and Elbaum showed Martin a partial list of the fighters who would be in the tournament and explained how each one was tied to King, Flood, Braverman, or Ort and was not qualified in terms of merit.

Elbaum also explained that honest managers of promising fighters were afraid to enter the tournament because they feared King would steal their fighters away, either through an option/first refusal clause King was putting into contracts, or just with a promise to get a fight on national TV.

Elbaum also told Martin that the *Ring* ratings were "becoming a joke," demonstrating how obscure preliminary fighters—with certain connections—were suddenly getting rated in the top ten, followed by tournament invitations.

Schwartz also stressed that his competing tournament, which would be syndicated to local independent stations, had already signed up some of the best young fighters excluded by King. Among those Schwartz named were Eddie Gregory, Vito Antuofermo, and Mike Weaver, all of whom went on to become world champions in a few years.

Martin passed along all this information to others at ABC Sports. "I told Spence, but it was like talking to a stone wall," he says.

On October 21, aware of the criticism, King employed his jailhouse attack bravado; he met with Spence and asked for an additional $500,000 to be added to his contract because of "budget miscalculations." Arledge agreed.

Around this time King felt so secure with his ABC connections that he began to hint to executives, including Martin, that ABC should give him a national late-night talk show, so he could compete against Johnny Carson.

On October 26, Henry Grooms, the Michigan manager of Greg Coverson, was mailed an invitation to enter the tournament. As of that date, Coverson had had only six professional fights. There were probably one hundred boxers at his weight more deserving of invitations. When the *Ring Record Book* was published in April 1977, Johnny Ort had added two wins to Coverson's record. These weren't fixed fights—they were fictional fights.

In November, ABC's corporate lawyers approved the form of the contracts the fighters would be asked to sign with Don King Productions. The contract contained a clause that said if the fighter won the tournament, King would have the option to promote all of the fighter's matches for the next two years.

This language—approved by ABC—was the cornerstone of King's shrewd grand design. With ABC's money, he would be able to monopolize young fighters after they had enjoyed a year of television exposure at ABC's expense. After losing Ali to Arum, King's goal was now *quantity*—numbers of fighters, inventory, product—as many fighters as possible under contract to him.

Also King contrived to have as many white fighters as possible in the tournament, knowing their commercial value, recognizing the commercial success of the film *Rocky*. When some at ABC questioned the ability of these white fighters, like Biff Cline (Chris's son), Pat Dolan, Tom Prater, John Sullivan, and Casey Gacic, King's rebuttal was always "The public wants to see fights between white and black fighters," which was certainly true.

It was also in November that King gave Johnny Ort his second cash payment—$3,000. But only after King wrote a check for $5,000 to Ort, which King then ripped up for some nefarious accounting reason.

In November 1976, Alex Wallau was twenty-seven years old, less than a year on ABC's payroll, working in sports producing on-air promos, publicizing future events. He would go on to become a star, an excellent on-air boxing analyst and a top ABC sports executive after he survived and conquered a 1988 diagnosis of cancer.

But in November, Wallau was a kid, on the road in San Francisco, when he first began to hear grapevine gossip about how King was manipulating the tournament. Although Wallau was not directly involved in boxing then, he loved the sport, going to as many fights as possible, visiting gyms, and he knew most of the idealistic reformers in the sport, a tight little network.

"When I got back to New York," Wallau recalls, "I saw the list of fighters in the tournament. I could tell many of them were stiffs, prelim fighters who didn't belong on national television. The first person I went to was Bob Greenway of ABC Sports and told him this is a mistake, ABC will get embarrassed. He told me it couldn't be stopped, and later told me that Jim Spence wanted my views in writing.

"Suddenly I felt like my ass was on the line. What if I'm wrong? I'll get fired. Evaluating talent is so subjective, how could I prove my impressionistic opinion was sound?"

So Wallau took a few days to document his opinions by trying to reconstruct the career records of some of the fighters in the tournament who he thought did not merit entry.

Wallau turned to Malcolm Gordon for help. Flash, as he was called by friend and foe, was a twenty-seven-year-old reclusive hippie boxing freak who published his own mimeographed boxing newsletter he sold to subscribers and fans for 35 cents, and who attended the club fights around New York.

Flash loved to paint trains and smoke pot and looked like Woody Allen with a ponytail. But he kept the most accurate and thorough records of fighters' past performances by clipping out-of-town newspapers and having a few excellent sources in gyms around the country. He also had a radical, artistic sensibility, and was sometimes given to conspiracy theories that lacked precision.

Flash lived in a small apartment in Sunnyside, Queens, with a printing press in his bathtub. His whole apartment was filled with boxing files. Flash knew.

Wallau invited the reclusive Flash over to his house for dinner in early December, telling him to bring as much of his documentation as he could carry.

"We were two schmucks trying to pretend we were Woodward

and Bernstein," Wallau recalls. "We were trying to piece together the accurate history of certain fighters in the tournament out of two shoeboxes. We spread all this information out on my living-room floor. I had some information on index cards, but Flash had a lot more. We made calls all over the country to get more facts about these guys."

Flash showed Wallau how important it was to take the research to a second level, to study the records of the fighters beaten by the fighters in the tournament, to audit the level of the competition. Flash showed Wallau how many of the wins recorded by tournament boxers were over fighters who had lost most of their fights, fighters who had been knocked out ten or twelve times in a row. Flash proved that even a winning record on paper was proof of nothing, how a protected fighter can be matched with tomato cans, retirees, and hospital cases to pad a record with paper wins.

One of the tournament fighters Wallau and Flash researched thoroughly was Anthony House, who was managed by Ort's pal Biff Cline and had almost no talent. While preparing his first memo for Jim Spence, Wallau called Johnny Ort at *Ring* to ask about the record of House, who seemed to have wins that were never reported by any newspaper in America.

"I personally saw House knock out Joe Kulawitz at Sunnywide Gardens in 1975," Ort told Wallau, not realizing he was talking to a fan who had attended every boxing show at the Sunnyside Gardens in 1975.

Wallau told Ort he couldn't remember the fight, or any fighter named Joe Kulawitz. He then called the New York State Boxing Commission, which confirmed no fighter by the name of Joe Kulawitz had been licensed to box in New York in the last decade, and that House had never boxed in New York.

Wallau now knew for a certainty this fight never happened.

Wallau then called Ort back and asked about Ike Fluellen. Ort told him Fluellen had knocked out "Pepe Alvarez" in Mexico on

November 7, 1976, and had won a decision over "Armando Chavez" in Juarez, Mexico, on October 24. No such matches had ever taken place.

Wallau composed two memos for Spence and his other bosses at ABC, the first dated December 10, and the second dated December 21. Both memos were so detailed and convincing that they should have stopped the tournament even before the first televised matches.

The December 10 memo, covering only the fighters scheduled to appear on the first elimination telecast in January, said of Hilbert Stevenson: "An unknown, unproven nonentity, who had been inserted into the tournament only because he is managed by Chris Cline . . . Ort's reaction to Stevenson's knockout by James Busceme was to raise Stevenson up to sixth in the U.S. rankings. . . . Stevenson has done nothing to justify his inclusion in the U.S. championships."

Of Tom Prater, who was in the tournament only to make sure Larry Holmes reached the finals, Wallau wrote, "He has no right to be in the tournament on the basis of his record."

Of Paddy Dolan and Johnny Sullivan, Wallau observed, "They are white club fighters who have never fought a main event, or an opponent of any reputation. . . . They are two disgraceful examples of King handing $15,000 to Paddy Flood and his friends."

Of Juan Cantres Wallau wrote, "He is the biggest embarrassment in the first quarter-final. He has never gone more than six rounds and has never scored a professional KO."

Wallau's memo also named some of the excellent American boxers whom King had excluded from the tournament, including "Marvin Hagler, Marvin Johnson, Matthew Franklin, and Eddie Gregory"—all of whom went on to win world championships.

Wallau handed his memo to Jim Spence as Spence was about to fly to Moscow. Spence would later tell investigators he read only the first page of the six-page memo. Spence returned from Moscow on December 22, when he received Wallau's second memo covering all the fighters in the tournament under contract so far, not just those on the first telecast.

This document was even more insightful and sarcastic than the first, and included a clipping from *The Washington Post* documenting Johnny Ort's ties to King and Chris Cline. This memo said that twenty-five of the more than fifty fighters in the tournament were qualified, naming Larry Holmes, Bobby Cassidy, Willie Monroe, Saoul Mamby, and Edwin Viruet among them. The memo identified eleven boxers as "marginal," and named fourteen fighters as "disgraces" or "jokes." Wallau was right about all fourteen, six of whom were white.

Of Anthony House, Wallau wrote: "None of his opponents are listed in the *Ring Record Book,* although I do know that one, Willie Crockett, had a record of 1–10, and had been knocked out seven times when he faced House."

Of Johnny Sullivan he wrote: "Sullivan is handled by Cockeye Dom Buffano, Al Braverman's partner who used to work in Wepner's corner. . . . In Sullivan's 17 fights, 10 were against opponents unlisted in the *Ring Record Book*. Of the seven who do have records, two were in their first professional fight, and three were in their second after unsuccessful debuts. Sullivan managed to lose two of these fights despite Dom's best efforts."

Of Tommy Rose, Wallau wrote: "To understand Tommy Rose, one must understand his manager until a couple of months ago, Bill Abel. Abel is a graduate of the Danbury Federal Prison where he completed a two-year course in nine months. In a *Daily Mirror* column in 1962, Dan Parker called him 'a 24-carat phony.' The April 1963 WBA newsletter contained this warning: 'An ex-con, Bill Abel, has been attempting to book youngsters using phony records, etc., to make a fast and easy buck. This boxing bum has been denied a license in New York and Florida.'

"Abel matched Rose in 13 fights in 1974–75. Five opponents were unlisted in the *Ring Record Book.* The others included Mach Reed (0–2, including a loss to the pathetic Jose Resto), Charley

Kitteredge (knocked out three straight times by nobodies, he went the distance twice against Rose in the space of six days), and Roland Sigmon (winless bum kayoed twice by Rose). None had winning records."

Jim Spence said he never had time to read this memo.

Meanwhile, in mid-December, Flash Gordon published the first of his many rants against King, *Ring,* and ABC. Here is a taste of Flash's dense, colloquial style in his newsletter, which was read by about four thousand hardcore boxing fans across the country:

> . . . ABC-TV will be sold a bill of goods most likely by King-Ort as to the merits of a "packed house" of boxers either directly managed, co-managed, booked, or on a kickback scheme, of: Pat Flood, Al Braverman, Don King, Johnny Ort, Chris Cline and Henry Grooms, all of whom will laugh all the way to the bank on another of King's con jobs.
>
> There are few topnotch fighters in Don King's Tournament from what our sources stated, and no question at the semi and final stage, these class USA boxers will prevail over the stiffs being slipped into what Don King claimed was, "A Tournament comprised of the best fighters in the USA". . . .
>
> So when your kid informs you that you stink, and Don King can take me places, we told you so here.

Flash also proposed a letter-writing campaign to Arledge at ABC, and reminded managers that the rival Schwartz-Elbaum tournament would air a stronger and more deserving group of fighters than King. He referred to King as "Dung King" and Ort as "Johnny Bought."

Despite all this inside churning and chatter, the mainstream sports press remained oblivious, continuing to give King's tournament ample and favorable free publicity.

On January 3, 1977, *Sports Illustrated* published a four-page puff piece on King's tournament by the usually dazzling and acerbic writer Mark Kram.

Kram's article quoted—without any apparent irony—Johnny Ort as saying of the tournament, "It's going to bring fresh air to the game."

"There are American champions to be made—honestly," Kram wrote. "The last word is so important; the champions here cannot be made in the back room, they must be made in the ring.

" 'This is a non-connection tournament,' says Flood."

Kram concluded his article by quoting a cocky Don King as saying, "I'm here to tell Madison Square Garden, its stockholders, Teddy Brenner—God bless them—that boxing is back, Jack. The sport of the dispossessed will be climbing the mountain. Don King doesn't need the Garden. The Garden needs Don King."

Alex Wallau recalled, "The *Sports Illustrated* article destroyed my credibility inside ABC. The timing saved King. I was just a kid. How could I know more than the most respected sports publication in the country?"

Several months after the article was published, *Sports Illustrated* quietly forced Kram to resign for accepting gifts and gratuities from Don King. A senior *Sports Illustrated* executive told me, "Kram took money from King. One of our own writers, Bill Boyle, found out about it. King claimed it was a loan. We had to let Kram go, although we never made a public announcement about it."

Neil Leifer, *SI*'s famous photographer, says, "Kram was a victim. Don saw a weakness in him and took advantage. Mark was in debt from two divorces and had some other vices. King used him. I don't know that Mark's intention was dishonest, but the result was dishonest. Mark was a wonderful writer. He needed counseling, and should have been suspended, but not fired."

But it wasn't just Kram. Almost all of the sports press was writing upbeat pieces about the tournament, leading up to the first quarterfinal eliminations, held on the deck of the U.S.S. *Lex-*

ington, in Pensacola, Florida, on January 16, 1977.

On January 15 in Pensacola, there was an ugly preproduction meeting in King's hotel suite, on the eve of the first telecast featuring the Larry Holmes–Tom Prater mismatch. Director Chet Forte mentioned that some of the discrepancies in some of the fighters' records still needed to be clarified. (Forte was the producer who devised the eleven-camera concept that helped make Monday night football so popular on ABC.)

At that innocent remark, all the other participants began to gang up on Alex Wallau, the most junior member of the ABC team in the room. King, Flood, Braverman, and Ort all took turns attacking Wallau in the most personal terms, meant to ruin the man's livelihood and intimidate him.

Braverman accused Wallau of criticizing the tournament because he was "on Teddy Brenner's payroll." Wallau had never met Brenner at that point.

Braverman then pointed his stubby finger at Wallau and said, "In the old days we knew how to take care of enemies like you. Bums like you used to be found laying in the gutter."

At the same time King was shouting at Wallau, "You are the enemy."

Director Chet Forte heard these remarks as a serious threat and became concerned for Wallau's safety. ABC director Larry Kamm also heard through an open door the Braverman comment about being found in the gutter and also feared that King's men might try to harm his co-worker.

"I was definitely concerned," Kamm told me. "I thought this was going to be a routine production meeting where we decide which fights we pretape, what the sequence of fights would be. Suddenly I was hearing these threats about Alex ending up in the gutter. I wasn't prepared for that."

"From that meeting on," Wallau says, "King kept telling Spence to fire me, or take me off the tournament. I was nervous about my job. Nobody in the daily press was picking up on what

Flash was writing. *Sports Illustrated* and *Ring* were one hundred percent in King's corner. I was perceived as an isolated crank."

On January 16, the first tournament card was aired from the U.S.S. *Lexington,* a wonderful visual backdrop of sailors and blue sea. The fights were undistinguished, all going the distance. Holmes methodically won every round against Tom Prater. Hilbert Stevenson, Pat Dolan, and Juan Cantres lost their fights. Bobby Cassidy won a close decision from Willie Taylor.

Bobby Cassidy told me years later, "Ray Elson and I were both managed by Paddy Flood. I know Biff Cline got into the tournament only because Paddy thought Elson could beat him, and Paddy could get a double payday that way. He told me I had to fight Willie Taylor because Elson couldn't lick him. All the opponents were handpicked. It was not a legit operation. But that's how boxing is. Paddy didn't do anything different than the Duvas or Arum. He just had a good thing going with no rules to stop it. Sure Paddy put in the fighters he managed, and his friends managed. It's always who you know. That's how life works. Braverman did the same thing, and I know how bad Braverman was because I dumped him as my manager to go with Paddy."

When I asked Cassidy how he really felt about the likable Flood (who had died two years earlier), Cassidy replied: "I loved Paddy. I just didn't trust him."*

The first tournament telecast received a rave review in *Ring* magazine from Johnny Ort, who never told his readers he had been paid $5,000 by Don King and was hardly an objective reporter. The headline over Ort's article was US TOURNAMENT MAKES SPECTACULAR DEBUT. Ort called King "the Mike Todd of boxing," which was how King was describing himself in those days.

King's second tournament telecast was staged on February 13

---

*Cassidy's son, Robert Cassidy, Jr., has emerged as one of the best young boxing writers in the country, authoring a searing profile of Sandy Sadler in *Newsday* in July 1994, filled with the reverence for an old champion that the son of a gutsy contender has in his genes.

at the U.S. Naval Academy. Again it was on federal property, outside the reach of any local boxing commission. King's staff picked the judges and referee.

The heavyweight main event was between Scott Le Doux and Johnny Boudreaux, who was managed by Flood. To even things up, Le Doux had to pay Braverman 10 percent of his purse as a "booking fee." Flood also worked in Boudreaux's corner, making the whole affair a quinela of conflicts.

Le Doux seemed to clearly win a dull eight-round decision. He knocked Boudreaux down in the third round, and Boudreaux appeared converted to pacifism by that experience. The television commentators, Howard Cosell and George Foreman, both made it clear they thought Le Doux was winning the fight.

But the unanimous decision went to Boudreaux, with Cosell shouting in disbelief, "They gave it to Boudreaux!"

One of the judges was Harold Valan, whom I once saw give a decision to Chuck Wepner (the Flood-Braverman fighter) over Ernie Terrell when it looked to me that Terrell had won almost every round. In that 1973 match, Valan was the sole and deciding official.

The unjust verdict—less outrageous than many others in history—led to one of the most bizarre scenes in television history, a classic moment of postmodern kitsch.

Le Doux lost control of his emotions, tried to kick his opponent, but instead kicked Cosell's toupee off his skull on live national TV. When Cosell retrieved his hairpiece, he momentarily put it on backward.

After Cosell got his toupee back on the right way, he did a quite professional interview with the still enraged Le Doux. The fighter told the national audience the whole tournament was fixed to favor fighters aligned with King, Flood, and Braverman. He said he had been warned not to take the fight with Boudreaux because of his opponent's financial ties to Flood, but he felt they couldn't steal a decision on national TV.

Cosell then interviewed King, who dismissed Le Doux's views as "absurd," and assured Cosell he had taken every possible precaution to make the tournament "an open, honest competition." (A fight manager once told me, "If bullshit were poetry, Don King would be Shakespeare.")

But Le Doux's sincere anguish on live television finally brought the tournament's underground sewer stench out into the open. A much bigger universe now knew about the allegations of rigged results and conflicts of interest. (The fight did draw an impressive rating, as did most boxing shows in this era.)

ABC was finally beginning to feel some pressure. This was no longer just some wacko mimeographed newsletter biting them in the ankle. Every national boxing writer, and millions of living-room fans, were now aware of the complaints. Two days after the fight, the top staff of ABC Sports held a lengthy meeting in Roone Arledge's office. Present were Arledge, John Martin, Chet Forte, Alex Wallau, and Jeff Ruhe, Arledge's sharp twenty-three-year-old assistant. Spence was absent, on vacation.

Wallau made a point of criticizing the booking fees the fighters were paying to managers, pointing out how, in theory, admission to the tournament was based on the *Ring* rankings, so why were any booking fees necessary? Arledge declared that from now on, all fighters and managers would be required to sign affidavits beforehand, swearing they had not paid any booking fees. (By the end of the tournament at least ten fighters would swear they had to make such improper payments to get into the tournament.)

In the same meeting, Wallau, by the far the most knowledgeable boxing person in the room, also emphasized how the contract clause giving King control over future fights* was a significant

---

*The venerable Philadelphia middleweight Bennie Briscoe says this option clause, giving King future control, was the reason he decided not to enter the tournament. Briscoe was some fighter: He held Carlos Monzon to a draw in Buenos Aires, knocked out Joe Shaw, Billy Douglas, George Benton, and Vicente Rondon.

reason why some good fighters were not participating—their managers felt they would be signing away all rights to King, who had done nothing to discover or develop the fighter.

Wallau also summarized some of the fictional fights he had discovered in the records supplied by Johnny Ort. Arledge asked Wallau to put this information in writing and, with wishful thinking, suggested *Ring* magazine would now "shape up."

The next day King was summoned to a meeting at ABC with Arledge, John Martin, Jeff Ruhe, and several lawyers. King was asked to respond to some of Wallau's criticisms, even though Wallau was not invited to the meeting to offer counterrebuttals.

King said that booking fees were routine in boxing and there was nothing wrong with them, although he agreed to eliminate them from now on in the tournament, since they contradicted the stated premise of *Ring*'s ratings being an automatic ticket in.

On the option/first refusal contract clause, King claimed they were used to satisfy the terms of his own contract with ABC. He also claimed that if any fighter objected to them, he dropped the clause from their contract, although this was not the case with Bennie Briscoe and other boxers.

King and Arledge met again the next day, February 17, and at this meeting Arledge asked King to provide him with a complete list of all the invitations sent out, and a chart showing all the matchups for the tournament in future fights. ABC was starting to apply oversight scrutiny to the runaway tournament.

Also on February 17 Arledge received a letter from Madison Square Garden president Michael Burke containing the latest issue of Flash Gordon's newsletter. It was yet another densely detailed, abusive rant against King and ABC. Burke's covering note to Arledge said: "This arrived in my mail without identification. Like most anonymous material, it's probably garbage."

On February 22 Wallau alerted Arledge to the fact that the CBS-TV network program *Who's Who* had interviewed Flash for an investigative segment being prepared on King and the tournament. Wallau also gave Arledge a copy of Flash's February 9 newsletter, yet another exposé of falsified records, favoritism, attempted extortion of fighters, and exclusion of independent managers.

On the same day, Goody Petronelli, Hagler's co-manager, wrote his letter to Arledge, alleging that Hagler had been intentionally blacklisted out of the tournament by King and explaining that Hagler had already knocked out Johnny Baldwin, and that Baldwin had gotten an invitation but not Hagler. Petronelli also included Flash's newsletters dated December 17, 1976, and January 5, 1977. This meant that between Wallau, Burke, and Petronelli, Arledge now had a complete set of Flash's indictments of himself. Between these newsletters and Wallau's two December memorandums, he had all the information he needed to terminate the tournament contract at this point.

But instead of terminating King, Arledge terminated Wallau—in a fashion. At the end of February, Wallau was notified by Chet Forte that he was being "taken off" the next boxing tournament telecast. The reason given was that he had a disruptive personality conflict with Howard Cosell, which was, in fact, the case.

King was exultant, rightly or wrongly believing he had gotten rid of his most dangerous critic as a result of his own pressure tactics. King later took the credit for Wallau's removal in an interview with lawyer Michael Armstrong, who investigated the tournament for ABC. Of wanting Wallau out, King told Armstrong, "I wanted to see the bullet in front of me, not behind me."

After about a week of feeling deserted and abandoned, Wallau was called in by Arledge and told his independent research had improved his career prospects at ABC, and Arledge wanted him to continue to scrutinize King's methods and practices. But he was still off the tournament telecasts.

The third tournament telecast was held on March 16 from the gym of Marion Prison, before thirteen hundred armed robbers, rapists, and murderers. It was billed as King's "homecoming to my alma mater." For the occasion, King got off one of his best malapropisms, saying he felt he was returning "like Walden to Thoreau."

King strolled through his old prison yard wearing a $30,000 diamond ring, a $9,000 watch, and his usual wad of $5,000 in his pocket, "so I don't feel naked."

But King appeared jittery, perhaps because Roone Arledge himself was in the production truck, keeping close track of everything. Or perhaps because the fights themselves stank. They were later described by Mark Jacobson in *The Village Voice* as "a bunch of smelly mismatches and slow waltzes, causing one guy to yell, 'Hurry up, I only got 20 years.' "

Some of the reporters at Marion asked King pointed questions about the tournament, and in almost self-parody, he replied, "I will not wither in the face of this salvo after salvo of invective and vituperation. This tournament is as honest as the day is long, as clean as a spring afternoon."

Paddy Flood's defense was more prosaic and fatalistic. He told Mark Jacobson: "Look, I can find ten guys who are willing to call you a crook. But because I'm in boxing, I can find 100 guys who are willing to call me a crook. That's boxing."

By now King knew his $2 million deal with ABC was in jeopardy, and with it, the power the deal gave him. King went back to his instincts from the jailhouse and the numbers business—attack first and ask questions later. He had prevailed against Wallau, and now he decided to play the race card.

King's press spokesman at the time of the tournament was Irving Rudd, one of the most beloved men in sports. Out of Brownsville, Rudd had starting doing public relations for Joe Louis in 1937, gone on to work for the Brooklyn Dodgers, and done some Ali fights. Reporters loved and trusted him, giving him the nickname of Unswerving Irving.

"Right after the Marion prison show, King flew in about a dozen black newspaper editors, put them up at a hotel, and gave an all-black press conference," Rudd recalls. "I told him this was wrong, but he ignored me. I pleaded with him not to make this a black-white confrontation, and to answer everything factually. But he yelled at me, 'Don't fuck with my mind.' He was determined to get the message out that he was the victim of a racist conspiracy to keep blacks out of power in boxing.

"Don felt that if he made himself look like an innocent victim, the black community would stick with him, no matter what the facts were. And that way he could survive anything. He was always thinking ahead. He was a great survivor. And he was right."

King stimulated statements of support from the Reverend Jesse Jackson and Manhattan Borough President Percy Sutton, who was then running for mayor of New York. The black press also published stories making King look like a martyr and the victim of a lynching by jealous whites.

His defenders did not notice that Marvin Hagler was black, or that Ernie Butler, who discovered Larry Holmes before King, was black.

At the same time, Al Braverman began to give out copies of an anonymous newsletter called "Boxing Beat True Facts." It was a personal attack on Flash Gordon, written in Flash's own style but with less fidelity to fact. The newsletter read:

Known to boxing troops as Degenerate and Sick Gordon . . . a sewer mongrel and beatnik pothead with Body Odor to boot . . . refuses to bathe . . . never goes out with girls (detests them) but goes out with BOYS . . . he stinks like a skunk . . . hates blacks and Puerto Ricans . . . born liar. A faggot.

But such juvenile nastiness by Braverman was futile. It could not suppress the truth, which was now flowing out of a dozen different places.

In mid-March, Jeff Ruhe found out that tournament fighter Kenny Weldon had paid a $2,500 "booking fee" to George Kanter. ABC acknowledged that this had occurred but did not make Kanter's name public in the press release it distributed.

On March 23, fight manager Jack Stanton wrote directly to Arledge making the case that his son, Larry Stanton, should have been included in King's tournament. The father pointed out that lightweight Pat Dolan, managed by Flood, was in the tournament, but his son had knocked out Dolan in 1976.

Jeff Ruhe, although only twenty-three, had Arledge's confidence, and he now began to make the case against King.

"I was in a few meeting with Roone and King in late March and early April," Ruhe says, "where King just tried to bullshit Roone. He came up to our offices wearing a white ermine coat and gold chains, and just was not making a good impression. By now we were getting affidavits signed by fighters like Weldon, and from managers, and King was losing his last shred of credibility. Cosell was now against King. Alex was being vindicated. King's only defender left was Jim Spence."

On April 6, Ruhe saw a phone message from Ike Fluellen, the Houston policeman Ort had rated in the top ten. Assuming Fluellen was calling about when he was finally going to get a fight in the tournament, Ruhe called King's offices first, before returning the call. But King's staff told Ruhe that Fluellen was being dropped because he had been idle for over a year and a half, even though *Ring* now ranked him in the top ten without fighting.

When Ruhe relayed this information to Fluellen, who had been training for months, the police officer told Ruhe the whole story of his involvement with Cline and Ort, and offered to sign an affidavit. "If I had stayed retired, I could have become champ," Fluellen joked. The next day, Fluellen signed the affidavit, and this became the next-to-last straw that broke the back of the scandal.

The last straw was the publication of the 1977 *Ring Record Book* the next day. This was the smoking gun that would prove the phony fights, padded records, and rigged admissions to the tournament.

Alex Wallau and Flash Gordon went to the offices of *Ring* magazine together, purchased several copies, and then rushed to ABC's offices to look up the career records of fighters like Fluellen, House, Biff Cline, and a dozen others.

"This is it! We have them!" Wallau shouted as he went through the book. "This is a fraud on paper! This is something we can prove. King can't talk his way out of this."

Wallau and Gordon compared the 1975, 1976, and 1977 *Ring Record Book*s. They saw fictitious fights, listed as taking place in 1975, that were not listed in the 1976 book, but were listed in the 1977 book.

Before the morning was over, Wallau was able to show the top executives of ABC Sports that at least fifty phony wins were attributed by Johnny Ort to fighters in the tournament, to justify ranking prelim kids as "the best in America."

The 1977 *Ring Record Book* contained five fake one-round knockouts in Biff Cline's record; four phony wins for Richard Rozelle; two phony wins for Pat Dolan; four fictional knockouts for Anthony House; two imaginary wins in Mexico for the retired Ike Fluellen. Johnny Baldwin was given one phony win in Mexico following his knockout by Hagler, to make him look qualified. Hilbert Stevenson was given five phony wins, plus a draw with Anthony House, both of whom were managed by Chris Cline. Ort couldn't even make up results that didn't have a conflict of interest.

On April 16 ABC finally killed King's tournament and retained the prominent attorney Michael Armstrong to conduct an in-house inquiry for the ABC Corporation.

ABC also canceled the fight—the heavyweight final—scheduled to be telecast that weekend between Larry Holmes and Stan Ward, both of whom were managed by Don King. King couldn't lose the final, no matter who won. The hippie with the ponytail had decked the promoter with the diamond ring.

ABC gave Alex Wallau a $4,000 raise and a $10,000 bonus for being the Serpico of the Sweet Science.

New York Governor Hugh Carey suspended James Farley as

boxing commissioner for accepting expense money from King to certify the integrity of fights held outside New York. Farley never returned to the job.

The collapse of the tournament sent a panic through the offices of television and advertising executives. As a result, the competing tournament run by Schwartz and Elbaum was canceled, even though they had tried to warn ABC about King and staged honest, competitive fights themselves.

Predictably, King was the agile survivor. He blamed everybody except himself for the fraud, shouting, "I'm a nut on the truth bit!" King made a big show out of "suspending" Flood and Braverman, saying they "were not acting in the best interests of the sport we all love."

King called Ort a "Judas," saying, "I am shocked, saddened and appalled that the *Ring* is no longer the bible of boxing." (Teddy Brenner quipped, "If the *Ring* is the bible, then boxing needs a new testament.")

Ort blamed devious managers for sending him inaccurate fight results.

The May 2 edition of *Sports Illustrated* atoned for the Mark Kram suck-up piece on the tournament by publishing a comprehensive exposé by Robert Boyle. Boyle also revealed for the first time that an unnamed writer for *Sports Illustrated* may have been "on the take," and that "*SI* is investigating the allegations against the staffer." (This was a blind reference to Kram.)

In September, on the quiet, lazy Sunday of Labor Day weekend, ABC released a summary of Armstrong's 327-page report. The report itself was never made public on grounds of confidentiality, although sources at ABC did slip out a few copies to reporters on the sly.

The Armstrong Report was not quite a whitewash. The facts were all there, but they were presented in the blandest possible way. Overall, the report was timid in its conclusions and protective toward ABC, which was paying Armstrong a big fee. The report was artfully political and did not go much beyond what

Flash Gordon and Alex Wallau had found out, on their own, months earlier.

Armstrong found "no criminal conduct," but did find "a good deal of unethical behavior by individuals involved in the administration and organization of the tournament."

The ABC press release stressed that Armstrong "concluded ABC was not guilty of any wrongdoing. ABC's presentation of the tournament and response to various charges could not be characterized as grossly negligent in any way." This was a friendly inoculation against any future lawsuits by managers or fighters against ABC.

The worst thing Armstrong said about King was that his $5,000 cash payment to Johnny Ort "seriously compromised the integrity of the selection process." The report also said that Ort admitted receiving money from managers whose fighters got into the tournament.

But the report did not hold King responsible for any of the documented kickbacks paid to get into the tournament, or the takeovers of fighters, or the bribing of *Ring,* or the blacklisting of fighters who wanted to remain free agents, like Hagler. It did not propose prosecution of Flood and Braverman, who seemed guilty of extortion and fraud.

The Armstrong Report essentially said everything went wrong, but nobody violated any laws. Once again, Don King was the unsinkable survivor.

A good idea had been implemented in a crooked way, when it could just as easily have been executed in an honest way. When King was caught, he just blamed his subordinates, tried to get his critics fired and screamed racism. That habit would repeat itself.

The ABC scandal should have been the Early Warning to the legitimate corporate world that King was a grifter in his heart. But in a few months it would all be forgotten, and King would be back doing business with ABC, HBO, and the hotel-casinos of Las Vegas and Atlantic City.

In September 1977, Don King celebrated his comeback with a

lavish party to mark the opening of his new corporate offices at 32 East Sixty-ninth Street, in a million-dollar townhouse he had purchased on one of Manhattan's most fashionable blocks, between Park and Madison avenues. More than one thousand people were invited.

The invitation contained a quotation from Robert Kennedy—"Only those who dare to fail greatly can achieve greatly."

It also contained a message from Don King: "I dare to fail greatly. I believe in America. . . . Only in America could a Don King happen, and I am not about to let America down."

CHAPTER 7

The Stealing of Larry Holmes

Ernie Butler first met Larry Holmes in 1968. Butler was then a forty-four-year-old ex-fighter, and Holmes was an eighteen-year-old living in the poor south side of Easton, Pennsylvania, a dying factory town with no future.

Butler worked in a shoeshine parlor and Holmes had been working at the Jet Car Wash ever since he dropped out of school in the seventh grade. They got into a dispute, and the cocky kid with a temper told the older man, "I'll kick your ass, man."

"You'll find me at the PAL gym," Butler told the teenager.

A few days later Larry Holmes swaggered into the gym and asked Butler to go a few rounds with him. The former pro showed the tough kid some of his moves—a triple jab, dipping his head at just the right instant to make a punch miss.

"After that afternoon I started coaching Larry," Butler said in 1993. "We began training at the gym and Larry was fast. We started pointing toward the 1972 Olympics."

Butler had been a solid professional with over one hundred fights. He had fought future lightweight champion Joe Brown in Newark in 1947. He had given away nine pounds to middleweight contender Rocky Castellani, and lost a close decision in Wilkes-Barre. And he remembers fighting Jimmy Doyle in Doyle's last fight before Sugar Ray Robinson killed him in a match in Cleveland in 1948. Butler had been around and knew a few things.

By the time of the 1972 Olympic trials, Butler was optimistic about the chances of young Larry Holmes, a quick learner with a work ethic. But in the trials Holmes had an episode of panic and disgrace. He quit and was disqualified in his match with Duane Bobick. Holmes was knocked down and tried to crawl out of the ring, an event that was videotaped and replayed several times. It was to haunt Holmes for years to come.

Managers frozen by first impressions, and writers looking for a lazy pigeonhole, called him a quitter with no heart for years afterward. He hated it, but it would lead many people to under-estimate him. Holmes was similar to the young soldier in *The Red Badge of Courage* who surrenders to fear and runs away in his first combat experience but redeems himself later by proving he has courage.

Not only would Holmes have to live down the "quitter" label, but many boxing experts would also write off his future because of his physiology. "Spindly ankles and thin calves" became a mantra with an echo, as experts decided that Holmes's upper body was too heavy for his coltish legs, and that he would never be "a real heavyweight."

But Ernie Butler never lost faith in Larry Holmes. They kept working together in the gym in Easton, even after the loss in the trials, while Holmes drove a truck to earn money, contributing to the support of his eleven brothers and sisters.

On March 21, 1973, Holmes had his first professional fight. He overcame fear and nerves to win a four-round decision from Rodell Dupree in Scranton. He earned $63, and Butler took $10

Sam Garrett lies dying on the sidewalk in Cleveland, after Don King—
one hundred pounds bigger—stomped and pistol-whipped him. Garrett's
last words were "Don, I'll pay you the money."

Photo inscribed from Jimmy Carter to Don King: "To my great friend" *BOXING ILLUSTRATED*

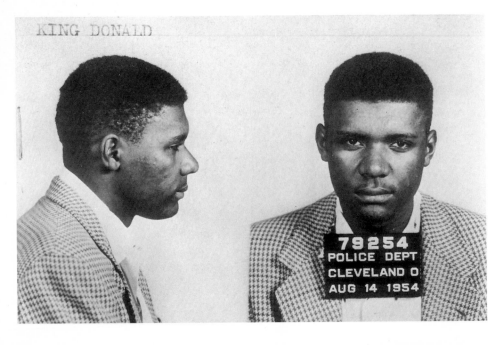

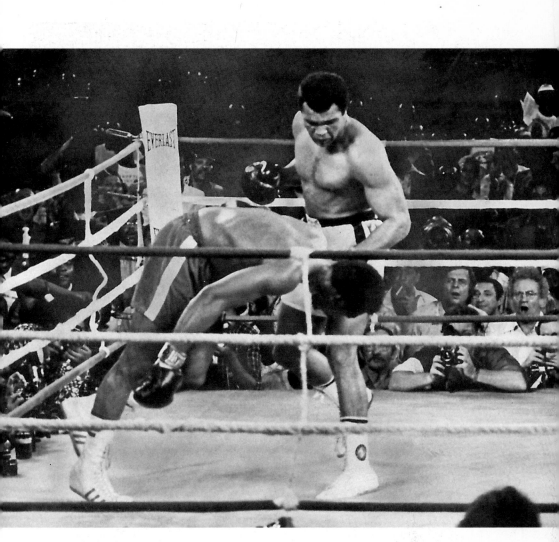

Muhammad Ali knocks out George Foreman in Don King's master-piece, "The Rumble in the Jungle." Norman Mailer and George Plimp-ton can be seen in the second row, their mouths open as Foreman falls.
BOXING ILLUSTRATED

Don King, dressed in white fur, posed outside Dewey Wong's restaurant in February 1986. *BOXING ILLUSTRATED*

Malcolm "Flash" Gordon, the hippie muckraker who first exposed Don King's ABC-TV boxing tournament in his mimeographed, 35-cent newsletter JANIE EISENBERG

Music legend Lloyd Price. He introduced King to Muhammad Ali and gave King the original idea for his distinctive electrified hairstyle. *NEW YORK POST*

An exuberant Don King at Madison Square Garden in October 1978. Larry Holmes, the heavyweight champion, was under contract to him, and so were seven of the top ten contenders. He was at the peak of his monopoly. JAMES HAMILTON

Mike Tyson at eighteen, before he met Don King. Tyson's first boxing family *(from left)*: Cus D'Amato, Tyson, Jose Torres, and Floyd Patterson *BIG FIGHTS*

Former two-time heavyweight champion Tim Witherspoon. King paid him $1 million to settle a lawsuit for fraud and conflict of interest. Witherspoon says, "Don's specialty is black-on-black crime. I'm black and he robbed me." ARLENE SCHULMAN

of it and opened a bank account in Holmes's name. The next day Holmes reported for work.

In May, June, and August Holmes won three more four-round fights in Scranton. After each one, Butler remembers, they slept on a couch, or on the floor in a friend's house, to save the expense of renting a motel room they couldn't afford.

In the summer of 1973 Holmes and Butler were a team. They laughed together, partied together, sweated together, dreamed together, traveled together, and practically slept together.

"I always wanted Larry to spar with fighters better than him, so he would learn," Butler says. "So I had him up at Deer Lake, boxing with Ali, Jeff Merritt, and Roy Williams. So one day I drove him down to New York City, to Bobby Gleason's gym, to get him some good sparring. I was also hoping some important people might notice him, and he could get a fight in Madison Square Garden."

The day Butler and Holmes arrived at Gleason's, Shavers was there, preparing for his match with Jimmy Ellis at the Garden. Shavers needed someone to spar with him who could move, jab, and smother punches like Ellis. Young Holmes volunteered for the assignment as an Ellis impersonator.

Holmes went three rounds with Shavers that day, feeling quicker than Shavers, feeling he could hit Shavers with his jab. But Shavers did connect with one big right that Holmes would never forget, despite his protective headgear. He felt Shavers's power and filed away the memory.

It turned out that Don King was in Gleason's that day as Shavers's co-manager, making a grand entrance after their sparring session had finished. King had a flunky with him who was giving out photographs. They were not pictures of Shavers, but of King himself, who was then unknown in New York.

Butler had heard about King from Jeff Merritt during his visits with Holmes to Deer Lake. Butler remembers introducing himself to King, who was "acting like a big shot already," and trying to tell him what a valuable prospect Holmes was, that he was going to be champion one day.

Holmes remembers that he went up to King that first day and asked him to autograph one of the pictures of himself. It said, "Best wishes, Don King."*

That day in Gleason's, Holmes also talked to Richie Giachetti, who had watched him spar with Shavers and liked what he saw. Giachetti was a trainer of King's fighters and a compadre going back to the Cleveland rackets, which was how he acquired the scar on his face. He also had a better eye for talent than King, and he began to tell King to pay some attention to Holmes, that the kid could box.

King never really became a believer in Holmes, but he trusted Giachetti's judgment enough to get interested. Over the next year King basically stole Larry Holmes from Ernie Butler, even though Butler had a five-year managerial contract with Holmes, dated March 21, the day of Holmes's first pro fight.

In June or July 1973, Giachetti called Holmes at home and asked him to come to New York—without Butler—and meet privately with him and King. Holmes drove the ninety minutes to Manhattan and King told him he wanted to become his manager. Holmes reminded King that Butler was already his manager, and King assured him that he would work out everything directly with Butler and not to worry about it.

"I'd like to keep Ernie in my corner in some way," Holmes told King.

"We'll work that out, don't worry," King soothed Holmes.

Then Holmes, King, and Giachetti went down to the New York State Athletic Commission—in King's limo—and signed papers

---

*Some of the details in this chapter come from a never-published manuscript by professor and author Sam Toperoff, who was generous enough to let me read it. The text was a collaboration between him and Holmes for a book to be published under Holmes's name in the first person. But the book, finished in 1988, never came out for several reasons. One was that Holmes had wavered on including several details about King after he received some threats. "The book contained what Holmes told me was true," Toperoff says.

making King Holmes's legal manager in New York State.

Butler says that in December 1973 he entered into a contract with King under which the two men would be co-managers of Holmes, sharing the manager's end of purses as fifty-fifty partners.

"I never got any money from the contract with Don King," Butler says. "I had a little contract with Larry, but they told me it wasn't any good. Don told me it wasn't written on commission paper. I know it was drawn up by a qualified lawyer, but Don told me it wasn't exactly legal. . . .

"I was with Larry for his first twenty fights, but Don was pushing me out, telling Larry I didn't know anything, that I didn't have the right connections to move him up.

"I took Larry to Ali's camp and let him stay there. He boxed with Ali every week through 1974. In fact, he went to Zaire with Ali as his sparring partner, and came back when the fight was postponed.

"It was up at Deer Lake that King started talking behind my back to Larry. He started making Larry all kinds of promises. King can talk real fast. I was working as a guard at the county jail that year and it was sixty miles to Deer Lake. I couldn't get there all the time. I had to raise my two children. Don just wormed his way in while I was working and being a family man."

In the August 1977 issue of *Sport Magazine*, Sam Toperoff published an article thoroughly exposing the King-ABC tournament. In the course of researching the article, Toperoff had interviewed Butler back in April 1977, since Holmes was in the tournament and King was saying any criticisms of the tournament were based on bias against black people. So Toperoff went to see the black person King had victimized to get Larry Holmes.

Toperoff quoted Butler as saying: "I picked the kid [Holmes] off the streets when he was 17, 18 years old. Taught him everything. Bring him along slow, the right way. Just when he's ready to be something, Giachetti shows up and tells him Don King is interested in promoting his career. But he's got to sign with them.

There's no way to keep a kid then. They tell me I'm going along with them since I developed him. But when it came down to it, they didn't take me."

By the middle of 1975, Butler was completely eased out of the picture, no longer even asked to carry the bucket in the corner or help in the gym. In October 1975 Butler filed a lawsuit against Holmes for breach of contract.

As soon as he filed the lawsuit, Butler says, he began receiving threatening and harassing phone calls in the middle of the night. He later told the FBI that Holmes's lawyer, Charles Spaziani, delivered threats to his lawyer, Frank Van Antwerpin, that the lawsuit better be dropped "or else." Butler also got anonymous telephone threats warning him to stop complaining about not getting paid his managerial share of Holmes's purses.

Butler told Ed Howarth, a Philadelphia matchmaker, that King altered their December 1973 contract and forged Butler's name to a new contract, and later Howarth gave this information to the FBI.

Butler is resigned to what happened to him, and still bitter about it. "Me and Larry, we're still friends," he said. "I see Larry all the time, he lives a mile away. I can't stay mad at Larry and I can't blame him for what happened. If I was in Larry's shoes, I might have done the same thing. Maybe I was holding him back. Larry had a chance to make some big money and maybe I wasn't the best manager to get him those big fights.

"But King didn't deal with me right. He sent those threats on my life. Don promised me I would stay with Larry as a trainer, even after Don became the manager and promoter. That would have been fair, that would have been nice. But as soon as the real money started coming in, they got rid of me. They should have let me stay part of Larry's team because I did discover him and teach him a few things.

"After 1974, I got nothing. I would see Larry fight on TV and feel bad I wasn't with him. I got an old scrapbook about me and

Larry, but I never look at it anymore. I was depressed for a long time over how I got dumped. I was hurt worse than in any of my hundred and four fights."

Holmes told Toperoff, "Ernie cared for me too much and protected me too much," meaning Butler was reluctant to match Holmes with tougher, riskier opponents, out of genuine affection. Holmes felt he didn't have the luxury of coming along slowly, that he had to prove himself quickly against better opponents if he was going to erase the stigma of the Olympic trials disqualification. He knew that behind his back the boxing crowd was still whispering "dog," and "yellow."

While Giachetti saw something in Holmes, Al Braverman and Paddy Flood did not. And their bad-mouthing seemed to reinforce King's lack of confidence in Holmes. King was getting Holmes some fights, but they were insignificant preliminary fights.

This inferior treatment began to feed a streak of resentment and hurt feelings deep inside Larry Holmes, who was more sensitive than most fighters. He always felt like a stepchild in King's camp. He felt like he was regarded just as an Ali sparring partner, that King always preferred the other heavyweights in his herd— Merritt, Shavers, Kevin Isaac, Roy Williams, and later Michael Dokes, Ossie Ocasio, and Greg Page.

King would eventually promote fights matching Holmes against Isaac, Williams, Shavers, and Ocasio in an attempt, at least in Holmes's mind, to use him as a stepping-stone for another fighter's career. King, who had bet his prison cigarettes against Joe Frazier, never really appreciated Holmes's talent, and Holmes would tell reporters for years that King lost a lot of money betting against him when he fought Shavers in 1978.

On November 28, 1973, King put Holmes in the ring with Kevin Isaac, in a preliminary to the Jeff Merritt–Ron Stander main event in Cleveland. Isaac was a bright prospect and Holmes was just a sparring partner. But Holmes survived a first-round knockdown and stopped Isaac in the third, displaying both power and passion. But the knockdown only made King think Holmes had a weak chin; he didn't notice the strong heart.

Shortly after this fight Holmes asked King for a $50 loan. King told him he didn't have the money, but Holmes had just seen him flash his customary cash wad of thousands.

During 1974 Holmes fought only three times, each time for very little money in Scranton. He felt King was neglecting him while focusing on making, and then holding together, the Ali-Foreman deal.*

In 1975 King used Holmes, as befitting a fighter stereotyped as just a sparring partner, in preliminary fights underneath Ali-Wepner in Cleveland, and Ali-Frazier in Manila. In Cleveland, Holmes knocked out the badly washed-up light heavyweight Charley "Devil" Green, and in Manila, he knocked out Rodney Bobick, Duane's brother, in revenge once removed.

In December, King put Holmes on the undercard of a Roberto Duran fight in San Juan. The opponent was the mediocre Billy Joiner and King promised Holmes $1,000. There was no negotiation because Holmes did not have an independent manager to represent his interests. King dictated the compensation. After a fight he would pay Holmes in cash from the large roll in his pocket with no official accounting.

Holmes says that just before the fight started, King told him to "carry" Joiner—not try to knock him out because he needed to fill time before the Duran fight went live on television. But Joiner was not clued into the scenario for a long, easy fight. He stung Holmes with punches in the first two rounds. Holmes, worried about looking bad, worried about maintaining his unbeaten record, went out and finished Joiner in the third, messing up King's TV timetable.

When it came time to get paid, King peeled off three $100 bills and gave them to Holmes, not the promised $1,000. Holmes

---

*On the way to Zaire, King asked Holmes to carry his bags at the airport. Gene Kilroy interceded, saying a sparring partner had too much dignity for such a task.

couldn't believe the most powerful man in boxing would cheat
him out of $700. He went crazy on King and the two men were
screaming insults at each other in the runway outside the dressing
rooms. The argument came close to violence before King backed
down and paid the promised $700.

In the unpublished Toperoff manuscript, Holmes said about
King's treatment of fighters: "I've had a lot of time in recent years
to think about why Don does what he does to fighters. With Don
it was making money off them, sure, but there was something
more to it. He really uses money as a form of power and control
over fighters. I believe that deep down Don King hates fighters,
is jealous of them, because we can do what a fat old bullshitter
like him can't do—and that's fight. That is why he wanted to
have such power over us, to humiliate us."

In April 1976 Holmes was staying at a motel in Bethlehem,
Pennsylvania, to be near his future wife, Diane Robinson. He
thought nobody knew he was there. But Don King, who has the
skills of a private detective, located him and told him he was
fighting Roy Williams, *in a week*!

King told Holmes the fight would be a preliminary to Ali's title
defense against Jimmy Young, but Holmes did not want to take the
fight. He was in love. He had just won a fight two weeks before and
was resting. And he knew Roy Williams very well from the gym at
Deer Lake. He was six feet six inches, 240 pounds, and so good nobody wanted to fight him. Holmes had seen him give Ali a hard
time in sparring sessions. Williams had already beaten Jimmy
Young, and Young was fighting Ali in the main event.

Roy Williams was one tough man who had never gotten a
break in his life, so he had become a sparring partner instead of
a contender.

"No way, Don," Holmes said. "I need a lot more than a week
to get ready for a guy like Roy Williams."

"If you don't want to do this thing," King explained, "you can
become like a needle in a haystack—h-a-a-a-a-a-r-d to find."

Holmes suddenly felt he had no choice, that this was a threat of blacklisted unemployment if he didn't do what King wanted. When Holmes asked how much he would get paid, King said $2,500, which was a humiliation, since Holmes had gotten $5,000 to fight the much easier Rodney Bobick in Manila.

Holmes always felt that Al Braverman was behind the decision to throw him in with Roy Williams on short notice, and later told him so. Braverman was then managing his own heavyweight, a white hope named Dino Dennis, who was undefeated although not much of a fighter. Dennis was being coddled because he was white, and an unbeaten white heavyweight is the most precious commodity in boxing. Holmes suspected that Braverman had talked King into making the fight with Roy Williams in order to knock him off and make Dennis the heavyweight star of King's stable.

Holmes won the fight, partly because by then Williams's fire was gone, snuffed out by years of neglect and the mentality of being a sparring partner too long. But in the first round Holmes broke his right thumb, proving again to the doubters he could work his way through severe pain and not quit. Despite the excruciating agony, Holmes won the fight with one hand, his left jab, and his lateral movement on those spindly legs.

After the fight King refused to pay Holmes's medical bills for the broken thumb, another psychic injury that went into Holmes's memory vault of grievance.

But Holmes was smart and he used the life of Roy Williams, who ended up in prison for a murder, as a cautionary tale, and as a reverse role model of what not to let boxing do to him. He respected Williams as a fighter, and liked him as a man, and he saw what the sewer politics of boxing had done to him. He promised himself never to become an interchangeable pawn in Don King's overstocked inventory.

After the Williams fight, Holmes quit as Ali's sparring partner, and his lawyer, Charles Spaziani, took care of his medical bills.

Holmes's thumb was cracked in two places at the base and he

couldn't go to the gym for three months. At night he developed secret terrors that it would break again in future fights, that this was a career-ending injury, that he had to develop employable skills for the real-world economy. He worried about how he would earn money during this period of inactivity.

The first day he went back into the gym, Holmes rebroke the thumb as he was testing it on the heavy bag. This time doctors implanted four pins at the base of the finger and told the fighter to give the thumb complete rest for four months. His arm was set in a cast that stretched from his shoulder to his fingertips.

Holmes would be idle for nine months because of the injury in a fight he wasn't allowed to refuse. He was twenty-six years old, and this should have been his prime. Instead, he had all this time to brood, about whether his thumb would be a chronic injury, and about why he never had any choice about whom he fought or how much he got paid.

Holmes's first fight after the hiatus was the easy one with Tom Prater in the ABC tournament. Howard Cosell told the nation that the winner of the first-round heavyweight match was getting paid $15,000. But Holmes got paid only $7,000 by King, who took a manager's share even though he was also the promoter, getting his $250,000 fee from ABC. Holmes had to swallow the subtraction since he was counting on two more paydays from the tournament, and this was his first income in nine months.

So when the tournament was killed, on the eve of Holmes's fight with Stan Ward, Holmes got dejected, and then very angry. He had just lost a potential $100,000 because King wasn't playing it straight with ABC. Holmes was now a year older and still undefeated, but his career was drifting without momentum. And the future of his manager-promoter seemed jeopardized by possible indictment. Holmes even thought about going back to driving a truck.

But whenever King gets into trouble, he just puts his head down and keeps on promoting bouts as if nothing is wrong. In March he put Holmes into a semifinal in San Juan against journeyman Horace Robinson. Holmes won easily but noticed that King had signed another young heavyweight to fight on the same card, Ossie Ocasio of Puerto Rico. It made Holmes feel like he would never be King's favored son, that there would always be a new face like Ocasio, or an ex-champ like Foreman, or an old war-horse like Shavers, or a white hope like Dennis to displace him, no matter what he did to prove himself.

Foreman lost the main event on that show to Jimmy Young and retired after hallucinating a vision of Jesus in his dressing room.

In June 1978 Holmes got a call from King's arch-rival, Bob Arum, offering to promote a fight on national television between Holmes and Young Sanford Houpe, who was managed by the comedian Redd Foxx. Holmes told King about the offer in an attempt to entice the two promoters into a bidding war for his services, an instinctive impulse toward free agency.

Arum offered Holmes $75,000 and King offered him $10,000 for the same fight. Holmes was thinking about getting married and told King he had to go for the best money. "Don't you try to put a gun to my head just because I got these other troubles," King told his fighter. "You'll regret it if you do."

A few minutes later King was playing the violin of nostalgia and loyalty, reminding Holmes, "I signed you when no one wanted to touch you. I gave you the chance when no one else would." Then he begged Holmes, "You stick with me on this, and I swear I'll make it up to you later."

Then he reverted back to threats, telling Holmes his contract with him was valid, he would sue him if he fought for Arum, and he would never get another fight again. King the virtuoso played the chord of every emotion to sway Holmes.

Holmes asked his lawyer, Spaziani, what to do, and Spaziani suggested he could always challenge the contract with King by saying he was under duress when he signed it. Holmes then went back to King and asked for more than the $10,000 he was offering. King said he couldn't, but promised Holmes a title shot and other big money opportunities if he would just go along this one, last time.

Then, according to the Holmes-Toperoff manuscript: "I said I wanted to talk to Arum again. I never saw Don's face get the way it got, like he was in pain. His eyes turned cold and empty. He said real quietly, 'If you do, I'll have your legs broke.' Not for a single minute did I think he was kidding. Not for a single minute did I think it wasn't a real threat. And not for a single minute did I doubt Don could find the people to do the job. . . . The first thing I did when I got back to Easton was pick me up a .22 caliber Smith & Wesson."

King loves the thrill of the threat as much as the thrill of the deal.

Trapped in his neurotic love-hate marriage to King, Holmes capitulated and rejected the better offer from Arum, although he would always resent the way King coerced him into the decision. Later Holmes would tell me, "Don can talk a rattlesnake out of biting you."

On September 14, 1977, Holmes knocked out Young Sanford Houpe in seven rounds on national television. And his thumb did not crack. Holmes was now confident he was the future champion in King's expanding harem of heavyweights.

The world got a good sample of Don King's audacious tactical imagination and deal-making in February 1978 when he stole not a fighter but the heavyweight championship of the world.

On February 15, Leon Spinks upset the aging Muhammad Ali and won the title. Bob Arum promoted this fight and he had a contract giving him options on the first three title defenses by Neon Leon. This was not good for King, since it gave Arum control of the title, and most experts anticipated the raw, wild Spinks, who hated to train, would lose the title in an early defense, so Arum could have a monopoly for some time to come, with option contracts.

Spinks revered Ali, as most of Ali's rivals except Frazier did, and he promised Ali an immediate rematch in September. King saw this honorable gesture as an opportunity to play boxing politics.

King called Jose Sulaiman, the president of the World Boxing Council (WBC), one of the comic regulating authorities, based in Mexico City, and convinced him to strip Spinks of his title for the crime of giving Ali an immediate rematch, instead of fighting the Number 1 contender, Ken Norton.

By stripping Spinks without due process or a fair hearing, Sulaiman created a second version of the heavyweight title, a great advantage to King, who had all the other contenders under contract.

King, with an assist from Sulaiman, broke the sacred, lordly line of succession that had stretched back from John L. Sullivan, through Jack Johnson, Jack Dempsey, Joe Louis, Rocky Marciano, Sonny Liston, and Muhammad Ali. It was like dividing the Kentucky Derby, or creating an alternative World Series.

Just seven days after Spinks won the title in the ring, where all titles are supposed to be gained and lost, King held a press conference and announced that Earnie Shavers would fight Larry Holmes in a "WBC title elimination." Since King controlled both fighters, this was using loaded dice and calling it public interest.

King announced that ABC—the network he had just fleeced the year before—would televise the fight; Shavers would get $300,000, and Holmes would get $200,000, of ABC's money.

King called himself the "former manager" of both fighters, and that's how *The New York Times* described him. King had long ago erased any distinction between the roles of manager and promoter for both these fighters.

Thirty-one days after Spinks won the title, from Madrid, Spain, Sulaiman officially announced that the WBC had stripped Spinks of that title. One reason Sulaiman gave was that Spinks had signed a multifight contract with Top Rank, Bob Arum's promotional company.

The WBC designated Norton as the interim champion because he had beaten Jimmy Young, and mandated that Norton must fight the Holmes-Shavers winner within ninety days for the title.

During the WBC convention that stripped Spinks, British promoter-manager Mickey Duff gave an emotional speech in favor of suspending the rules and granting Ali the rematch "because of all that Ali had done for boxing the last eighteen years. Boxing owes this to Ali."

Right after the speech Duff encountered King, who was with Norton.

"There's Mickey Duff, he doesn't like black people very much," King said, addressing Norton but wanting Duff to hear his insult.

"Don, you're a professional nigger," Duff replied, and King just laughed.

Don King couldn't lose. He had Norton, Shavers, and Holmes all under contract to him, as well as Jimmy Young and George Foreman, whom King was still trying to talk into a comeback to fight for what in reality was the Don King-ABC heavyweight championship.

(Stripping Spinks would be the first of dozens of crucial, rule-bending, inconsistent favors Sulaiman would perform for King, as he became more King's junior partner than his independent regulator.

(When King-controlled champions Carlos Zarate and Wilfredo Gomez went more than a year without fighting their mandatory Number 1 contenders, Sulaiman did not strip them. He let Tyson go more than a year without fighting Evander Holyfield when he was the Number 1 contender. When Buster Douglas beat Tyson, Sulaiman tried to force Douglas to give Tyson an immediate rematch, the same offense he stripped Spinks for.

(When Julio Cesar Chavez wanted to fight top contender Roger Mayweather for a promoter other than King, Sulaiman refused to sanction the fight—until King became the promoter.

(When middleweight champion Julian Jackson wanted to leave King, Sulaiman said he would revoke Jackson's license because he had two detached retinas. When Jackson reconciled with King, Sulaiman approved his license, although his eyes were the same.)

King's bold stratagem of breaking up the heavyweight title would have a revolutionary impact on boxing, leading to more than twenty different champions over the next eight years, as revolving mediocrities like Tony Tubbs, Trevor Berbick, Gerrie Coetzee, Bonecrusher Smith, Mike Weaver, and Pinklon Thomas would hold one version or another for a few months and then lose it in their first defense.

This revolving door continued until King managed to talk HBO into investing $16 million of its money in 1986 to begin a new tournament to reunify the title, a sequence of seven fights co-promoted by King and Butch Lewis, leading back to a single, undisputed champion of the planet. King got a $3 million fee for this series of fights from HBO.

King was just as convincing arguing for the morality of splitting the title in 1978 as he was arguing for the morality of reunifying it in 1986. In 1991 he would even organize a new campaign to divide the title again by stripping Holyfield for not fighting Tyson.

In March 1978 Holmes won almost every round against Shavers, employing his now trademark style of long, stiff jabs, quick rights, and plenty of movement. Shavers couldn't land one damaging blow. For years after this fight Holmes, who had to accept the short end of the money, told reporters that King had bet $35,000 on Shavers to win.

On June 9, Holmes confronted Ken Norton in Las Vegas in one of the most stirring heavyweight title fights of the modern era. The fifteenth round was an unforgettable display of tenacity, with the fight scored even going into the last three minutes, both men exhausted, and Holmes in pain from a torn ligament in his arm that he never told anyone about before the fight.

Holmes fought the last round like his whole life depended on it, which it did. The theatrical drama of boxing is watching two athletes, naked before the world, decide their own fate with their own skill and will. One second, one punch, one minute can determine a lifetime of success or regret.

There are no excuses in boxing. In baseball, the pitcher can say the catcher gave him the wrong sign for the pitch that became a home run. In basketball, the center can say the point guard didn't get him the ball when he was open under the basket. In football, the fullback can say the quarterback didn't call his number on the big play.

But in boxing, the athlete is totally alone. And the final round of a dead-even heavyweight title fight is the existential moment when a fighter must create his own destiny.

And that's what Larry Holmes did. The kid they called a quitter just would not quit. Norton hurt him several times early in the round, but Holmes would just not stop punching, just would not accept defeat, and with one last assault in the last thirty seconds, he pulled out an agonizingly close split decision.

Larry Holmes, the black sheep of Don King's heavyweight harem, had become champion of the world.

And Don King was back at the top of the world because Larry Holmes had carried him there. A year after his ABC disgrace, King was back in the cockpit of boxing. He seemed incapable of embarrassment or guilt.

Starting with Holmes's victory, King would control the richest prize in sports for twelve consecutive years, becoming a millionaire many times over, until Tyson lost to Buster Douglas in 1990. He had a monopoly not only on the championship, but on the entire division, never losing his appetite for more inventory, so as never to be dependent on just one fighter's loyalty. Because he lacked the patience and perception to scout amateur tournaments, King felt the need to tie up everyone, to be safe.

After losing his control over Ali, King's guiding principle seemed to be that all fighters were interchangeable. He once told Stan Hoffman, the manager of heavyweight James Broad: "My philosophy is that all fighters are two-dollar whores. Never fall in love with your fighter. My rule is fuck the fighter before the fighter can fuck you. Never let the fighter become bigger than the promoter."

In December 1978 King put his monopoly on paper. He sent a letter to Gil Clancy of Madison Square Garden, listing all the heavyweights he controlled. King wrote:

> Please contact me for the services of the following fighters:
> Larry Holmes, heavyweight champion
> Ken Norton, number one contender
> Jimmy Young, number two contender
> Earnie Shavers, number three contender
> Leon Spinks, number four contender
> Alfredo Evangelista, number six contender
> Scott Le Doux, number ten contender
> Stan Ward, number fifteen contender
> Michael Dokes
> Kevin Isaac

Larry Holmes was a splendid champion who dominated an era. He won his first eight title defenses by knockout. He was an electrifying fighter when hurt, getting off the floor to win against Mike Weaver and Renaldo Snipes, and in his rematch with Shavers. He demolished Leon Spinks, Ossie Ocasio, and Gerry Cooney. He remained undefeated until he lost his title on a dubious decision to Michael Spinks, in 1985, after a seven-year reign as champion.

But for all his ability, Holmes never attained the level of icon and national hero. He had the misfortune to follow Ali and suffered from the comparison with Ali's amazing grace. Holmes just didn't have the charismatic personality or dazzling style to vanquish Ali's ghost, even after he did beat the faded Ali himself in the ring.

Every generation seems capable of falling in love with just one great fighter. And Holmes was in the same position as Gene Tunney, who defeated the beloved Dempsey, and Ezzard Charles, who

defeated the beloved Joe Louis. They were admired but never beloved themselves; they never penetrated the mass imagination or
mass culture.

Perhaps the public unconsciously resented Tunney, Charles,
and Holmes for beating the first loves of each generation of fans.

This was just one more snub, one more disrespect, that Holmes
stored up in the furnace of his memory—and probably used to
motivate himself in moments of crisis and fatigue. It was not anything he or Don King could do much to change. He just lacked
a certain crossover charm—like O. J. Simpson's.

Holmes just came across as angry blue-collar, not middle-class
like the athletes who get all the commercial endorsements—Joe
Montana, Michael Jordan, Magic Johnson, Ken Griffey, Jr.,
Grant Hill, Shaquille O'Neal. He didn't have the actor's glib
grace, or the Olympic glamour of Oscar De La Hoya and Sugar
Ray Leonard. Holmes also lacked the dramatic punching power
that can excite the mass of marginal fans. He was a dish only for
boxing gourmets.

Don King, meanwhile, had his best chance to expand beyond
boxing during the years Larry Holmes was champion. He con-
vened sporadic meetings in Las Vegas to create a diversified black
entertainment and sports conglomerate, but they never went
very far.

King did promote Michael Jackson's 1984 national tour, but
all the talk about movies, records, a black cable network, pay-
per-view events, and other ventures, like agenting for NBA players, never materialized into a coherent business plan, or into a
formal organization.

King understood that boxing was entertainment. King knew
how to raise the capital for any project. He had the contacts with
the biggest black entertainers who would follow him. But Don
King was a soloist. He couldn't delegate. He couldn't create a
structure he could operate within. He wouldn't hire the best
agents, lawyers, accountants, writers, experts. He didn't trust any-

one else because he assumed a stranger would hustle him, just like he would hustle any stranger. So he was stuck with Al Braverman and stepson Carl as his thuggish assistants.

King had the potential to build a sports and entertainment empire and become another David Geffen, or Berry Gordy, or Quincy Jones. But he lacked the sense of collaborative enterprise and institutional stability to accomplish that.

King talked a lot about doing this, but his learning curve leveled off. He could navigate the transition from numbers to boxing, but not the harder transition from boxing to corporate entertainment. He had the ideas, but not the discipline. He had the talk, but not the capacity to listen. And he had alienated the man who could have helped him make the music and entertainment transition, Lloyd Price, who was an astute businessman, as well as a songwriter and performer.

The stormy championship partnership between Don King and Larry Holmes lasted five and a half years before it broke up over money that was missing from Holmes's paychecks.

King just finds it hard to maintain permanent, stable relationships, either with business associates like Price, Elbaum, and Schwartz, or with fighters like Ali and Holmes.

Such long-term alliances are rare in boxing, but sometimes an authentic bond of trust and friendship is created that survives all the pressures and lasts for a career. Joe Louis had this with John Roxborough. Muhammad Ali had it with Angelo Dundee and Herbert Muhammad. Jose Torres had it with Cus D'Amato; Joe Frazier with Eddie Futch; Sugar Ray Leonard with Mike Trainer; Riddick Bowe with Rock Newman; Mark Breland with Shelly Finkel; Marvin Hagler with the Petronelli brothers; Michael Spinks with Butch Lewis.

But Larry Holmes is a material man, and King is a con man, and Holmes became convinced that King had cheated him out of his just compensation in every major fight. In 1988 Holmes told Wally Matthews, then *Newsday*'s boxing writer, that over the course of his career, King cheated him out of $10 million. Holmes said that throughout his career King took 25 percent of his purses as a hidden manager, and that Giachetti took 12½ percent and Spaziani took 12½ percent; and since King also took expenses off the top, Holmes ended up with less than 50 percent of his money on every fight.

Holmes told me he got only $150,000, not his contracted-for $500,000, for his brutal fight with Ken Norton, waged with a torn ligament in his arm. He said he got paid only $50,000, not the announced $200,000, for his first fight with Shavers.

For his Tex Cobb title defense, he says King first cut his purse from $2.1 million to $1.6 million, and then cut him by another $200,000 after the fight. Holmes says King underpaid him by $250,000 for the Leon Spinks match. He says he got underpaid by $2 million for beating Ali.

The fight that most enraged Holmes was the Gerry Cooney contest in 1982. King gave the white hope "parity" in the announced share of the revenue, but Holmes—and most others with access to the records—say that King actually paid Cooney at least $2 to $3 million more than Holmes, when all the closed-circuit revenues were divided.

"Gerry got his full share, but I didn't get mine," Holmes says. "I had to sue Don over the accounting and auditing of the Cooney fight."

Holmes adds, "I never saw a contract for the Cooney fight."

Holmes resented this all the more deeply because King promoted the Cooney fight as a racial Armageddon, stressing the black-white element and helping to create a racially polarized atmosphere. Cooney's co-manager, Dennis Rappaport, internalized this cynical strategy to the point of calling Cooney "America's fighter" and shouting "Win for America!" from the corner during the fight.

Holmes was understandably enraged when he discovered just before the fight started that Secret Service agents had installed a telephone in Cooney's dressing room, so that President Reagan could call and congratulate him in case he won. No such phone line was placed in Holmes's dressing room at Caesars Palace.

Holmes was also understandably upset when vandals put up racist graffiti on his property in Easton after the fight, and somebody blew up his mailbox. He felt the racializing of the fight was a no-win situation for him and damaged his popularity. To then find out that his promoter, who is forever talking about black brotherhood, paid more money to the white challenger than the black champion, was a deep wound.

But despite all this, Larry Holmes still covered for King when he testified several times before a federal grand jury in 1981. Holmes was bitter at King, but he still gave no testimony harmful to him.

The final break between King and Holmes came in December 1983, with King trying to have Holmes stripped of the WBC title by Jose Sulaiman for not fighting Number 1 contender Greg Page. Page was then King's favorite heavyweight, King having swiped him from Butch Lewis in the superficial belief he was the next Ali.*

Holmes was fed up with seeing King secretly root for the fighter in the other corner, which he had seen with Kevin Isaac, Earnie Shavers, and Ossie Ocasio, and felt he would relive that experience with Page, even though he was still the champion.

So Holmes resigned as WBC champion on the last day of the WBC convention in Las Vegas, and accepted the championship belt of a new, rival sanctioning organization based in New Jersey, the International Boxing Federation (IBF).

After the final break, King told Newark-based promoter Murad Muhammad, "I'm going to get Larry Holmes and break him. I'm going to make him crawl."

Murad says Holmes told him, "You got to be careful. Don's a killer. He threatened me many times, saying, 'Don't let me go back to jail.'"

---

*Lewis sued King over this pilferage and won a settlement of $280,000 plus 33 percent from Page's title fights. King had gotten Page's loyalty by paying for the burial of his father and weeping over the grave. Lewis also charged that King gave Page $200,000 under the table to sign.

* * *

In June 1988 I had the luck and pleasure to sit next to Larry
Holmes at the Tyson-Spinks fight in Atlantic City. For two hours
the former champion entertained me and my friends with anecdotes and one-liners about King.

"Don looks black, lives white, and thinks green," Holmes began. "I was loyal to Don for ten years but he was never loyal to
me. Don was my automatic partner. After every fight he would
say, here's ten dollars for you, here's twenty for me."

As Buster Douglas and Mike Williams were fighting the semifinal, Holmes kept up his sardonic chatter and repeated lines he
seemed to have been sharpening for years.

"When I see Don, I see the devil," he said. "The reason he
wears his hair so funny is to hide the horns. The only mistake I
made my whole career was getting tied up with Don. I had more
fights with Don than I had in the ring. Whenever I wanted to
leave him, Don told me he would get my title stripped like Spinks,
or my legs broken.

"My first million-dollar purse was supposed to be Alfredo
Evangelista, but I got a lot less. My second million-dollar
purse wasn't a million either. He robbed me against Ossie Ocasio, who was his fighter. I made a lot of money, only I didn't
get it."

When King himself was introduced from center ring, Holmes
stood up and booed, along with most of the fourteen thousand
other fans. And some fans in our ringside section applauded him
for booing King.

Holmes was feeling particularly hostile to King on this night
because King had just skimmed his pay for his recent failed comeback fight against Tyson. In January 1988 Holmes had been
knocked unconscious by Tyson in four rounds—and then short-
changed $300,000 by King.

Holmes was retired in the fall of 1987 when Don King pulled
into his driveway in Easton in a big white limo. King settled into
Holmes's house, ordered Chinese food from his favorite restau-

rant in New Jersey, and started selling Holmes on a comeback fight with Tyson.

After ten hours of nonstop evangelical rap, King had talked Holmes into taking the hopeless fight for $3.1 million.

"You know I get ten percent of that," King told Holmes.

"No, you don't," Holmes shot back.

"I don't even need you to sign," King countered. "I've got your signature on the last page of a lot of contracts."*

King and Holmes continued to argue about this 10 percent "finder's fee" all through training and even in the dressing room minutes before the Tyson bout.

After Holmes lost, King deducted the $300,000 for himself from Holmes's share of the purse.

"I'll sue you," Holmes shouted at King.

A few months after I listened to Holmes's wonderful monologue in Atlantic City, he reached an out-of-court settlement with King. King paid him $150,000—half of what he was entitled to—and Holmes signed a legal agreement promising he would stop giving reporters negative information about King.

Only in boxing can a champion sign away his free speech rights to get back half the money that was skimmed from him.

But Don King signed no such gag order. In March 1991, King was quoted in *New York* magazine as saying, "Whatever I got from Larry, I deserved it! He couldn't draw flies to a dump. I had to work with Larry on his personality to make him a big star."

King did not mention Ernie Butler, who is still living in Easton, now seventy, still teaching a few kids how to box for free, still doing what he did on the day in 1968 that he first found Larry Holmes.

---

*Contract fraud was such a habit with King, he could joke about it. Ernie Butler says King forged his name to a contract. Butch Lewis accused King of forging a contract with Greg Page. And the U.S. government charged King with forging a contract with Julio Cesar Chavez to defraud Lloyd's of London.

Tim Witherspoon says King made him sign blank contracts and duplicate contracts with different percentages for Carl King.

The Betrayal of Muhammad Ali

Don King was not the only promoter trying to induce Muhammad Ali out of a restless retirement in the spring of 1980. There was also Bob Arum, Harold Smith, Murad Muhammad, and the government of Egypt.

Ali had retired after recapturing the title for an unprecedented third time by defeating Leon Spinks in September 1978. After that he had been honored at a series of retirement dinners and public celebrations.

Gradually his weight ballooned up to 270 pounds. His speech became slightly slurred and slower. And he was starting to feel a little bored, a little concerned about where his next few million dollars were coming from.

The honors at these dinners were nice, but Ali was an addict of fame. He yearned for the solo spotlight of center stage. He loved people, he loved attention, he loved having the press around him all the time, looking for a quote, writing down his rhymes, his nicknames for opponents, his predictions, his political ideas, his sermons.

Ali was missing the unmatchable high of seeing himself on television every night, and of fifty thousand people chanting his name on the way to the ring.

Nobody put a gun to Ali's head to make him come back. It was his own decision. But people did put a lot of temptation on his table.

Bob Arum wanted Ali to fight WBA champion John Tate, but Tate was unexpectedly knocked out in the fifteenth round by Mike Weaver on March 31. And since Larry Holmes had already knocked out Weaver, he continued to be recognized by most fans and writers as the legitimate champion.

Harold Smith, not yet detected as the embezzler of $21 million from Wells Fargo National Bank, came to Easton to see Holmes with an offer to fight Ali. Smith's promotional company was called MAPS (Muhammad Ali Professional Sports), but Ali was only being paid a fee to lease his name to the company; he was not part of the company. Smith arrived in a stretch limo and in the company of two beautiful women.

Like so many people in boxing, going back to Jack Kearns and Tex Rickard, Harold Smith was a likable rascal. He had already signed up Tommy Hearns and Aaron Pryor with huge cash signing bonuses transported in pillow cases. He had also signed up Saoul Mamby, one of Holmes's best friends in boxing, giving him a $75,000 signing bonus that he told Holmes about.

Smith had attempted to sign up Holmes a year earlier, when he had a physical confrontation with King inside Holmes's hotel suite in Las Vegas. Smith says the pushing and shoving stopped when King pulled out a pistol. This is quite possible since King did frequently carry a weapon.

Mort Sharnik, who was the boxing consultant for CBS-TV in the early 1980s, recalls a dispute he had with King in San Juan in 1980, after Michael Dokes, managed by Carl King, was given a draw in a fight most observers thought was won by Ossie Ocasio. As they argued, "a pearl-handled pistol fell out of the breast pocket of King's tuxedo," Sharnik recalls. "The gun had to be illegal because King didn't have his pardon yet."

A gun also fell out of King's pocket in 1987, as Bob Arum was wrestling with him to prevent him from jumping into the ring right after the Sugar Ray Leonard–Marvin Hagler fight that Arum had promoted and King had nothing to do with.

Larry Holmes had no desire to fight Muhammad Ali. Ali was his idol and he loved the former champion. Holmes had been Ali's sparring partner from 1973 to 1975, an experience he would treasure the rest of his life. Ali had given Holmes his first quality boxing equipment when he saw the falling-apart junk his sparring partner was using. The first week of sparring Ali had given Holmes a black eye, and Holmes was so proud to have it, he wouldn't let anyone put an ice pack on it. He wanted to be able to show it off to his buddies in Easton. A shiner from the Greatest was a trophy of honor to the young Larry Holmes.

Now Harold Smith was sitting in his office in Easton offering him millions to fight his idol. Holmes was thinking Ali at thirty-eight was in no condition to fight anyone, much less himself at his peak. Holmes had sat next to Ali at a lot of boxing functions lately and seen the gray in his hair and the bulge around his middle.

But such was the remorseless cycle of boxing history. Rocky Marciano had to knock out his hero, Joe Louis, to get to the top. The young Ray Robinson had to beat his hero, an old Henry Armstrong. The ritual slaying of fathers is another reason boxing is the cruelest sport. Holmes had every impulse not to do it, but he also had been instructed it was his job to do it, as heavyweight champion.

Harold Smith seemed direct and confident as he made his offer to Holmes, and Holmes's lawyer, Charles Spaziani. They were sitting in Holmes's office in downtown Easton, in a building

Holmes owned as part of his dream of being the Bugsy Siegel of
Easton, constructing a commercial strip in the middle of no-
where—a disco, a motel, a gym, a restaurant, an office building.

"I'll give you five million dollars to fight Muhammad Ali,"
Smith said. "I'll give you two million now for signing, and three
million later. If I can't get Ali to sign, you keep the two million."

This was the offer Holmes had always dreamed about getting.
Now it was on the table, and he started to waver and stall. Before
the meeting he had, on some peculiar compulsion, called Don
King in Manhattan and told him Smith was about to arrive in
Easton, and told King to get there fast himself and match any
offer. Holmes knew King was driving ninety miles an hour and
would arrive shortly to play out a scene in a B-movie Holmes was
directing without an ending in mind.

Smith handed Holmes two checks, each for $500,000, drawn
on the Wells Fargo Bank of California.

"If they don't clear, we don't have a deal," Smith said. "Take
them. What have you got to lose?"

Holmes felt dizzy from temptation and indecision. He was
sweating and remembers walking over to the window to catch a
breeze on a warm May afternoon.

Then Harold Smith brought out his magical leather pillow case
and showed Larry Holmes what he said was $1 million in cash.
The pillow case was full of old bills—hundreds, fifties, and twen-
ties. Spaziani looked at the money and was speechless.

"Here's one million in cash if you agree to the fight," Smith
said.

A few minutes later Holmes heard Don King's limo screech to
a halt outside the Alpha Building. He had gotten to Easton in
record time. Nobody outworked or outhustled Don King.

The two promoters threatened and cursed each other, with
King screaming Smith's money was "drug money." Smith claimed
he had investors who were oil millionaires in the Middle East.

Holmes summed up the confrontation this way in his unpublished memoir: "Don tried physical intimidation, but Smith didn't scare. That impressed me."

But in the end Holmes didn't take the million in cash, or the million in Wells Fargo checks. He was nervous about the origins of the money. It didn't feel like the way real businessmen made serious propositions. And King still had a strong emotional control over him.

Don King had talked him out of fighting Young Sanford Houpe for Bob Arum in 1976 for more than seven times the money King was paying him. And now he was willing to fight his idol for half the money Harold Smith was offering him.

It would take almost three more years, and getting short-changed in the Gerry Cooney and Tex Cobb fights, before Holmes was strong enough to walk away from Don King.

But once he rejected the $5 million offer from Smith, it became inevitable he would let King promote the fight with Ali, although Murad Muhammad would tempt Holmes with a $3 million offer to fight Ali in Egypt. But Holmes did not want to give Ali the home court advantage of a country that had such a large Islamic population.

Harold Smith left saying, "The money is good and it's always there for you, Larry." Neither would prove to be the case. But that's boxing. Nobody tells the truth, not even nice guys who would like to be good guys.

By the end of June Don King had put the deal together. He promised Ali $8 million, Holmes $2.5 million, 25 percent of which King would take back for himself. King negotiated a site fee from Caesars Palace, but for the first time he had to place his own money at risk to make the fight. This investment was new, and King never forgot it for a moment. He cut corners to save money every possible way, even serving skimpy ham and cheese sandwiches at press conferences, forgetting, or ignoring, the Muslim religious injunction against ham that Ali and part of his entourage obeyed.

For a few days King considered putting the fight into Cairo, even telling reporters, "We're going to dedicate this fight to peace in the Middle East." But Holmes balked and Caesar's came up with the money.

After the fight was announced, King told boxing writer John Schulian, "You see, as an afoxidando [sic] and a good friend of Ali, I didn't want him to come out of retirement and fight Holmes. Ali couldn't believe that. He told me he was fighting for equality and justice, for the future of our children. When I heard that, I said, 'You're right, Ali.' And I promised him I would help make the fight, which is what my businessman's instincts had been telling me to do all along."

Ali should never have taken the fight. He never seemed right from the start. His long-term personal physician, Dr. Ferdie Pacheco, told him to stay retired and would have nothing to do with the fight.

In March, Ali was sparring in the gym with Jeff Sims, a slow heavyweight. Ali spat out his mouthpiece to taunt his foe and Sims smacked him in the mouth. The punch sliced an inch-long gash that needed ten stitches to close. If Dr. Pacheco's counsel needed a second opinion, this punch should have been it.

Instead, without one tune-up fight, Ali dyed his gray hairs, closed his eyes to all of nature's messages, and signed to fight Larry Holmes in October.

He went to Deer Lake and hired Tim Witherspoon, then a kid with seven pro fights, to be one of his sparring partners. After a few days in the gym Ali asked Witherspoon not to hit him in the body.

"I hit him in the head pretty easy," says Witherspoon, another who still idolizes Ali. "They never asked me to stay off his head. I feel bad about it now."

Many of the writers who visited Ali in Deer Lake came away disturbed. Some had not seen him for two years and they could perhaps better notice the deterioration in his speech and reflexes.

In the gym he seemed lethargic and easy to hit. Some of the same writers thought they saw the same conditions before he beat Foreman in Zaire, so they were reluctant to believe their own eyes. Was he letting a kid like Witherspoon hit him for a reason?

But enough of the writers did stories questioning the wisdom and morality of the fight so that the Nevada State Athletic Commission required that Ali get a full neurological and renal examination at the Mayo Clinic, as a precondition for licensing Ali to fight. Ali spent two days at the famed Rochester, Minnesota, clinic, on July 23 and 24. The doctor's report, sent to the Nevada commission, is written partly in medical jargon. It said: "A CT scan of the head was performed and showed only a congenital variation in the form of a small cavum septum pellucidum."

This is a hole in the membrane separating the ventricles of the brain that can be enlarged by blows to the head.

Other parts of the report are in plain English: "He does not quite hop with the agility that one might anticipate, and on finger-to-nose testing there is a slight degree of missing the target" and he had "some difficulty with memory."

This is about Muhammad Ali, whose genius was agility and eye-hand coordination, the Ali who dodged all of Liston's punches during the round he was blinded in one eye, who landed seven straight punches to Foreman's head to knock him out, who could see Frazier's punches coming and turn his head, whose jab couldn't miss the moving target of Leon Spinks's head two years earlier.

The report also said Ali suffered from "occasional tingling of the hands in the morning." The Mayo report also noted that Ali "claims that he has always had some mild slurring of his speech for the past ten or twelve years."

This was Ali conning a doctor, who should have looked at videotape of Ali in 1970 or 1974 to see that Ali was the greatest talker in boxing history. There was a drastic decline in Ali's speech clarity and speed that any sixteen-year-old could have noticed, much less a Mayo clinic specialist.

But the doctor's report recommended Ali get a license and the Nevada commission gave him one.

Dr. Pacheco thinks the doctor's report was scandalous. He says: "Just because a man can pass a physical examination doesn't mean he should be fighting in a prize ring. That shouldn't be a hard concept to grasp. In fact, most trainers can tell you better than any neurologist in the world when a fighter is shot. You watch your fighter's career from the time he is a young man; you watch him develop into a champion; you watch him get great; then all of a sudden he doesn't have it anymore. Give him a neurological examination at that point and you'll find nothing wrong. . . . Anybody in the gym can see it before the doctors can, because the doctors, good doctors, are judging these fighters by the standards of ordinary people, and the demands of ordinary jobs."

The Nevada commission refused to make the Mayo report available to the press. Reporters who doubted Ali was healthy enough to fight were told they were substituting their layman's opinion for that of the premier medical institution in America. But the fact is, the report raised more questions than it answered; it should have been made public; and the Nevada commission should have gotten a doctor experienced with fighters to follow up on the hole in Ali's brain, on his difficulty with the hand-to-nose test, the tingling in his hands, and his slurred speech and loss of memory.

In the weeks before the fight Ali fooled some people into thinking he had a chance because he got his weight down to under 220. He looked slim and fit and he talked the old talk. The odds against him dropped from 3 to 1 to only 13 to 10.

But Marty Monroe beat him up every day in the gym. Ali had no reflexes. He couldn't get out of the way of punches anymore. His own punches had no snap, and his legs had no spring.

Gene Dibble was one of those who loved Ali unconditionally. He had served as his financial adviser during the 1970s and had done his best to protect Ali from the swindlers and leeches Ali always let into his life and would never get rid of or confront. In his biography, Tom Hauser quoted Dibble on his feelings on the eve of the fight: "Before Holmes, things just weren't right. He was slow and debilitated physically. He couldn't run. Hell, he could hardly stay awake. My brother and I saw him the day before the fight. And my brother, who's a physician, took one look at Ali and said there was no way he should fight. That was enough for me. I said, 'Ali, why don't you postpone this thing?' But he shrugged it off. . . ."

Ali was not only suffering from the neurological symptoms described by the Mayo Clinic doctors. He was also suffering from the side effects of a medication given him by Dr. Charles Williams, the doctor of his manager, Herbert Muhammad.

Gene Kilroy was the first to notice the medicine given Ali by Dr. Williams was having a terrible effect on him. Kilroy told me: "Ali was in good shape coming out of Deer Lake. But in the middle of September I was in his room at Caesars when Dr. Williams came in and told him he had some thing to give him that would make him strong. I told Ali please don't take it, but he did. Right after that Ali started urinating all the time and being dehydrated and sleepy. He started losing weight too fast. He couldn't run in the morning. I was scared to death. I saw him getting weaker as the fight got closer. I felt so bad I told him one day, to build him up, that I was betting everything I had on him to win. And Ali told me not to do it, that something was wrong."

What was wrong was that Dr. Williams had misdiagnosed Ali's underlying malady as a thyroid condition. He prescribed a potentially lethal drug called Thyrolar, and instructed Ali to take one tablet a day, starting three weeks before the fight.*

The drug actually put Ali's life in danger. It accelerated his

---

*Without consulting his physician, Ali tripled the dosage. He says he "thought the pills would be like vitamins."

heart and prevented him from sweating, causing dehydration. It could have caused a stroke or bleeding inside his head. The truth is: There was no medical evidence that Ali had a thyroid deficiency, and Dr. Pacheco says, "Ali is lucky he lived through the Holmes fight."

The day of the match there were three giant cardboard cutouts hanging over the entrance to Caesars Palace. They were life-size pictures of Holmes and Ali, and an even bigger one of Don King, who dominated the two champions. It was the crude Las Vegas version of King in Gleason's gym, giving out photos of himself after Holmes and Shavers had sparred in 1973. King would always be the greatest modern self-promoter, even better than Madonna.

The fight itself was like watching the public torture of an international hero. Ali just took a sickening beating. He winced, and shuddered, and cringed under the blows. It was like watching a middle-aged impostor who'd invaded his body and stolen his face. He could not punch, he could not move, he had no strength, he was fatigued after the first round. All he had left were pride and stoicism.

Holmes did not know what to do. He didn't want to hurt Ali, but he also wanted to put him out of his misery as quickly as possible. He felt like he was beating up his father. He tried to make it a mercy killing at some points, but at others he just stepped back and took it easy, hoping the referee would have the sense to stop it.

In the fourth round Holmes hit Ali with a powerful right to the kidney and heard his hero moan. Ali started to fall, but wouldn't go down. In describing the kidney punch in his unpublished memoir, Holmes wrote: "There's not another man on earth who would have stayed on his feet after that punch. That same pride is why he took so many beatings in fights, even in the fights he won. And it was why he was one of the greatest fighters of all time. In my opinion, the greatest."

By the ninth round a tear stained my notebook and I had to look away. Ali had come to carry so much meaning for me that I couldn't bear to watch his end.

Ali had come to represent the Zeitgeist of the sixties, the purest personification of a decade and a state of mind. In the decade of black assertion, he was black power. In the decade of antiwar protests, he was the most famous and punished resister to the war. He had more styles than Dylan and he was more fun than the Beatles. In the decade when fame killed Joplin, Hendrix, and Jim Morrison, he rode fame like it was a skateboard. He symbolized change, rebellion, and liberation in an era defined by those qualities.

Now he was a hollow shell, taking a beating, when he belonged under a doctor's care. It was the public flogging of a generation's youth and idealism.

I had seen Ali upset Liston with his speed, beat Cleveland Williams with his power, Foreman with his imagination, Frazier with his bravery, and Spinks with his memory. And now he was being pummeled in the parking lot of a casino, so other men could make money.

After the tenth round Herbert Muhammad made a gesture that was the prearranged signal to stop the fight.

"That's all," Angelo Dundee told referee Richard Greene.

"One more round," begged Bundini, tears in his bulging eyes, as he grabbed on to Dundee's sweater.

"Fuck you, no!" Dundee screamed, and the massacre was stopped.

As soon as the fight was over, Larry Holmes started to cry, right in the ring. He went over to Ali, slumped on his stool, and kissed him.

"I respect you, man, I love you," Holmes said between his own tears of mixed emotions. "I hope we're always friends."

After the fight Ali was too sore and weak to even take a shower. He was helped to his room at Caesars and he lay down on a bed still wearing his trunks and robe. Only his shoes were off, and the room was dark.

Holmes told Gene Kilroy he wanted to see Ali and that was how Holmes, feeling only sorrow in victory, saw his mentor an hour after the fight.

"I didn't want to hurt you out there," Holmes said. "Please don't fight again. If you need any money I'll give it to you."

After a long silence, Ali sat halfway up in the bed and cupped his hands around his mouth. He started to mimic the collective sound a big fight crowd makes.

"I . . . want . . . Holmes. . . . I . . . want . . . Holmes," Ali began to chant. "I fed you, I taught you how to fight. And look what you did to me. I'm coming back to whip your ass."

Ali was smiling now, although his swollen face and shut eyes made him look like a gargoyle. He saw Holmes was depressed, and he was trying to cheer up Holmes by playing around despite his pain.

"Gimme Holmes, gimme Holmes," Ali was play-acting as Holmes prepared to leave the darkened room.

Later Holmes would tell Ali's biographer, "I want people to know I'm proud I learned my craft from Ali. I'm prouder of sparring with him when he was young than of beating him when he was old."

Like many others, I believe that the point-blank beating Ali took in this fight has a direct causal relationship with the decline in his health and his current medical condition.

Interviewed by Tom Hauser nine years after the fight, John Schulian was still emotional: "I hated Don King for promoting that fight . . . that lying, thieving motherfucker. That he could stand there and say, 'Oh, Muhammad, I love you, I'm with you, Muhammad; you're the greatest!' And then make a fortune off Ali getting brutalized that way. Well, fuck you, Don King. The man is a total scumbag. . . . They sacrificed Ali. That's what it was, a human sacrifice for money and power. That night went far beyond Ali. One of the great symbols of our time was tarnished. So many people—blacks, whites, Muslims, Americans, Africans, Asians, people all over the world—believed in Ali. And he was destroyed because of people who didn't care one bit about the things he'd stood for his entire life."

And *Daily News* boxing writer Mike Katz told Hauser: "I don't know what happened behind the scenes in Vegas. I just know that it was essential to Don King for Ali to go ahead with the fight. This was one of the few times King had his own money on the line, as opposed to someone else's. If Ali-Holmes had fallen through, or failed at the gate, King would have been in trouble."

But the worst was yet to come.

When the fight was over, and Ali got out of the hospital, Don King paid him $1,170,000 less than the signed contract stipulated. The contract called for Ali to be paid $8 million and it contained a clause saying there could be no amendment except in writing, and there had been none.

About a week before the fight King had started to tell Ali that the expenses had been high, and the closed-circuit ticket sales were not as brisk as he had hoped, and his own money was at risk, and that Ali might have to accept a $1 million cut in his earnings.

Ali had retained Michael Phenner, a corporate lawyer from Chicago, of impeccable integrity, and in the days before the fight, Charles Lomax was following him all around Caesars trying to amend the contract down to $7 million. Phenner flatly refused and warned Lomax not to let King cheat Ali on his purse. Despite King's anxieties, the fight made a substantial profit.

After the fight Phenner talked to Ali and they agreed the contract had to be enforced as written. When Ali was shortchanged by almost $1.2 million, he asked Phenner to file a lawsuit against King for the money he had surely earned with his torn flesh, lost platform, and diminished dignity.

On June 9, 1982, Muhammad Ali sued Don King in the Northern District Court of Illinois. The suit asked for "statutory interest and reasonable attorney's fees" in addition to the $1,170,000. By the time the suit was filed, Ali had permanently retired and his health had deteriorated considerably.

This lawsuit scared Don King. To be perceived as cheating Ali would be a damaging blow to King's stature and credibility in the boxing universe, especially with fighters. King feared the Muslims and didn't want any more conflict with them. He had reported to the FBI a death threat from a Muslim earlier in 1982, and he had been beaten by four Muslims in the Bahamas in December 1981, at the direction of another Muslim, James Cornelius.

And King knew that Ali was standing on firm legal grounds, backed by a top-of-the-line corporate lawyer. Phenner and most legal experts expected Ali to win a quick summary judgment verdict.

That's when King called on Jeremiah Shabazz. King had a sixth sense for the weaknesses people had, who could influence whom, how to make someone yield to his single-minded purpose. He knew Shabazz was a person he could trust, a person Ali *did* trust, and that he would be the best possible intermediary to get Ali to drop his lawsuit.

Shabazz was now the Muslim minister in Philadelphia, but King knew he had been the minister in Atlanta and Miami who first introduced Ali to the Nation of Islam, back in 1961, and had been important in Ali's conversion to the Islamic religion. Shabazz had always been part of Ali's camp and Ali saw him as a religious leader as well as savvy about boxing.

Shabazz lived by his wits and King had paid him over the years for various services. In the spring of 1982 King had called Shabazz in a panic because he believed that some Muslims from New Jersey, affiliated with a rival promoter, had a murder contract to kill King. Shabazz had rushed up to New York and helped defuse a potential assassination of King. King had taken the threat seriously enough to notify the FBI and have his office filled with agents and bodyguards when Shabazz arrived to work the phones.

"I saved his life," Shabazz recalls. "He relied on me that day more than he did on the government people."

So in late July 1982, Don King asked Shabazz to come to his office on East Sixty-ninth Street in Manhattan. When Shabazz arrived, Don King had $50,000 in a suitcase on his desk, all in cash.

"I want you to give this cash money to Ali," King said, "but only after you get him to sign this document."

King showed Shabazz a letter to himself ending the lawsuit, releasing King from all legal and financial obligations, and containing a space for Ali's signature at the bottom. King also gave Shabazz a first-class, round-trip airplane ticket to Los Angeles, and promised Shabazz a sum of money for himself if he returned with Ali's signature on the document.

"Don definitely owed Ali that one million," Shabazz says now. "But Don had gotten Herbert Muhammad to tell Ali that the lawsuit wasn't worth fighting. Don had gotten Herbert to see it his way. Ali was ailing by then and mumbling a lot. I guess he needed the money."

The last thing King said to Shabazz was to repeat, "Don't give him the money until after he signs the paper."

King always operated on the premise that any fighter would be more impressed with $10,000 in cash in his hands than with a bank check for $1 million. He had dazzled dozens of fighters with fresh green cash from casino cages and bank vaults, to get them to sign pieces of paper.

He knew even the great Ali was vulnerable to the magic powers of cash money in stacks. Especially in failing health and retirement.

So Jeremiah Shabazz flew to California with the suitcase held tightly on his lap. He did not let it out of his grasp during the five-hour flight.

When Shabazz arrived in Los Angeles, he hired a notary public for $100 and took her with him to see Ali, who was in the UCLA Medical Center, receiving treatment for his failing health.

The notary read Ali the letter and asked him if he understood what he was signing, as she and Shabazz sat at his bedside.

Ali mumbled yes and signed the piece of paper Shabazz had carried from King's office. The letter said:

"I acknowledge receipt by me and Muhammad Ali Enterprises, Inc., of $7 million as full and complete consideration of Don King Productions, Inc., and Don King's obligation to me under the Bout Agreement dated June 25, 1980, and hereby release Don King and Don King Productions, Inc., from any and all monies due to me, or for which I may have been entitled under the said Bout Agreement."

The letter Ali signed even gave King the right to promote any future comeback fight Ali might decide to engage in. The last paragraph read: "I further agree that you shall have the exclusive first right of refusal to promote any and all bouts referred to above subject to the terms and conditions agreed upon by my manager Jabir Muhammad."

Ali had taken the beating of his life to earn this money. Now he had taken $50,000 from a friend and given up the right to collect $1.1 million.

"I regret what I did very much," Shabazz told me. "I got used."

When Ali told Michael Phenner he had signed a release ending the lawsuit without telling him, the tough corporate litigator sat in his office and cried.

CHAPTER 9

The

Teflon

Don

On July 11, 1980, FBI agents Joe Spinelli and John Pritchard, in the company of former boxing champion Jose Torres, drove the two hours up to Catskill, New York, to see Cus D'Amato. It was a happy ride, full of old stories and shared experiences because all three men were good friends. Spinelli was the godfather to Torres's Puerto Rican son and Pritchard's black son.

This journey marked the beginning of the FBI's investigation into professional boxing as an industry. It did not start as an investigation into Don King, and it never concentrated exclusively on King. It was an inquiry into a derelict system.

The only boxing person who would go to jail as a direct result of the probe would be King's assistant, Constance Harper, who was convicted by the same jury that acquitted King of tax evasion. The investigation did develop information that led to the conviction of the mobster Michael Franzese, and it did accumulate a lot of evidence of King's associations with organized crime. It also turned the Reverend Al Sharpton into an FBI informer for a while.

But on the humid summer day it started, Jose Torres was making the introductions to his old manager, vouching for the dedication of the two agents to the demanding and somewhat paranoid D'Amato.

As history would have it, July 1980 was also the first month that D'Amato began working with a fourteen-year-old kid named Mike Tyson, although the agents did not glimpse the prodigy on this visit.

D'Amato, then seventy-two, suggested James Cagney in his looks and intensity. He sat at a picnic table in his yard and gave the agents a three-hour lecture on the history of larceny in the cruelest game. They barely had a chance to ask any questions. D'Amato just kept rolling along. He seemed like he had been waiting for these two visitors for forty years.

D'Amato had been active in boxing since the 1930s and he was like a professor of history. He described how the gangster Owney Madden controlled Primo Carnera when he was heavyweight champion, and how the novel *The Harder They Fall* is based on Carnera.

He described how the feared killer Frankie Carbo ruled boxing in the 1950s, controlling virtually every welterweight and lightweight champion, and most of the top contenders.

He stressed the commercial side of boxing, calling multifight option contracts "legalized extortion." He lectured on the hidden ownership of fighters, the manipulation of rankings, and the sport's own lack of regulation.

If anything, D'Amato seemed more hostile to Arum than to King. When Spinelli asked him which one was worse, D'Amato replied, "How could God have made the same mistake twice?"

At the end of the country seminar, Pritchard asked who else they should go see at the start of their education. D'Amato suggested Flash Gordon, and provided the address of his phoneless apartment in Queens. He also recommended Alex Wallau at ABC.

Nothing D'Amato said came close to usable legal evidence. But the day had been well spent as an orientation and history lesson.

On the drive back to Manhattan, Spinelli, who had the streak of the social worker beneath his law enforcement mask, felt he was embarking on a socially redeeming adventure, not merely another routine FBI investigation.

Joe Spinelli had been a boxing junkie ever since his grandfather took him by subway, when he was just six years old, to see Rocky Marciano fight Archie Moore at Yankee Stadium in 1955. That brisk September night, with its roaring crowd, electric atmosphere, and bright lights, became one of those childhood memories that remain vivid forever.

His grandfather had come from the same small town in Italy as Marciano's family, and the grandfather had a reverential feeling about Marciano that he was able to communicate to his young grandson.

Also, Spinelli's father had been a successful amateur boxer, fighting in "smokers" across the Bronx for a few dollars. His father had given Spinelli a populist view of boxing, from the perspective of the fighter as working stiff, who took the blows but usually ended up with less money than the promoters who counted the house.

So from the outset Spinelli felt his job was to clean up boxing for the protection of the fighters. He brought an uncommon passion for systemic reform to his mission, not merely a relentless lock-up-the-bad-guys cop mentality. Although Spinelli had this, too.

After a few months, the FBI investigation began to focus on King, mostly because he was the dominant promoter in boxing and the ABC tournament had left behind a paper trail and some bitter, talkative boxing folk.

Also, on September 10, 1980, the Cleveland office of the FBI sent Spinelli an airtel memo citing some of King's long-term relationships with Ohio mobsters. The airtel said:

Organized crime figures in Cleveland who King would most likely remain in contact with are black numbers operators Virgil Ogletree and Richard Drake. Source information from July of 1978 indicates that King returned to Cleveland at that time to bring back into line several subordinate numbers operators in the Cleveland area. . . . In the early 1970s King kicked back part of his numbers profits to Alex Birns, aka Shondor (killed in the bombing of his vehicle in 1975) and LCN member Anthony Panzarella.

Panzarella was a career hoodlum, first jailed for robbery in 1929, who dabbled in numbers, gambling, and Teamster Union rackets and pled guilty to tax evasion in 1968, a case based on his unreported income from the numbers. He provided King with protection in exchange for his kickbacks, and when he died of natural causes in 1989, some old-time Cleveland mobsters were offended that King did not attend the funeral and pay his respects.

Spinelli's first breakthrough came on January 21, 1981, when Richie Giachetti turned over five tape recordings he had secretly made on his own initiative of his telephone conversations with King, and one with Larry Holmes. Giachetti had made the tapes to have a weapon to use against King in case the two old friends became enemies. Giachetti was starting to feel that King was cheating him out of money and he wanted some leverage with King. The tapes Giachetti made were dated November 18, 1978, December 12, 1978, two on January 14, 1979, and June 1, 1980. One was undated.

Giachetti had first told Spinelli about them six months earlier, claiming they contained proof of crimes. He asked Spinelli to serve a subpoena on him for the tapes, so he could say he had no choice in turning them over. Giachetti, who was experienced in dealing with law enforcement, said he wanted immunity for himself before he testified before any grand jury.

In these preliminary conversations Giachetti also told Spinelli and Assistant U.S. Attorney Dominic Amorosa that he had copies of "double contracts" signed by Larry Holmes that would prove how King was taking 25 percent of Holmes's earnings as an illegal undercover manager.

Giachetti kept promising Spinelli and Amorosa he would provide the tapes as soon as he was paid from Holmes's fight with Ali in October 1980. Giachetti was expecting $500,000 under his contract that gave him 12 ½ percent of Holmes's purses, but King paid him only $350,000, keeping the rest for himself. This accounting eased Giachetti's guilt about becoming a "rat" and breaking the code of silence he had lived by ever since he was a runner in King's numbers empire in the 1960s.

But when Spinelli finally heard the tapes he had negotiated over for six months, he was a little disappointed. They contained no direct proof of any indictable offense. But there was a colloquial admission by King of his ties to the mob.

On one of the tapes King recounted a sit-down with a mobster sent by a rival promoter. King told Giachetti: "They put the mob on *me*! What he [the rival promoter] had hoped was that I would start mouthing off and yelling at this guy, but I was too smart. I knew if I did that, I would end up in the fucking lake. So I told this guy who *I was with,* and he said, 'Oh, OK, I understand.' "

On June 3, 1981, Spinelli got the convicted California bank swindler and Don King wannabe Harold Smith to do some undercover work for him, in hopes of getting a lighter sentence for his Wells Fargo Bank embezzlement. He arranged for Smith to call Giachetti and consensually record the conversation.

"What's happening, Richie?" Smith began.

"That fucking King," said Giachetti, "he sent a hit man to Las Vegas to tell me to lay off him. . . . You know that I got tapes of King that I made."

Later in this same call Giachetti claimed that King "pays off" Jose Sulaiman and journalists.

Smith's taped conversation seemed to confirm information Spinelli had received three weeks earlier, from two separate FBI informants, that King was, in fact, trying to arrange for Giachetti's murder.

On May 15 an FBI informant told Spinelli that he had found out from King that King was planning to go to Philadelphia four days later to meet with Frankie "Flowers" D'Alfonso "to discuss the killing of Giachetti." D'Alfonso was one of King's mob friends, and King had steered him the lucrative closed-circuit rights to the Holmes-Ali match for Philly and Atlantic City, and would later get him the rights to the Holmes-Cooney fight. D'Alfonso himself would be executed in a mob hit in 1985.

A second FBI informant, based in Baltimore, told Spinelli that King's meeting had to be canceled at the last minute because D'Alfonso suspected he was under surveillance at the time (which was true), and he didn't want to be seen with King.

King found out about Giachetti taping him from Holmes, who heard the tapes when they were played for him during a grand jury appearance in the Southern District. Holmes and King fired Giachetti the next day.

Giachetti is a genuinely tough man who boasts he never lost a street fight. But he was in fear for his life after the hit man visited him in Vegas on May 27, 1981, and told him King had put out a contract on him.

Giachetti was so scared that he told the whole story to Mike Marley, who splashed it all over the back page of the *New York Post* on August 8, 1981. "I am fearful for my life," Giachetti confessed to the *Post*'s boxing writer. "I'm scared to go to the bars I used to, my old hangouts. . . . I think they would try to make it look like a mugging. A bombing, an outright killing would be too obvious."

Marley quoted Giachetti as saying, "The mob guys have come to see me. . . . My family is very scared and my two kids are upset. I make sure I don't go out alone. I sneak in and out of Vegas and New York now."

The *Post*'s story continued: "Giachetti said he was paid a visit by a New York man who is deeply involved in organized crime. 'This guy said King told him I put a contract out on King,' Giachetti recalled. King tried a reverse tactic."*

Somebody a lot tougher than even Giachetti was also afraid of King—Larry Holmes, the heavyweight champion.

Early in 1981 Spinelli went to Holmes's house in Easton to give him a grand jury subpoena and try to talk him into cooperating with the investigation. Spinelli used his empathy with fighters and knowledge of the sport to make human contact, and soon Holmes was relaxed, and they sat around the pool talking boxing for an hour. Spinelli told him how impressive he was in that fifteenth round with Norton.

Holmes started out in a jovial mood, at one point calling his lawyer, Charles Spaziani, and laughing, "I got the FBI here and they have subpoenaed my ass. And they have a subpoena for you, too, so you better go hide."

The mood of the conversation turned when Spinelli got to his message.

"You know there are plenty of deserving fighters who never got to own a nice house like this because they got ripped off by promoters," Spinelli told Holmes. "You know the fighters, and you know the promoters, and you know exactly how they do it. That's why we want you to testify. We're hoping, Larry, that you would appear before the grand jury as a friendly witness, someone who really knows the story and come forward willingly."

"Look, Mr. Spinelli," Holmes responded, "I'm just a fighter trying to turn a couple of bucks in the few years I have."

"No, you're not, Larry. You're more than that. You're the heavyweight champion of the world. And that gives you a certain credibility and responsibility that goes along with it."

---

*Giachetti eventually reconciled with King, who assigned him to train Mike Tyson in 1991. Marley quit the *Post*, where he wrote favorably about King, and went to work for King in 1992.

After quoting that report by Spinelli in his unpublished manuscript, Holmes wrote: "I knew he was right, and I really did want the sport cleaned up. But I didn't volunteer a thing. . . . Joe Spinelli began to come across to me as a pretty decent guy. Spinelli made it a point not to single out Don King when he talked about going after promoters. . . ."

Those were Holmes's thoughts in reflected tranquillity. But what he said to Spinelli that day in his house was something very different: "King's got a lot of bad friends. I've got to make a living. I have a family. I'm scared for my family. I've got to be careful. He can hurt me."

Spinelli remembers, "Larry looked as frightened as any man I've ever seen."

The lions were still afraid of the rats.

Another exceptional fighter who broke Spinelli's heart was Saoul Mamby, who was gifted, intelligent, screwed by King, but wouldn't testify.

Mamby was the best fighter nobody ever heard of in the late 1970s and early 1980s. The Bronx-born black Jew became a vagabond because no one was willing to fight him during the seasons of his prime. He displayed his subtle skills in Curaçao, Quebec, Venezuela, Kingston, and Santo Domingo. Even when he was champion he never got a chance to perform before his hometown fans in New York.

Mamby boxed the way Sarah Vaughan wove a melody, the way Tony Gwynn hit a curve ball. He was a smooth, economical craftsman. He didn't have a big punch, but he was harder to hit than the number.

A cooperating witness had taped a conversation in which Mamby described how King skimmed his purses and had forced him to retain his stepson Carl as his manager. He told the story of how, when he finally won a world title at age thirty-three, in Seoul, South Korea, Carl King didn't even go with him, but took part of his earnings when he got home.

In an interview with Spinelli that was not under oath, Mamby told him that Don King took 20 percent of all his earnings. But on July 20, 1981, when he was under oath before the grand jury, Mamby denied what he told Spinelli and what he had said on tape. He would say nothing derogatory about King.

The next day the cooperating witness taped Mamby admitting he had not told the grand jury the truth. Spinelli probably could have gotten a perjury indictment of Mamby, but he didn't even try.

"I saw Mamby and Holmes more as victims than targets," Spinelli said years later.

In December 1992 I interviewed Mamby. He was then almost forty five years old, broke, in debt to the IRS, and still fighting. Very few boxing lives have happy endings.

"I defended my title five times with Don King as the promoter, and every time I was paid less money than the signed contract guaranteed me," Mamby said.

"In three of my defenses I found out after the fight Don or Carl also managed my opponent. I defended my title against a tough guy, Esteban De Jesus, in Minnesota. Afterward I found out his manager was Connie Harper, Don's secretary.

"I defended my title in Indonesia against Thomas Americo. My purse was supposed to be $350,000, but Don took $50,000 off the top for expenses. Don promised me I was getting paid $250,000, but after I won the fight I got a check for $135,000.

"Then I went to Nigeria to fight Obisia Nwankpa, who I later was told was managed by Carl. I was supposed to get paid $300,000, but I actually got paid less than half of what I was entitled to. Don double-billed me for travel expenses. He billed me for the plane tickets and hotel rooms for his employees. After all those deductions, I got a check for $118,000.

"After that I left Don and signed to fight Aaron Pryor for Harold Smith. Smith did give me a generous signing bonus, and this fight was supposed to finally be my big payday. But the fight never came off. Pryor got shot by his girlfriend and then Smith got indicted for the bank fraud.

"I still like Harold. At least he just robbed banks, not fighters.

"So then I had to crawl back to Don, and he matched me with Leroy Haley in Vegas, and I lost my title in a split decision. Right after they announced the judges' scoring, right in the ring, I saw Carl King hug Haley. That's when I realized he was Haley's manager, too.

"But Carl and I are still friends. I don't blame him for anything that happened. He just did what his daddy told him. I don't think he ever kept any of my money. I think he gave it all to his daddy."

When I asked Mamby why he hadn't told the grand jury the truth back in 1981, he said, "I couldn't do it. I was still fighting. I needed to keep working. So I didn't tell the grand jury anything. Afterward, Don asked me what questions they asked me, and I told him."

In the fall of 1982, Spinelli began getting FBI informant and surveillance reports of King having dinners in public places with some of the leading gangsters of New York.

On September 14, King dined with John Gotti, then a fast-rising capo in the Gambino family, with interests in boxing. The dinner took place in Patrissy's Restaurant in Little Italy.

On September 29, King had dinner at Abe's Steakhouse with Genovese capo Matty "The Horse" Ianiello "and two other members of Ianiello's crew."

On December 6 King dined with both Gotti and Ianiello at Abe's Steakhouse. An informant's report on this meeting said, "Gotti and fight promoter Don King were engaged in a heated discussion and it appears to the source that King was in serious trouble with Gotti."

Gotti later told a friend that he had slapped King during this meeting because King "was not paying his debts to us on time."

The informant's report added: "Source advised that Ianiello

was heard to say that 'that guy's got to be taught a lesson and John will take care of it.' "

On November 8, 1991, King was quoted in an Associated Press wire service story as saying, "Categorically, I never met John Gotti."

But on July 8, 1992, King walked into Room 192 in the Russell Senate Office Building in Washington to be questioned in an executive session by a Senate subcommittee looking into boxing. Dan Rinzel, chief counsel to the committee's Republican minority, asked King under oath if he had ever met John Gotti. King replied, "I respectfully decline to answer the question on the basis of the protection offered under the Constitution."

Rinzel then read King his categorical denial to the AP reporter while not under oath.

"Where are you telling the truth?" Rinzel asked.

King invoked the Fifth Amendment again.

And he took it five more times in response to questions about meetings with other major mobsters, including Gambino family godfather Paul Castellano, whom, the committee had been told by capo Michael Franzese, King had met with.

King also took the Fifth about his meeting with Franzese, and that meeting was recorded by the FBI.

All these meetings with ranking gangsters were titillating and vaguely sinister, but they were not against the law. They whetted Spinelli's appetite, but did not help him make a case.

It should be repeated here that Don King did not invent the link between organized crime and boxing. Indeed, King has always denied that any such link exists, at least as far as he is concerned. However, the alliance between boxing and the mob flourished before King was born.

In the 1930s, the mob owned heavyweight champion Primo Carnera. In the 1950s, Sonny Liston was co-owned by Frankie Carbo, who was convicted for one killing and acquitted of three others, and by St. Louis mob boss John Vitale.

Carbo, and his accomplice Blinky Palermo, dominated boxing

during the 1950s by using millionaire businessman James Norris
as their front man. Norris had a television monopoly and was a
willing dupe for the gangsters. This cartel controlled many champions, including Johnny Bratton, Johnny Saxton, Virgil Akins,
and Jimmy Carter.

They sometimes fixed fights—including the LaMotta–Billy Fox
bout in 1947—to stage betting coups. Sometimes they bribed the
judges when the fighters wouldn't accommodate them.

Carbo had to act as an undercover manager because of his
manslaughter conviction, but Palermo was the licensed manager
of Saxton and the great 135-pound champion Ike Williams.

In 1960 Williams testified before Estes Kefauver's Senate committee and explained that he received no money at all from Palermo
for two title defenses, against Beau Jack and Jesse Flores, but that
he still had to pay taxes on the $65,000 of unpaid purses. Williams
also testified that Palermo offered him bribe money to throw his
fights with Kid Gavilan, Jimmy Carter, and Freddie Dawson.

In his old age, Williams was virtually penniless. When he died
in Los Angeles in September 1994, he was living on Social Security payments of $600 a month.

Jimmy Carter, the talented, mob-controlled fighter who beat
Williams for the lightweight title, passed away the same week that
Williams did. Carter died in his hometown of Aiken, South Carolina, and his family was so destitute that charity was needed to
pay for his funeral expenses.

Carbo and Palermo were both eventually convicted in the same
case for trying to extort control over welterweight champion Don
Jordan through threats of violence against his legitimate manager.

In terms of pure gangsterism and Mafia monopoly, the Carbo-
Norris era was much worse than anything to come under Don
King.

In mid-1981 the prosecutor Spinelli was working with—Dominic
Amorosa—left the government to go into private practice. His

replacement, Roanne Mann, and the U.S. attorney, John Martin, decided together to withdraw Amorosa's offer of immunity to Richie Giachetti. This decision meant Giachetti's six homemade tapes were no longer of any value to the investigation, and Giachetti took the Fifth before the grand jury. Spinelli bitterly opposed this judgment, but he was overruled.

Then Holmes and Mamby also balked before the grand jury. Spinelli started getting threatening calls at work. A workaholic, Spinelli began to drive himself even more, traveling and working twelve-hour days. He became so stressed out and overworked that he developed a case of Bell's palsy, which paralyzed one side of his face. He had to spend two weeks in bed.

While recuperating in bed, Spinelli got an idea. He realized the only way to really make a case against someone as smart, as intimidating, as insulated as Don King was through a costly undercover operation—a sting.

Spinelli had gone undercover himself a few times, and he had been probing Congressman John Murphy on the fringes of ABSCAM—the massive sting that captured on videotape seven members of the Congress taking bribes. Actually going into the marketplace of boxing would be the only way to secure proof beyond a reasonable doubt against King, he reasoned.

Through a series of memos and meetings, Spinelli convinced the FBI to allocate a substantial sum of money to fund an elaborate sting operation that was much broader than just targeting King. A Group I undercover operation was approved on March 23, 1982, and became fully operational by October.

A phony company called TKO Promotions was set up in an office near Madison Square Garden. A luxury apartment was rented near Lincoln Center. A Rolls-Royce was leased.

And one of the best undercover agents in the country, Victor Quintana, was recruited out of the Los Angeles office. Quintana was Dominican, bilingual, a black belt in karate, a graduate of the FBI's acting school. He had been an agent for fifteen years and before that, a police officer for seven years in Compton, California.

A scenario was created: Victor was an ex–South American drug trafficker looking to launder and legitimize $3 million of drug money through doing some boxing co-promotions. The plan was to try to get a license in New Jersey, sign up some fighters, and eventually promote some fights with the license.

Spinelli dreamed about managing a world champion and taking down a network or casino executive, someone in the corporate world who let all the boxing corruption go on because it was "just boxing."

Don King, meanwhile, was thinking his usual five moves ahead. He knew Spinelli was his adversary, so he decided he would try to get to know Spinelli, perhaps charm him a little.

On December 5, 1981, King was in Freeport, in the Bahamas, trying to get an injunction to prevent the Ali–Trevor Berbick fight. King was saying he had a valid contract with Berbick and he wanted $100,000 from the promoter, James Cornelius, if the fight was going on as planned. King wanted his promotional rights for Berbick to be paid for.

That night Cornelius and four large men, all Muslims, came into King's room at the Bahamas Princess Hotel and administered a professional beating to King. They broke his nose and knocked out some teeth. As soon as he got back to New York, King called up Joe Spinelli and announced he wanted to file a complaint with Spinelli himself about the assault.

As case agent on the boxing probe, Spinelli, along with agent Jim Kossler, went to King's office on East Sixty-ninth Street and conducted a formal interview, with King as crime victim, not suspect. They could see King's still-swollen eye, stitches in his mouth, a large welt on his temple.

King soon had Spinelli laughing out loud. He put on a performance. King began by looking at his adversary and saying: "This is like Victor Hugo's *Les Misérables*! I wake up every morning, I look at the ceiling and I know Joe Spinelli is listening! I walk down the street and look over my shoulder, and I know Joe Spinelli is following! I know the *motherfucker* knows more about me than me!"

As he said that, King stood up and pointed his finger at the FBI agent, who couldn't hold back a smile at the funky flattery.

"Four of them was beating me up," King explained. "But as they were working me over, I got two of them, named Omar and Luke, on the side. I slipped them two hundred dollars each and asked them to take it easy on me, not to kick me so hard. Right away Omar told Cornelius, 'I think we done enough,' and I knew my money was working for me already."

King described how right after the beating stopped, Cornelius ordered him to leave the island immediately or he would be killed. A bloody King went directly to the airport and flew to Ft. Lauderdale. There his fighter Michael Dokes drove him to the emergency room at the Broward County Medical Center.

After completing the narrative of his complaint, King attempted to charm his foe.

"I ain't such a bad guy, Joe," King said. "There's worse in boxing than me. I just play by the rules that exist. I'm just a twenty-four-hour-a-day guy. Nobody can outwork me. That's why I'm on top. Nobody can outwork me and I play by the rules. The problem is, you don't like the rules."

Spinelli admitted to himself that King was making a fair point, that the rules had to be changed, that Cus D'Amato was exactly accurate when he called option contracts "*legalized* extortion," that King himself was more the symptom than the disease.

King then got Spinelli laughing when he declared, "At least when you're dealing with the gumbahs [Italians] you know where you stand. These Muslim guys are *irrational,* my little Italian brother."

A second way King was thinking ahead was that he began a public campaign to get an official pardon in Ohio for his first-degree manslaughter conviction. This way, if he were to be convicted in the current investigation, he would not have a predicate felony on his record to assure him a severe sentence. A pardon would also help him get licenses in Atlantic City and Las Vegas and make him appear less unsavory in corporate boardrooms. A pardon would also be a display of his political power to fighters and other witnesses who might be wavering on whether to testify against him.

Clarance Rogers was the attorney handling King's petition for a pardon, and Rogers was law partners with the powerful George Forbes, president of the Cleveland City Council. And Forbes was close to Governor James Rhodes, even though Rhodes was a Republican and Forbes a Democrat.

Among those whom King got to write letters on his behalf to Governor Rhodes were Cleveland's Republican mayor, George Voinovich; Indians' president Gabe Paul; Browns' owner Art Modell; Coretta Scott King; The Reverend Jesse Jackson; and even Cleveland police officer William Hanton.

But retired police detective Carl DeLau, who supervised King's arrest, wrote to the parole board urging that no pardon be granted.

Lame-duck Ohio Governor James Rhodes, who had received several campaign donations from King and had given King his direct-line phone number, granted King his pardon during his last week in office, on January 4, 1983. The pardon restored all of King's citizenship rights and prevented his conviction from being held against him in any future legal proceeding.

The next day an exuberant King staged a combination "pardon party" and press conference, with big trays of shrimps and ribs for the press and his friends. King called Governor Rhodes "a great American who cares," proclaimed, "Only in America," and observed, "No one in the history of sports has accomplished what I have."

King had also shrewdly hedged his bets. The previous September he had made a $10,000 contribution to the incoming Democratic governor, Richard Celeste—just in case Rhodes did not come through. King personally handed Celeste the check, according to the *Plain Dealer*.

The only negative word to be found in the Cleveland papers about the pardon came from Sam Garrett's two stepchildren, who had known their father only for a few years.

"I don't see how those people could have backed him. What if it was someone in their family who was killed?" said Lauree Howell, who was twelve when her stepfather was stomped to death by King. She said King had never apologized to the family.

Ellen Harper, Garrett's other stepdaughter, was interviewed holding the flag that had been draped over Sam Garrett's casket. She said the pardon made it feel like her stepfather had never lived.

"It hurts because it's not fair," she said. "Sam cared about us."

Shortly after the pardon, Don King hired the son of Governor Rhodes as a "consultant."

By November 1982, the sting operation—code-named Crown Royal—was progressing to the point where Quintana, dressed in his gold chains and designer jeans, was hanging out with Columbo family capo Michael Franzese. They had first met at a fight in Atlantic City, and although the yuppie-ish Franzese was more interested in movies, gasoline, and offshore money, he also had an 8 percent piece of middleweight Davey Moore. Quintana wanted a meeting with King.

In one conversation taped by Quintana's hidden wire, Franzese explained: "Don King is not with my family. He's with some cousins. I've got to call the cousins to get their approval before I can introduce you."

This was standard mob protocol. And since Franzese was a mob prince, the son of the legendary street capo John "Sonny" Franzese, he was acutely aware of all the underworld etiquette.

To prove his bona fides, Quintana had Franzese call a bank in

Illinois where the FBI had set up a paper account. Franzese was told Quintana held $15 million in his account. That's when Franzese called Corky Vastola.

On November 3, 1982, Quintana and Franzese were invited to the back room of Gargiulio's Restaurant in Coney Island, to meet with Vastola and Jimmy Rotundo, two heavy New Jersey mobsters in the DeCavalcante crime family.

Vastola asked Quintana, "How much money you got? You got to do business with Don King, you gotta have the money. You don't want to see the man, and the man is out of your league."

"Three million dollars. Cash. Right now," Quintana said.

A few days later Vastola told Franzese the Cleveland family approved his meeting with King.

A few days after that, as Quintana gently pushed Franzese to arrange the meeting with King, Franzese started to warn the undercover fed about the feds.

"We have to be very careful with King," Franzese said. "A lot of people in Cleveland are telling me that the heat he's under from the feds is enormous. Don't get too close to him, Victor. You should keep that in mind in dealing with King. You don't want to get jammed up with the feds."

As Spinelli waited for the face-to-face meeting with King to be set up, he thought about all of King's Mafia affiliations. In Cleveland, in New Jersey, in Philadelphia, with each of the five families in New York City. And he formed a working hypothesis—one of the reasons King skimmed fighters' earnings so ruthlessly was that he had to kick back a portion of his own profits to organized crime—the mob had become his hidden partner. That seemed to be the significance of his confrontational meeting with John Gotti.

On January 12, 1983, Michael Franzese and the Reverend Al Sharpton finally got a wired Quintana in to see King for a short meeting. King agreed to do a co-promotion with Quintana and the FBI's undercover company.

Before King sat down with Quintana and Sharpton, he first

held a private premeeting with Franzese. In this meeting Franzese told King that his family was "very interested" in seeing this deal go forward, and that if it proceeded successfully, Franzese himself would invest a substantial amount of cash in the promotions. King assured Franzese he should not be concerned about losing any money on any "family situation."

Franzese also assured King that he had checked through Vastola, and "the Cleveland family" had sanctioned this deal going forward.*

After this was all clarified, only then did King invite the others in for the larger meeting. King told Quintana, "You must be serious about doing a co-promotion, or you wouldn't be coming here with Michael."

Spinelli now had a promise of co-promotion, and the proof on tape that King would knowingly do business with a well-known mobster like Franzese. But his excitement would be short-lived. Right after this meeting, the FBI chiefs in Washington decided they could not approve the bureau's undercover participation in promoting a real professional boxing match.

In November 1982, Duk Koo Kim of South Korea had died as a result of brain injuries he suffered in a nationally televised fight with Ray Mancini. Spinelli's supervisor informed him, "The bureau can't do it. They're worried about the liability. What would happen if some fighter got killed and it came out later that the FBI was behind the promotion?"

Don King was lucky again.

"I was really disheartened by that decision," Spinelli says now, "but the Bureau was right in making their decision. . . . We were right where we wanted to be, doing a co-promotion with King. We were at the top of the mountain. And when we got that decision from Washington we were suddenly kicked down to the

---

*Michael Franzese's account of the premeeting with King is based on his August 12, 1992, testimony before the U.S. Senate permanent investigations subcommittee public hearing on mob penetration of boxing.

bottom of the mountain. I tried to argue we could get around the liability problem with insurance and other precautions, but the risks were just too big."

The covert phase of Crown Royal had reached a dead end. There would be no ABSCAM-like partnership with Don King. The FBI would never get its chance to be on the inside with hidden cameras, as fighters were paid, bank accounts opened, Jose Sulaiman talked to, blank contracts filled in, the judges chosen, the rankings determined. Spinelli would never find out why King was so close to so many capos and dons.

A few months later Quintana taped a conversation with Danny Pagano, a soldier in the Genovese family. When Quintana mentioned that he had gotten a meeting through Michael Franzese of the Columbo family, Pagano asked incredulously, "What did you go to Michael for? King's with us."

A colorful subplot and historical footnote to the Crown Royal sting was the ensnarement of the Reverend Al Sharpton, the Falstaffian preacher-without-a-pulpit who seems like a character right out of Ralph Ellison's *Invisible Man*. In 1982, long before he became notorious for the Tawana Brawley rape hoax, Sharpton was trying to juggle his incompatible roles as street hustler, mob front, social activist, and media manipulator.

Victor Quintana was introduced to Sharpton, then just twenty-nine, by Michael Franzese in December 1982, as the best intermediary to set up a meeting with Don King. Sharpton—funny, a compulsive talker, gossip, and name-dropper—soon became the star of a series of FBI recordings.

Sharpton kept mentioning how close he was to Danny Pagano, whose father, Joey, was a top-level hoodlum and the rumored hit man who killed Joey Gallo at Umberto's Clam House.

Sharpton kept telling the wired Quintana of his exploits in the record industry with King, and passed along ribald gossip about singers Dionne Warwick and Shirley Bassey. He also made references to his odd alliance with South Carolina Republican Senator Strom Thurmond, possibly the most antiblack member of the Senate.

In one taped meeting Sharpton described how he had gotten his friend James Brown to do a radio commercial boosting Thurmond's reelection, and how he had called in that favor to ask Thurmond to use his influence with the Republican Justice Department to block any indictment of King.

Sharpton might have been puffing about the meeting he says he set up between King and Thurmond, but the tapes do establish that he used Thurmond's office when he was in Washington, and that he spoke with Thurmond's assistant, Ted Kinghorn.

Sharpton also blabbed away in a meeting taped on March 4, 1983, with Quintana and Bob Ramn, who did video work for King. Sharpton delivered an informed lecture on King's mob connections, saying their origins go back to King's bond with the "Jewish Mafia of Cleveland," founded by Moe Dalitz. Sharpton even boasted—falsely—that he had checked with Pat and Don Maggadino of the Buffalo crime family to verify that King had "no problems with the Cleveland people."

On this tape Ramn said that King kept most of his money "offshore and in Swiss bank accounts."

During one of the meetings with Quintana taped by the FBI on CCTV, the talk veered away from getting a meeting with King, and to setting up a potential drug deal. Once again Sharpton couldn't keep his mouth shut.

"Let me see what I can do, I know some people," said the minister who did antidrug crusades in the projects.

Quintana, keeping with his script, stressed he was only talked about pot and cocaine, not heroin. Sharpton said he would mention the prospect to Danny Pagano.

"He's a Genovese guy, you know," Sharpton said, showing off his knowledge of crime family factions.

But when Quintana met with Pagano, Pagano told him, "I don't deal in drugs."

Spinelli watched the video of Sharpton volunteering to further a drug deal at least thirty times, trying to read his character, measure his potential to be flipped, to become his informant against King. Spinelli needed a breakthrough on Crown Royal. His six-month funding cycle was about to expire, and the probe was at an impasse.

In the portly, anxious-to-please image of Sharpton, Spinelli thought he saw a weak man, a bluffer, a blowhard—not a tough or sinister criminal. Spinelli thought he and Quintana could flip Sharpton themselves.

At 5:00 P.M. on June 30, 1983, Sharpton arrived at Crown Royal's $2,400-per-month luxury apartment, in a doorman building near Lincoln Center. Sharpton was making small talk with Quintana when Spinelli and another agent, Ken Mikionis, burst out of the bedroom, startling the minister.

Without saying a word they inserted a cassette into the VCR and started playing the video of the meeting where Sharpton offered to call Danny Pagano about the fictional drug transaction. Sharpton is as smart and as quick as Don King. After less than a minute he asked, "What do I have to do?"

Spinelli never got to deliver his your-life-is-at-the-crossroads speech he had been rehearsing in his mind all day. "I'll do whatever I have to do to stay out of jail," Sharpton repeated.

"Fine," Spinelli said, "but you better be straight with me. This is no game. This is very serious. You'll only get a chance to cross me once, and that will be it."

The next day Sharpton taped his first conversation with Don King for the FBI. King asked Sharpton to orchestrate attacks in the black media on Larry Holmes because Holmes had left him and signed to fight Marvis Frazier. King asked Sharpton to plant stories in the black media, including *Jet* and *Ebony,* depicting Holmes as an "Uncle Tom" for leaving him for "a white promoter."

"Put a fire under Larry's ass" was King's instruction.

Holmes's fight with Marvis Frazier (Joe's son) was being co-promoted by Robert Andreoli, who was white, and Murad Muhammad, who was black and a traditional Islamic Muslim.

On July 6 Sharpton recorded another conversation with King, who was in a cautious mood. King told him not to come to his office during daylight hours. King also asked Sharpton to call him the following week in Vegas, but to use the code name of "Roy Williams." Sharpton asked if King would help him out financially for helping to smear Holmes, and King, using some sort of code, said he would assist him "with the mail."

On July 8 Sharpton taped a conversation with Holmes, and Holmes admitted he had not told the truth to the grand jury out of loyalty to King.

Al Sharpton never taped a conversation of prosecutorial value with King. He generated background intelligence, embarrassing tidbits, character insights a novelist could use, and documentation of King's talent for three-dimensional deception. But no conversation where lawbreaking came up.

The whole thing was probably a double con. Spinelli had conned Sharpton into thinking his videotaped conversation was sufficient evidence to indict him for a drug conspiracy, which was not the case. And Sharpton never really tried to incriminate King.

After a few months Sharpton was passed along to FBI agents on other squads. He did help John Pritchard, the chief of the Genovese squad, gather information that led to the conviction of the mob's main man in the record industry, Morris Levy. He supplied the probable cause for a wiretap order on Danny Pagano. He contributed to the case against Michael Franzese involving a gasoline and tax swindle.

Years later, Pritchard, by then the Number 2 man in the New York transit police, said, "The Rev was a great bullshitter. I have to say he probably conned the FBI in terms of the boxing investigation."

In 1988 Sharpton talked his way out of his exposure as an FBI informer by admitting parts of the story and denying others. He also won an acquittal on charges of tax evasion, went on to run in the Democratic primary for Senate in 1992 and 1994 and become the subject of favorable profiles in *The New Yorker* and *The New York Times Magazine*.

During the 1994 campaign, Sharpton told me, "I'm running to get a more moderate and mainstream image. I'm now into coalition more than confrontation. I'm changing."

"Then why don't you change your hairdo?" I asked.

"You don't understand," the witty hustler said. "I was raised up by James Brown and Don King. By their standards my hair is normal!"

The covert phase of the FBI's boxing probe was over by August 1983. All the financial information Spinelli developed was turned over to the IRS, and the investigation into King evolved into a traditional tax-fraud case assigned to IRS agent Mark Schwartz. He worked with Roanne Mann, the assistant U.S. attorney.

Looking back on his boxing probe eleven years later, in 1994, Spinelli's assessment was: "Dom Amorosa leaving for private practice when he did hurt us. Not giving Giachetti his immunity agreement was a killer. If we had Giachetti as a witness, we could have had the tapes and the contracts and proven King was taking twenty-five percent of Larry's money. And stopping the covert co-promotion with King ended all our chances to make a substantive case."*

On December 13, 1984, the new U.S. attorney, Rudolph Giuliani, called a press conference to announce a twenty-three-count indictment for tax fraud and conspiracy against King and

---

*In early 1984, Spinelli was transferred to the New Haven office of the FBI. In January 1986, Governor Mario Cuomo appointed Spinelli the first inspector general for New York State. In November 1991, he published an article in *Sports Illustrated* detailing all the evidence of King's relationships with mobsters.

Constance Harper, the vice president of DKP but really King's personal assistant.

The indictment charged King with diverting and skimming $422,000 between 1978 and 1981 from DKP and not paying federal taxes on the money. In his press conference Giuliani said, "The scheme involved obtaining cash from casino cages on several occasions—on one occasion as high as seventy thousand—and not reporting it as income."

Giuliani said some of the money was used to pay King's personal gambling debt at Caesars Palace casino.

Connie Harper was charged with not paying taxes on $150,000 other income and helping to conceal King's skimming from DKP's accountants.

Don King, the master survivalist, prepared for another war in his epic life. He toned down his public act, wrapped himself in the flag more than ever, and made "Only in America" his trademark phrase. He retained Vince Fuller of Williams & Connally, then in his prime, to be his lawyer. And he hired—and paid—Andrew Lawler to be Connie Harper's lawyer.

King and Fuller quickly settled on a defense strategy—*blame the subordinates,* just as King had blamed Flood, Braverman, and Ort for the tournament scandal. King would not dispute the essential facts of the indictment; he would just depict himself as the innocent victim of his accountants, bookkeepers, and assistants, whom he relied upon in good faith. He would claim his intent was pure.

Because innocent intent was King's defense, the judge's procedural ruling became the turning point of the trial. Roanne Mann, the trial prosecutor, had evidence that King had committed tax evasion once before, in 1973, and wanted to present this evidence to the jury as "a past similar act." This would have undermined King's defense of no knowledge and no intent to mislead the government.

Roanne Mann had King's 1979 federal grand jury testimony

from Cleveland, plus other documents that indicated that King had not paid any federal taxes on his 1973 profits from the numbers racket. This evidence showed that King had maintained three bank accounts under fictitious names at the Quincy Savings & Loan in Cleveland, including a joint account with Virgil Ogletree, his partner in the numbers.

King had opened accounts under the fake names of "Henry George" and "Charles Brown," and the joint account with Ogletree for K & G Enterprises under the fake names of "Kenneth Donaldson" and "James Woods."

King had been given immunity by the grand jury and had admitted that he was getting from Ogletree "25 percent of the win, or thereabouts," which had to be well over $100,000.

Roanne Mann had the signature cards from the bank, and the handwriting samples from King, showing King making deposits into these three accounts. She also had his 1973 tax return that showed no taxes were paid on this money, while King claimed a total income for 1973 of $20,300. She also had King's own grand jury testimony admitting the unreported cash came from the numbers business. (At that time King was telling reporters he was out of the numbers racket and only doing boxing promotions.)

This degree of sophisticated tax evasion would have undercut King's trial defense of victimization by devious subordinates.

In a pretrial hearing, Roanne Mann told Judge Thomas Grisea: "According to his own testimony, he [King] would make deposits into the account, his associates or partners would make withdrawals, King would receive a percentage of the money. And we believe that that is consistent with part of the scheme in this case, in which a joint account was opened by the two defendants, and they channeled monies that had been skimmed from the corporation through that account. . . .

"They are going to claim that the reason it wasn't reported was due to the incompetence of King's accountants and bookkeepers. And certainly the fact that he engaged in a prior tax evasion— and in addition used a similar scheme to channel monies—I think is highly probative of knowledge and intent."

At first Judge Grisea ruled that the government could present all this evidence to the jury, as a past similar act. But after the trial began, Judge Grisea changed his mind and ruled all the evidence from the 1973 tax evasion was inadmissible.

This was crushing to the prosecution and another astonishing example of Don King's good luck.

Roanne Mann had already told the jury in her opening statement that she would prove that King had committed tax evasion in the past, and now she was disarmed of the proof of her promised past example, in midtrial.

This procedural ruling allowed King's lawyer to lay the responsibility off on everyone else, including his co-defendant and dear friend, Connie Harper.

Harper had been King's faithful employee for fifteen years.* She came from a prominent Cleveland family. She was so close to King that King had put fighters like Esteban De Jesus in her name, to hide his own ownership. But this loyal servant became the fall woman at the trial.

Fuller blamed the employees in King's Manhattan office, even though the critical documents dealing with King's cash advances from Caesars casino were kept in King's home in Ohio, not his Manhattan office.

Don King never took the stand in his own defense.

On November 19, after seven hours of deliberation, the jury acquitted King of all charges and convicted Harper of tax evasion. She served four months in prison and now has a job on the Cleveland Board of Elections, a job King has told friends he secured for her.

Reflecting back on the trial, Roanne Mann, now a lawyer in

---

*Connie Harper was probably more than a close associate—she was one of King's mistresses for years, according to most of King's employees. These co-workers believe that Harper—unmarried, plump, and short—was in love with King, and whatever she did was motivated by blind romantic loyalty.

Harper's presentencing rep would later describe her as an addictive personality, prone to obsessive shopping, eating, and sleeping. The report would conclude that Harper might have been "swept away by the excitement and glamour of Don King's world."

private practice, told me, "I underestimated the power King's personality had over a jury. He was a star, a celebrity. He was a folk hero to some of the jurors. Most of the women on the jury asked him for his autograph. They were fascinated by him."

She added, "Go reread the trial transcript. You will see how Andy Lawler's summation for Harper really helped King get off. It was a brilliant summation, but it wasn't for his own client."

Don King let a woman who loved him do the time for him.

Eight months after he was acquitted, Don King flew most of the jurors over to London, lodged them at a luxury hotel, and gave them free ringside tickets to the Tim Witherspoon–Frank Bruno heavyweight title fight.

Don King billed the promotion for the expenses.

CHAPTER 10

Only
in South
Africa

By 1983 the anti-apartheid revolution, both inside and outside South Africa, was gathering momentum. Nelson Mandela was starting his twenty-first year in prison. Protests—violent and non-violent—against the system of legalized segregation and denial of black voting rights were becoming more frequent. The whole civilized world was starting to mount boycotts of an outlaw nation based on minority rule and white supremacy. Nations were starting to impose economic sanctions and devise disinvestment strategies to weaken apartheid.

As part of this international upsurge, consciousness was starting to rise among athletes and musical performers in America that they had a contribution to make in the isolating of South Africa.

South Africa was banned from the 1964 Olympic games, invited to the 1968 games in Mexico City, and quickly disinvited when forty-one black African nations threatened their own boycott. In 1970, South Africa became the first nation expelled from the Olympic games.

In 1979, Bob Arum promoted a fight in Johannesburg between black American heavyweight John Tate and white South African Gerrie Coetzee. Although the audience was not officially segregated—except by the economics of the prohibitive ticket pricing—the fight was condemned almost universally, including by Don King, as morally abhorrent.

Arum's partner in the promotion was Sol Kerzner, a white South African who owned the country's largest chain of hotels. When Tate won by a knockout, there was dancing in the streets of the black township of Soweto.

In 1980 Arum came back to promote a fight between Coetzee and another black American heavyweight, Mike Weaver. This match was held in the phony homeland of Bophuthatswana, which was recognized by no other nation on earth as an independent country. Its specific site was the opulent Sun City hotel and casino, owned by Kerzner.

Once again Arum was appropriately lashed by King, the Reverend Jesse Jackson, and a group called ACCESS, standing for American Coordinating Committee for Equality in Sport and Society. ACCESS organized a letter-writing campaign to CBS-TV, which bought the rights to televise the bout, and King started calling Arum "The Apostle of Apartheid" at every opportunity.

King became such a crusader for boycotting anything involving South Africa that he even put out a press release denouncing an insignificant fight held in Miami Beach between a white South African heavyweight named Kallie Knoetze and Bill Sharkey of New York City. King's press release said: "The plight of black people, socially and economically, troubles me, and I wholeheartedly support the position taken by Jesse Jackson, who feels this country has an obligation to break cultural and economic ties with the repressive regime of South Africa, and feels a moral obligation to resist promulgation of their policies through sports figures. . . . It would be an unpardonable sin for Knoetze to have the opportunity to become a world champion. The heavyweight championship of the world is a coveted sports prize, a revered and symbolic title. It should not be used as a great propaganda tool to promote racial hatred."

By 1983, a movement was also developing among black American performers and civil rights activists to convince American stars not to perform at Sun City.

The South African resort was offering staggering sums of money to American performers to appear in the casino's six thousand-seat arena. Among those who did accept Sun City's money were Frank Sinatra, Liza Minnelli, the Beach Boys, the Osmonds, Linda Ronstadt, Cher, Paul Anka, Dolly Parton, Glen Campbell, Olivia Newton-John, and Ann-Margret.

Kerzner, who sounded more like a bouncer from Brooklyn than a South African entrepreneur, even convinced black performers like the O'Jays and Millie Jackson to accept invitations to play Sun City.

Millie Jackson unwittingly gave the international boycott movement a shot of adrenaline by her comments while in South Africa. A reporter asked her if she was going to perform in Soweto. "Soweto? Where is that place? I never heard of it," Jackson replied. When told she was breaking a boycott, Jackson said, "I'm not going to mix my career with politics. All I want is the money." After her remarks were publicized in the United States, black performers like Gladys Knight and Ben Vereen canceled their appearances at Sun City.

At the same time, boxers began to reject gigantic offers for matches promoted at Sun City. Sugar Ray Leonard rejected one mega-offer. And Muhammad Ali confirmed that he had rejected an offer by Kerzner to co-promote his 1978 rematch with Leon Spinks in South Africa.

Given this moral example by the two preeminent fighters of the era, very few black American fighters were prepared to follow Tate and Weaver into the eye of apartheid.

Also, Nelson Mandela, a former amateur boxer and knowledgeable fan, put out the word through the African National Congress that he believed the international boycott by athletes and artists was important and effective.

Soon an organization was formed called Artists and Athletes Against Apartheid. Its moving spirits were tennis great Arthur Ashe, singer-activist Harry Belafonte, and Randall Robinson, the executive director of Trans-Africa. Don King became a charter member of this group and a signatory to its founding principles.

Also in 1983, Gerrie Coetzee was moving into contention for another chance at the heavyweight championship. He decisively beat up and knocked down Renaldo Snipes, but didn't get the decision because the fight was held in Westchester, Snipes's home turf. And he acquired a hardworking novice promoter named Cedric Kushner.

After hooking up with Kushner, Coetzee knocked out Stan Ward in three rounds and fought an exciting draw with highly ranked Pinklon Thomas that was on national television. After this, the WBA rated Coetzee among the top contenders, making him eligible for a title fight.

Kushner is yet another one of those Runyonesque boxing characters—rowdy, colorful, a captivating storyteller about his own novelistic life.

Now a millionaire with offices in East Hampton, Long Island, Kushner started out as a sixth-grade dropout in South Africa. His first job was on a cargo ship to Europe, cleaning the cages of rhinoceroses.

On his twenty-second birthday, in July 1971, Kushner arrived in America with $400 in his pocket and an immigrant's burning desire to work. He became a laborer in Boston, a pool cleaner in Miami Beach, a Ferris wheel operator in Asbury Park, New Jersey, and a messenger in Manhattan.

"When I was in Miami, I used to stand in front of the Fontainebleau Hotel every night and just watch all the rich people coming in and going out, all dressed up, having valets retrieve their expensive cars for them. I just looked. That was my hobby."

At the 1972 Munich Olympics Kushner had a job as a bilingual ticket scalper. While scalping tickets he met a Texas businessman who gave him his card because he was impressed by the way Kushner negotiated ticket prices in both German and English.

Eighteen months later Kushner contacted the name on the business card, and the man staked him to $5,000 to get into the business of being a music-concert promoter. His maiden effort was a Steppenwolf concert on November 19, 1974.

After that, Kushner rose in the cutthroat music competition that is a fine preparation for boxing, promoting concert tours by Fleetwood Mac, Bob Seger, Rod Stewart, and Joni Mitchell.

By 1980 Kushner was a big-time rock and pop promoter when he was indicted for antitrust violations involving collusion with another promoter to monopolize territorial rights. Kushner was eventually given two years probation and fined $10,000. But in boxing, somebody with just one conviction is considered a reformer.

And by the summer of 1982 boxing was the next career Kushner had in mind for himself. He was a fan, and on a humid August night he traveled up to Westchester, bought a ticket, and watched Gerrie Coetzee, his fellow South African, beat up Renaldo Snipes but get robbed of the decision by the local judges.

Kushner, a short, bulky man with a walrus mustache, managed to shove his way into Coetzee's dressing room after the fight. He introduced himself to the bitterly disappointed fighter and told him in Afrikaans, "If I had been your promoter, you wouldn't have lost this fight."

It took Kushner three more months to finally arrange a meeting with Coetzee's manager, Peter Venison, who was a hotel management expert and traveled much of the time. When the two men finally met, Kushner was aggressive and spelled out a whole marketing and management plan to get Coetzee another shot at the title.

"Gerrie has to move to the United States," Kushner argued.

"He has to divorce himself from South Africa. Apartheid is becoming a burden to his career. He has to move his wife and kids to America. We have to Americanize him. He has to come across as a nice guy."

One part of the plan was easy: Coetzee loved America. The other part was harder. He was not such a nice guy. He was moody, temperamental, suspicious, disloyal, filled with self-doubt over his earlier defeats and the fragile bones in his right hand that had already required fourteen operations.

After a few weeks of negotiations a plan was agreed on. Kushner would co-promote Coetzee's fights with Bob Arum, with Venison remaining the manager. Kushner would baby-sit the fighter day-to-day, while Arum would make the fights and negotiate the television deals. Early in 1983 Coetzee's wife and two children moved into a rented house in Pleasantville, New Jersey, near Atlantic City.

Coetzee's first major fight for this new team was with Pinklon Thomas in Atlantic City. In the dressing room before the match Coetzee was in a paranoid fever. He was worried about his hand, which he had hurt again during training. He was worried about the officiating in New Jersey, feeling a white South African could not get a fair shake as a result of the bad decision in the Snipes fight.

Kushner was also apprehensive about the judging, but the day before the fight he had praised the New Jersey officials to reporters, saying he had "total faith in the integrity of the commission." Of course he didn't, but he thought the extravagant, if insincere, flattery was the appropriate reverse psychology in a no-win situation.

But a few minutes before the fight, Thomas's handlers used some of their own Freudian jabs. They came into Coetzee's dressing room and charged he had too much wrapping on his tender right hand to cushion it. George Benton demanded that Coetzee's hand be rewrapped in front of a commission member.

The uptight Coetzee stormed out of his own dressing room, saying he wouldn't go through with the fight if he was forced to rebandage his hands. Since the fight was on national television, and contracts had been signed and monies advanced, a sudden cancellation would be a calamity for everybody involved.

Kushner promised Jersey Joe Walcott and Bob Lee of the commission that he would "pacify and control" Coetzee and there would not be any cancellation. He gave the same assurance to Mort Sharnik and Gil Clancy of CBS. Then he found Coetzee, coaxed him back to the dressing room, and by then there was no time to examine or change the hand wrappings.

After the fight, which was legitimately a draw, Kushner filibustered for ten minutes, paying homage to the judge and the New Jersey commission for treating his fighter fairly and respectfully. It was smart politics. The papers carried Kushner's generous quotes, and Coetzee suddenly had some goodwill in New Jersey, where he was now describing himself to reporters as a happy resident of America.

In boxing the double-cross is as frequent, and as swift, as the right cross. And right after this fight Kushner and Arum had a falling-out. Arum says Kushner dumped him to deal with Don King. Kushner says Arum told him he would make a title fight between Coetzee and Larry Holmes, but that Kushner could not be part of the promotion.

Whichever version is closer to the truth, the split created the opening for Kushner to approach Don King about Coetzee getting a title fight with Michael Dokes, who was the WBA champion, controlled by King and managed by Carl King as a front.

Kushner was smart, tough, and aggressive, but he was no match at the negotiating table for King, who had outthought heads of nations and major corporations. Kushner had been in the boxing business only a year, and King had all the leverage. He controlled the champion, and he was able to hold South Africa over Kushner's head.

From the outset King had no reluctance to promote a fight with Coetzee. It might have been political immorality for Arum to promote Kallie Knoetze, but King recognized it was good business for him to promote Gerrie Coetzee. Not only was King willing to be his promoter, despite his South African citizenship, King began the negotiations by demanding three options on Coetzee should he win the title from Dokes.

Kushner told King: "I find this a little inconsistent. First you don't want to do business with me, or the fighter, because he's from a nation that practices racial apartheid. Now you tell me the only way you'll do business is if you have options."

By the time Kushner said he was willing to accept giving King three options, King had changed his position and demanded the contract give him options for the "lifetime of Coetzee's championship, should he win."

"What you're telling me," Kushner summarized, "is that if Gerrie is successful in the Dokes fight, and then he has five defenses, you have to be the exclusive promoter for all five defenses."

"Absolutely," King replied. "If you don't give me the options, there is no fight."

Recalling the negotiations now, Kushner says, "It was a total paradox. King was saying on the one hand, 'I won't fight him because he is a South African,' and on the other hand he was saying, 'If you don't give me the lifetime options that I'm asking for, I won't fight him either.' And I'm embarrassed to say those are the terms I finally agreed to. I can tell you that if you've only been in the boxing business for one year, and you're dealing with Don King, he's going to chew you up and spit you out for breakfast. . . .

"Coetzee was the mandatory challenger and according to the rules I didn't have to sign options with King to get the fight. But Don told me there would be no fight without lifetime options. I felt I had no choice. Coetzee was twenty-eight, and he had fragile hands. He had already lost two title chances. This was going to be his last chance. So King got everything he wanted."

Don King gave the white South African a chance at the title with a black fighter he called his son, who was managed by his stepson, and stipulated that should his surrogate son lose, he would become the exclusive promoter of the white fighter he should be boycotting, not monopolizing. Kushner never saw Carl King during the entire negotiations.

King set the fight for September 23, 1983, at the Richfield, Ohio, Coliseum, and sold the television rights to HBO. By the time the fight was signed, Dokes was a cocaine addict, but Kushner and Coetzee didn't know this.

The night of the fight there was a ragtag band of fifteen anti-apartheid pickets outside the arena, and about seven thousand people rattling around the twenty-two thousand seats inside.

Even though Dokes was born in nearby Akron, the fight, like many of King's promotions, never caught on with the public. The undefeated Dokes went into the ring a 5-to-1 favorite. He had knocked out Mike Weaver to win the title, and Weaver had knocked out Coetzee. The day before the fight Coetzee's own father had told boxing writers he gave his son "about a 2 percent chance to win."

But Coetzee dominated the whole fight. Dokes went into the ring with cocaine in his system and he was gasping for air by the fourth round. Coetzee knocked him down in the fifth and finished him in the tenth.

At the close of the tenth round, Dokes's hands were dropping and Coetzee clubbed him with two chopping rights. Dokes pitched forward on his face with his arm caught on the middle strand of rope.

The bell rang but the count continued, and Dokes rolled over on his back and was counted out.

Then came one of the defining, symbolic moments of Don King's boxing life. He jumped into the ring, in his tuxedo and bow tie and gold jewelry, stepping right over the fallen black champion he called his son to embrace the new white champion from the land he had condemned. King was hugging Coetzee before Dokes could regain his senses.

When Larry Merchant interviewed Coetzee in the ring for the HBO audience, the new champion thanked Don King first, and God second, for his victory.

King, always five moves ahead of the competition, immediately understood he had a money machine in Coetzee. He had the first white heavyweight champion in twenty-three years, since Ingemar Johansson. He knew he had a puncher who was controversial. He had seen the box office success of the *Rocky* movies, and of the Cooney-Holmes fight. And he knew that Dokes could not excite fans, that the Richfield arena was two-thirds empty for this fight. He anticipated a series of black-white "grudge fights" with Coetzee that would make millions on closed-circuit TV.

King had said it would be "an unpardonable sin" if Kallie Knoetze became heavyweight champion. But now he had just made a different white South African heavyweight champion and he was joyous over the deed. There was a holiday on King's face, thinking about future profits, as he hovered next to Coetzee in the ring.

A few minutes later King hugged Kushner, shouting, "Ced, my main man!" King invited Kushner into his limo and they drove back to Cleveland together.

"The whole ride back in the limo King kept telling me how much money we're going to make together," Kushner says. "I had never seen Don so happy. He kept saying how much money we could make with Coetzee in South Africa. Dokes was still woozy and Don was already telling me to go to South Africa and start negotiating with Sun City for Gerrie's first title defense. So I knew better than anyone else what a fucking fake and phony Don King is."

The next morning King woke up Kushner with a 7:00 A.M. call. King was already at his desk in the hotel, thinking about a title defense in South Africa and he asked the groggy Kushner to meet him right away to continue the conversation from the limo the night before.

When they met over breakfast in the hotel coffee shop, King told Kushner he would get paid a straight $250,000 fee for each title defense by Coetzee. Then he asked Kushner to secure for him permission to go to South Africa so he could negotiate directly with Sun City and Sol Kerzner over how to stage a co-promotion at the resort.

When King and Kushner met in New York a week later, King explained he couldn't be the "open, public promoter" of a fight in South Africa because it would look bad politically, but he was willing to sell his option rights on Coetzee to Sun City in exchange for a letter of credit.

King proposed as a challenger either Jeff Sims or Alfredo Evangelista, two fighters not serious contenders but already under exclusive promotional contracts to King.

Meanwhile, another promoter surfaced. Kenny Bounds wanted to match Coetzee with Larry Holmes in a unification title fight in Las Vegas. Bounds spent seven months trying to make this fight. He was an ambitious amateur with access to big money. He thought he could come right in, write checks, tie up all the players, make a $20 million killing, and become the new king of boxing. But in the end he would prove only how problematic it is to be a boxing promoter. His unrealistic math and negotiating inexperience would remind everyone how hard it is to be Don King, how hard it is to maintain longevity in boxing, how hard it is to outmaneuver all the competition year after year, how hard it is to make a big fight happen.

Kenny Bounds was a thirty-six-year-old Dallas real estate developer and former Georgia Tech football player. He was probably the most wholesome would-be promoter in boxing history. He had owned a health food store, had been the state director of the Fellowship of Christian Athletes, and was a dropout from a Baptist seminary.

Boxing is unstructured, like frontier gold prospecting, so Bounds first had to travel across the country buying up the various rights just to negotiate for a Coetzee-Holmes fight. He visited middlemen, managers, brokers, fixers, and lawyers. Soon he had made commitments of about $18 million just to get into the game.

Bounds guaranteed Holmes $12 million and gave him a non-refundable $3.5 million binder. He gave King $750,000 to sell his option on Coetzee for one fight, and signed an agreement to pay King an additional $6.7 million letter of credit by May 7 of 1984. This $6.7 million was then supposed to be divided, with $3.2 million going to Coetzee, $2.2 million to Kushner, and the rest to King. This meant King would get about $2 million for doing nothing. Bounds also contracted to pay Murad Muhammad $1 million as a finder's fee for delivering Holmes to the deal.

On top of all this, Bounds had to pay for travel, publicity, insurance, and undercard fighters. So going into the deal, he had a nut of about $20 million.

Bounds held a press conference on March 12 to announce that Coetzee and Holmes would fight on June 8 at Caesars Palace in Vegas.

"King can't stop this fight," Bounds told the press that day.

King was playing his usual double game. He was trying to kill the fight by pretending to go along with it and overpricing the value of his option in the hope the financing would fall apart. Although King was not on good terms anymore with Holmes, his real goal seems to have been to co-promote a Holmes-Coetzee fight himself in South Africa, with his arch-rival Bob Arum playing the out-front role.

In costing out the deal, Bounds made a series of rookie mistakes. He expected to sell the closed-circuit TV rights in South Africa for $5 million. But he forgot that June in Vegas was winter in South Africa with 35 degree temperatures and cold rains. Since the South African government didn't permit closed-circuit fights anyway, Bounds could sell only the home TV rights for $1.5 million to the government-controlled TV station.

Bounds also misjudged the value of the domestic TV sales. He was counting on selling the delayed-broadcast rights for $3 million. But he ended up selling the first delayed rights to HBO for $500,000, and the second delayed rights to ABC for $200,000.

He had budgeted the live gate at $6 million, but all he could negotiate with Caesars was $3.5 million. Down the line the numbers kept coming up short. With the fight five weeks away, Bounds had guaranteed revenues of $9 million, and $20 million in expenditures.

Two investors in Bounds's company started to panic and refused to put up other assets as a guarantee for King's letter of credit. King agreed to give Bounds a few extra days grace period and Bounds flew from Dallas to Vegas to California in search of additional capital. There was some interest, but nobody was willing to write a check.

Caesars announced the collapse of the fight on May 15, saying Bounds had breached his contract, apparently by failing to deliver the letter of credit to King. Bounds said he was unwilling to pull down his two other companies, AP Development (real estate) and KBK Energy (oil), in order to try to salvage the promotion.

The whole sobering experience cost Bounds about $5 million. Holmes and King kept their nonrefundable advances, and Bounds never had anything to do with boxing again. Real estate is a gentleman's game compared to the cruelest sport.

The disintegration of the deal also drove an irreparable wedge between Kushner and Coetzee. All the while Bounds was trying to hold his fight together, King was working on Coetzee, telling him to dump Kushner, come with him, and make some real money with a pro who knew how to put on a promotion and sell it with showmanship.

Just as King had turned Shavers against Elbaum, and turned Holmes against Ernie Butler, he turned Coetzee against Kushner. He has an instinct for the back stab equal to Iago or Kissinger.

As the Holmes fight was collapsing, King flew to California, where Coetzee was training, and offered him $650,000 to fight David Bey (managed by Carl) in Sun City, and to abandon Bounds and Kushner.

Kushner says, "Coetzee was awed by King. He was awed just having King in his home. He just dumped me and went with King. I had given Gerrie $100,000 out of my own pocket for living and training expenses. But Don convinced him that I was no good, and that he could make more money for him. Don then went to see Gerrie's prior manager, a disbarred South African lawyer named Harold Tucker, and they made a deal. I was out of the picture and my contract abrogated."

In January 1985, Kushner sued King for breach of contract in Manhattan Supreme Court. Kushner claimed that King owed him $225,000 out of the $750,000 that Bounds had paid King. The lawsuit also alleged that King had engaged in "intentional and malicious acts and conspiracy" to terminate Kushner's relationship with Coetzee and to "replace Kushner and obtain the valuable promotional and business relationship with Gerrie Coetzee."

In 1991, King settled the lawsuit and paid Kushner $150,000. The payment came about because Kushner was then Tony Tucker's promoter and King was making a Tucker–Mike Tyson fight.

Michael Dokes quickly became a forgotten person. King stopped calling him as soon as he became an ex-champ. Dokes slipped deeper into the velvet sewer of the cocaine trade, getting arrested several times for sale and possession, and going through several cycles of prison and rehabilitation.

In 1988 Dokes was in New York for one of his comeback fights and he spoke about his ruined career.

"I was using blow [cocaine] steady since 1982," he said. "It was good for training in the gym. But the first time I went into a fight with cocaine in my blood was when I lost my title to Coetzee. I can't remember the end of the fight. . . . Don King hurt me. One time I went to Cleveland to ask Don for some money when

I was in a jam with the IRS. He said he didn't have any money and I started to cry. I loved that man. I looked up to him like he was my daddy. I even tried to comb my hair so I could look like him. And he had this big mansion, and millions of dollars, and he wouldn't help me out just a little. I became suicidal, close to a nervous breakdown. And I was still doing drugs all the time."

When asked if King knew he was a drug addict while he was heavyweight champion, Dokes almost whispered, "I believe he knew it. He never tried to stop me. He let me do whatever I wanted. I ran wild and he made money."

Then he added, "You can't use any of this stuff until after I stop fighting. Carl has promised me a fight with Tyson and I need the money. I got nothing left. I spent it all on blow and lawyers. Blow is the most seductive drug ever conceived on earth."

After the collapse of the Coetzee-Holmes match, Don King made a quiet deal with Sol Kerzner and Sun City. He would sell his rights to Coetzee, and provide a suitable challenger from his stable, in exchange for $1 million. Sun City would be the promoter and King would not have to do anything in public to earn his money.

The first fighter King tried to convince to make the fight—and violate the international boycott—was an amiable, undefeated heavyweight named David Bey. King liked to call Bey a "half-breed" because his mother was white and his father was black.

Bey was then rated the Number 3 contender, having just beaten Greg Page in impressive fashion in July in Las Vegas. Bey had beaten James "Buster" Douglas in his first pro fight, and his record was now fourteen wins and no defeats. A former army boxing champion, he called almost everyone "Sir."

What made Bey an even more attractive candidate to King was that Carl King was his manager of record. Carl took 50 percent of all of Bey's purses, even though he did not negotiate in his interest, guide his career, or in any way earn his share. Moreover,

Bey had a warm relationship with both Kings, despite this oner-
ous financial arrangement.

As Bey recalls it, King invited him to his townhouse on
East Sixty-second Street in Manhattan and offered him the fight.
King promised Bey a $650,000 purse, plus $100,000 for
expenses, to fight Coetzee for the title at the Sun City casino in
December.

Bey read the contracts and saw that King was getting more
money than he was. Don King then told him that Carl King would
not be accompanying him to South Africa. Bey was also taken
aback when King asked him to sign a life insurance policy in case
something happened in South Africa.

"Don wanted me to go," Bey told me in an interview that was
videotaped as part of a television documentary. He said, 'This is
a big opportunity for you, a fight for the championship of the
world, and you'll bring the title back home to America.' "

But Bey was a little uneasy and he asked King if he could think
about it for a few days.

Bey was then dating singer Natalie Cole, and she strongly advised him not to go.

"I didn't know what apartheid was," Bey says. "I didn't know
anything about it. But my lady friend said it was a bad thing
to go."

A few days later Bey accidentally ran into Arthur Ashe and
Harry Belafonte at the Sepia Awards dinner at a Manhattan hotel.
He approached them and said King had made him this offer, and
he didn't know what to do because it was an opportunity to make
$650,000, and he had never made more than $50,000 in any fight
before this.

Belafonte, who was deeply involved with the ANC movement
in South Africa, and had been a close friend and adviser to Martin
Luther King, made a direct moral-political appeal to the fighter.
Belafonte remembers telling Bey: "Anything that gives legitimacy
to Sun City strengthens the system of apartheid, and worsens the

oppression of black people in South Africa. But nobody is better qualified to tell you what a trick bag you're in than Arthur Ashe, who is sitting right over there. Go talk to him. Arthur played in South Africa as a tennis pro in the 1970s. Afterward Arthur discovered that his whole point of view was wrong, that he had been used and exploited by the apartheid system."

Bey then spoke to Ashe, who was a little less blunt and passionate but made the same point—that it would be morally wrong to take the Sun City fight, and that Bey would have to make a sacrifice that was small compared to the sacrifice others were making to bring down a system of pure evil.

When Bey reported these conversations back to King, King told him he couldn't trust Ashe because Ashe "owned stores in South Africa." This, of course, was not true.

After a few more days of thinking Bey told King he couldn't accept the fight.

"As soon as I told him I wouldn't go," Bey says, "Don told me I had made the right decision, and how proud he was of me, and he gave me a big hug, and told me how brave I was."

King then turned around and convinced Greg Page to take the fight. Page was also managed by Carl, and had lost his last two fights—to Bey and to Tim Witherspoon. But King made sure he was still rated in the top ten and set the fight with Coetzee for December 1.

King was in control of both fighters' careers when the match was announced, but he was careful to keep a low profile and not publicize his $1 million fee.

But there are few secrets in the boxing subculture and soon word spread and got into the sports pages about what King had done.

On November 8, 1984, Michael Katz published a story in *The New York Times* revealing that King would soon be expelled from the executive committee of Artists and Athletes Against Apartheid for violating the charter of his own organization.

Katz quoted King as saying, "I'm not going to South Africa. All I did was sell my rights."

"Same thing," rebutted activist Franklin Williams in the same article.

Katz quoted Larry Holmes as saying, "I think King should be ashamed of himself. He's always talking about his principles. It seems he sold 'em. If a man's got principles, you can't buy 'em."

David Bey turned out to be an unsung hero and martyr to the anti-apartheid movement because Page, who went in his place, knocked out Coetzee and won the title. Bey had beaten Page in his last fight and likely would have beaten Coetzee, too. This would have meant several million dollars to Bey and an irrevocable piece of boxing immortality; being heavyweight champion is an honor you can never lose and it stays with you the rest of your life. And Bey gave it up for a principle that had to be explained to him by Ashe and Belafonte.

Before Ashe, Belafonte, and Randall Robinson could formally evict King from their anti-apartheid organization, King submitted his letter of resignation on November 16.

In his letter King claimed that he had tried to convince Greg Page not to accept the fight but that Page wouldn't listen to him. He further claimed that the only reason he finally accepted the $1 million payment from Sun City was that Coetzee had insisted on it.

"Coetzee felt a strong moral obligation to me," King wrote, "and only through his insistence did I receive any compensation for the assignment of my rights."

King wrote that he had tried to explain all this to the group's president, Arthur Ashe, but that Ashe "wasn't interested." The tone of the letter was that King still felt he had done nothing wrong. Ashe told me that King's account was "false," and Page told me King urged him to take the fight and not to boycott Sun City.

A year after his resignation, King made a public donation of

$100,000 to Randall Robinson's organization, TransAfrica, to get back in the good graces of the activist community. On June 22, 1990, Nelson Mandela delivered a memorable address to the United Nations, and Don King was his honored guest. King was photographed with Mandela and spoke about his devotion to the anti-apartheid cause.

King even told reporters he was planning to promote a Mike Tyson fight in South Africa to benefit the ANC. The *Sunday Star* of Johannesburg quoted King as saying, "It would be tremendous to go to Johannesburg, where our brothers have been shackled and fettered without compunction or remorse, and fight under Nelson Mandela's banner for freedom and equality." King said the fight could raise $100 million and proposed that a "large share of the profits would be donated to the ANC."

Even though Harry Belafonte spoke to King about such a fight in South Africa to benefit the ANC, King never made a serious effort to organize the promotion. He put Tyson's 1990 comeback fights into casinos in Atlantic City and Las Vegas.

King often speaks the lofty words of altruism and idealism, and every year before Thanksgiving he gives out turkeys in poor neighborhoods, like an old Tammany ward boss. But he has never really used his power to benefit the larger community or the poor. Back in Zaire, when George Plimpton asked him about sharing his profits with the dispossessed, King fell into a double-talk monologue to escape the implications of the question.

What King should have done was donate the entire $1 million he took from Sun City and give it directly to the ANC, back in 1984, when the ANC was struggling and Mandela was still in prison. That would have been one press conference where all of King's superlatives and self-dramatization might have been justified.

BLACK PROMOTER TAKES $1 MILLION FROM SOUTH AFRICA AND GIVES IT BACK TO LIBERATION STRUGGLE would have, at last, been a headline worthy of King's self-image of an epic life.

In March 1991 I flew to Las Vegas to try to interview King, both for this book and for a PBS documentary I was working on as the writer-correspondent. The occasion was that King was promoting the first Mike Tyson–Razor Ruddock match at the Mirage. King's office had accredited me and my PBS colleagues to attend the fight.

I was traveling with Charles Stuart, an independent producer who had won six Emmys; his cameraman, John Baynard; and ex-champion Jose Torres, who was a close friend of mine and a consultant to the documentary.

High on my list of questions for King was his 1984 deal with Sun City, since he was now leading a campaign to prevent *black* South African fighters from being ranked by the IBF and getting title fights, in a holier-than-thou boycott extremism.

I have had a strong involvement with the issue of South African liberation ever since I was an activist in the 1960s. I had once been arrested in a sit-in at the Chase Bank in a protest over the bank's loans to the government of South Africa. In the mid-1980s I had written several lengthy articles in support of economic sanctions against the South African regime.

I had even written about the video released by forty rock, rap, reggae, R&B, and jazz performers in 1985 called "Ain't Gonna Play Sun City." The video was an effective mix of music and politics that included artists like Bruce Springsteen, Miles Davis, Darlene Love, Bonnie Raitt, Eddie Kendricks, David Ruffin, Bob Dylan, Jimmy Cliff, Lou Reed, Herbie Hancock, and Ruben Blades.

The lyrics, composed by Little Steven Van Zandt, seemed directly relevant to what King had done:

Relocation to phony homelands
Separation of families I can't understand
23 million can't vote because they're black

We're stabbing our brothers and sisters in the back
I ain't gonna play Sun City.

The first thing you see when you get off the plane at McCarran
Airport are rows and rows of slot machines, even before you get
to the baggage-claim area. The first street you see is called Paradise Road, and the next is Rainbow Drive. And then you see the
neon signs for the casinos with those names that suggest fantasy
and opportunity—the Stardust, the Mirage, the Golden Nugget.

Las Vegas is Disneyland for high rollers and desperate dream-
ers. On the eve of a big fight, it also becomes a convention of
pimps, hookers, pickpockets, the princes of the crack trade, wise-
guys with gold chains, gold teeth, and gold rings.

We were there to cover the fight, hopefully to interview King,
and let John Baynard shoot the atmosphere of this grotesque wa-
tering hole of vices.

Two days before the fight, King was standing in the main ball-
room of the Mirage giving an interview to a cluster of print and
TV reporters after finishing a long press conference with the fighters for the contingent of five hundred journalists.

As I joined the group, King was beginning a personalized tirade
against Bobby Lee, the president of the IBF. The real reason for
King's anger was that the IBF had recently sanctioned a title fight
between Evander Holyfield and George Foreman, rejecting King's
demand that Holyfield fight Tyson or be stripped of the crown.

The issue King was raising was not the sanction but the IBF's
policy of ranking black fighters from South Africa and sanctioning
their right to fight for a world title if the fight is located outside
of South Africa. This seemed fair to me, since the point of protest
shouldn't be to deprive black South African fighters of equal opportunity.

"Bobby Lee has no dignity," King was almost shouting. "The
IBF is a bunch of ingrates and mercenaries. Bobby Lee is no longer
fit to be the president of an organization. He's dealing with South

Africa clandestinely and surreptitiously. He's putting fights on in Europe. How can a black man condone working with apartheid? He's a traitor, an Uncle Tom."

Since that's exactly what King himself had done, I couldn't resist the opening.

"What about the million dollars you took from Sun City, Don?" I asked.

Don King was not pleased to be reminded of his hypocrisy in the midst of his own oratory against Lee, with dozens of boxing writers and black fighters standing around.

Don King began attacking me.

"You ain't nothin' but a scumbag," he screamed. "You are dirt. You are nothing. You are a scumbag!"

For about two minutes Don King stood about three inches from me screaming insults, as a larger and larger crowd gathered, drawn by the roar of his rant. Two thoughts raced through my mind: Is my cameraman getting this? This guy has killed two people!

As King cursed me, I could hear Joe Frazier ask, "Who is that guy? What's he got on Don?"

Every thirty or forty seconds I interrupted just to say, "Don, you haven't answered my question; why did you take the one million from South Africa?"

Each time I squeezed in my question, he raised his volume with more insults.

"You are Goebbels! You're prejudiced!"

I knew King was trying to intimidate me, so I just stood my ground and kept repeating my question. I could now see that John Baynard was smiling and getting all this down on video.

After my third repetition of the question, King did something I had never seen him do before. He apologized, admitted he was wrong.

"Yes, I made the mistake of dealing," he recanted at the same decibel level at which he had ranted. "And I've suffered deep contrition for it. I stand reproved. I apologize."

Then he returned to the attack. "But you are nothing. You are an SOB. You are dirt."

King then took a few steps away and continued to attack me to another group of reporters.

"Newfield is the worst guy who ever lived," he said. "He's just like Goebbels."

But I was happy. For six years I had listened to him rationalize and sugarcoat his under-the-table payment from Sun City, and now we had his apology on videotape for our *Frontline* documentary.

But the good feeling didn't last long. A few minutes later one of King's goons, wearing a warmup suit, came up to me and whispered, "Better watch your back, Jack. This is Don's town."

A few seconds later, one of King's press aides, Joe Safety, grabbed my press credential, which was hanging around my neck, and took it.

King had never denied me press credentials for any of his fights before. Despite investigative stories I had written in the past, King often kidded me and laughed them off. He had never gone out of control before. It must have been the disclosure of his betrayal of the ANC in front of so many black journalists and fighters. He certainly didn't seem aware we were taping his tirade for public television.

I found Charles Stuart and told him what had happened, and he said, "Let's go to the press office and get your credentials restored. They knew who we were when we applied for the credentials. All you did was ask one question."

When we got to the press office, however, another press aide named Andy Olson confiscated Stuart's credential, too. Olson was apologetic and explained he was "just following orders." Olson advised us to have the executive producer of *Frontline* fax a letter to Don King Productions requesting restoration of our credentials to cover the fight, for which we had all flown to Las Vegas at considerable expense to PBS.

So we called the *Frontline* executives and lawyers back in Boston, and they did fax to us a high-minded letter about freedom of the press and the original intent of Madison and Jefferson. The next morning we took the fax to Joe Safety, but he refused to even read it. He said we were banned from coverage and ordered us to leave the press room.

John Solberg, King's top press aide, came out from behind his desk and ordered us to leave, saying all our credentials had been revoked.

"This is worse than Central America!" exclaimed Charles Stuart, who was then editing a documentary on Noriega's Panama.

"You're violating the First Amendment," I said. "I was just doing my job. I just asked one question."

"On what grounds are you denying our application?" Stuart asked.

"I don't have to give you a reason," Solberg said. "It's a privilege, not a right. Throw them out."

Solberg then placed the palm of his hand over the lens of the camera, in the classic gesture of censorship by a fool who doesn't realize the camera is still rolling.

"You are on private property! Take the tape out of this man's camera!" Solberg shouted to some of King's goons who were circling around us. But Jose Torres was standing next to Baynard, his hands clenched in a fist, and nobody made a move.

The private property we were on—the hallway—belonged to Steve Wynn and the Mirage, not King, and two Mirage security guards arrived at that moment.

"Take the tape out of the camera," Solberg repeated.

But the security men realized we had a legal right to be taping in the hallway and made no attempt to confiscate the tape from Baynard's camera.

As we started to leave, Carl King shouted to me, "I'm not as nice as my daddy. I'll kick your fucking ass."

Baynard caught that on tape, too.

"This is great," Stuart said. "Mike Wallace lives for shit like this."

Stuart was right. The confrontation with King made our documentary more dramatic and personal, and both Stuart and I won Emmys for the program. King's volcanic eruption, and his apology, might have been the most self-revealing interview King has ever given.

On the night of the fight, Gene Kilroy, Muhammad Ali's facilitator, sneaked me and Jose Torres into the ringside section, where we saw the fight and King saw us, not too happily.

A few hours after the confrontation ended, Jose Torres and I encountered Greg Page, who was still fighting, boxing an eight-round preliminary on the undercard against an opponent with a losing record.

We started to talk to him about his match with Coetzee at Sun City, when he won the heavyweight championship of the world, which should have been the best night of his career.

"Winning the title in South Africa has made my life much worse," he said, his sad, fearful eyes darting around the room. "I'm sorry I went. I'm sorry I let Don talk me into it."

After a pause he added, "Life ain't fair, you know. Some things are better left unsaid. But my story is even worse than Tim Witherspoon's."

"Can we talk about it?" I asked.

"Don's people are watching us," the former champion said. "I'm in room 2104. Call me later."

And he walked away.

When I called Page later in his room, he sounded just like Michael Dokes, another of the lost generation of Don King's heavyweights.

"I can't talk anymore," Page said. "I still have a few fights left and I need Don. It's like I told you, some things are best left unsaid."

Tim Witherspoon and the Lost Generation of Heavyweights

The first time Tim Witherspoon became conscious of Don King's presence in his life was in December 1981. Witherspoon was fighting Alfonzo Ratliff in Atlantic City when he heard that deep, commanding voice saying, "Terrible Tim, Terrible Tim, you're going to be all right."

Tim Witherspoon already knew about Don King, from his months as a sparring partner for Muhammad Ali, from watching television, from reading the sports pages. He knew King was the most powerful man in boxing, that he was "friends with presidents and Jesse Jackson," and that "stars like Eddie Murphy and Diana Ross hung around him." Tim knew it could be important if Don King was taking an interest in his career.

Once again Don King was the vulture on the ring post, starting to sing his song of seduction.

Nobody expected Tim Witherspoon to have a big pro career. Boxing was only his third favorite sport after football and basketball. Tim had been an all-city tight end in high school in Philadelphia, and was given a football scholarship to Lincoln University in Jefferson City, Missouri. But he quit college after one semester.

In 1978, he was working in a hospital, serving food to doctors, setting up rooms for parties, and preparing coffee and doughnuts for the surgeons, making $150 a week. He was also living at home with his five brothers and three sisters in a three-bedroom house.

As an all-around athlete, molded for competition, Tim started fooling around the local gym and discovered he liked boxing and had some natural ability. He tested himself in seven local amateur bouts, winning six and losing one to Marvis Frazier. He decided to turn pro and see what developed. He had no big-time connections. He certainly had won no amateur championships like Greg Page, Tony Tubbs, Michael Dokes, or Tony Tucker.

So Tim started far away from boxing's mainstream. His first pro fight was in Upper Darby, Pennsylvania. His second was in Lynchberg, Virginia. His third was in Commack, Long Island. His fourth was in McAfee, New Jersey. Tim's manager was Mark Stewart, although they did not yet have a written contract.

During 1980 and 1981 Tim kept winning, learning, and started earning extra money as a sparring partner, first with light heavyweight champion and friend Matthew Saad Muhammad, and then with Muhammad Ali at Deer Lake. Soon he was earning enough as a sparring partner to quit his job at the hospital.

In his ninth fight, Tim was thrown in with Marvin Stinson, a Philadelphia fighter who had been a big amateur star and was thought to have the potential for a successful pro career. Tim was considered just a stepping-stone. But Tim won a decisive ten-round decision in Atlantic City that made the insiders take notice of him for the first time.

After four more wins, Tim was matched with Alfonzo Ratliff on December 5, 1981. Ratliff was a capable fighter, who would go on to become a rated contender and fight Mike Tyson on

HBO. But with Don King shouting out encouragement, Tim stopped him in seven and entered boxing's major leagues.

In 1981 Don King did not have a promoter's license in New Jersey because he had not yet received his pardon for the murder of Sam Garrett. So he had to operate through fronts and behind the scenes.

King went to Mark Stewart some time in mid-1981 and acquired an interest in Witherspoon that Tim didn't even know about. King already had his hidden promotional rights to Witherspoon even before Tim heard his voice saying, "You're going to be all right."

Witherspoon signed a managerial contract with Mark Stewart on August 11, 1981. The contract gave Stewart 50 percent of Tim's purses and Stewart guaranteed Tim an annual income of $100,000 a year. The contract was approved by the Pennsylvania State Athletic Commission on August 18. This was four months before the Ratliff fight.

Stewart says he brought King into the picture and fronted for him as a promoter out of a sincere desire to further Tim's career. But sometime later, Stewart also sold a managerial share in Tim to Carl King, for $50,000. At that point Stewart needed money for lawyers because he was under investigation by the FBI and IRS.

Stewart was eventually convicted and sentenced to four years in prison for tax fraud involving the preparation of false returns for forty-seven people—many of them sports celebrities—who had invested in a phony tax shelter controlled by Stewart. The whole thing was a sophisticated scam.

Tim liked Stewart and still thinks he was decently motivated. But because of his own problems, Stewart did steer his own fighter into a spiderweb of arrangements and relationships without even telling him.

Witherspoon was a good-natured, happy-go-lucky jock. He tended to trust people and was not prepared for the way he was cut up financially outside the ring.

Tim had never been in trouble or arrested in his life. But here at the outset of his career he already had a manager who was committing tax fraud, and a promoter who had gone to prison for manslaughter. And Tim didn't even know any of this.

Witherspoon did not realize what was happening around him until August 1982. Don King had surfaced as Tim's promoter a few months earlier, promoting his victory over Renaldo Snipes in Las Vegas, where King was licensed.

Right after that match King told Witherspoon he was fighting another young contender, James "Quick" Tillis, in August, in a match to be televised nationally by CBS. Tim was excited and felt confident he could beat Tillis.

But about a week before the fight Tim developed an infection in his right ear. He went to the Good Samaritan Hospital in Pottsville, Pennsylvania, and was advised by a doctor to stop training and postpone the fight.

"The ear hurt, I felt weak, and the infection was hurting my sense of balance," Witherspoon recalls. "So I called Don in Cleveland and told him what the doctor said. But Don told me to forget about the doctor; the fight had to go on because he was getting a lot of money from CBS television, and he would lose credibility if he had to cancel the date.

"Don played a trick on me," Witherspoon says.

King told Tim to fly to Cleveland and "tell the reporters why you can't fight."

But when Tim arrived in Cleveland there was no press conference. Instead King took Witherspoon to the offices of the Cleveland boxing commission and ordered him to fight, regardless of the counsel of his physician. (There was no state athletic commission in Ohio till 1984.)

King had tipped off reporters and photographers to the meeting, and the next day pictures of Witherspoon facing the city commissioners were printed in the Cleveland papers.

Cleveland commissioners Mike Minnich and Eugene Pearson told Witherspoon they didn't believe his story, and they sus-

pended him indefinitely. Tim went home to Philadelphia confused, angry, and unable to earn a living without his license.

"I was pulling mothballs out of my pockets I was so broke,"
Tim recalls.

After a few weeks King called Witherspoon with an ultima-
tum—sign long-term exclusive contracts with him and his stepson, and he would get the suspension lifted immediately.
Otherwise Tim would be blacklisted and his career finished.

"I'm the commission, and the commission is me," Witherspoon
recalls King telling him. "Them guys ain't nothing. It's me. They
do what I tell them."

Witherspoon was quite willing to sign with King again to be
his promoter, but he didn't see any reason to pay Carl to be his
manager, since Carl could not possibly be an independent nego-
tiator for Tim against his own father.

(In 1989, in a deposition with prominent defense lawyer Tom
Puccio, King admitted he pays Carl "a stipend," which finally
proved Carl couldn't be an independent bargainer for his fighters,
against his father.)

After holding out a few more days, Witherspoon finally surrendered. King had effectively used his monopoly power in Ohio
to coerce the fighter into signing away his future.

Told he couldn't bring a lawyer, Tim went alone to King's
office in Manhattan and signed four contracts of servitude. The
first contract made Don King his exclusive promoter, which Tim
wanted. The second made Carl King his manager and entitled
Carl to 33 percent of all his earnings. The third contract was a
copy of the second—except that it entitled Carl to 50 percent of
Tim's earnings. That was the one that would be enforced. The 33
percent contract was "for show," to be filed with boxing commissions that prohibit a manager from taking half a fighter's
purse.

The fourth contract was totally blank. King could fill in any
numbers, any opponent, any date he wanted.

At the end of the meeting King gave Witherspoon a $1,500 signing bonus.

In June 1991, Don King would be asked about this meeting and the blank contract in a nationally televised interview with Sam Donaldson of ABC. King's double-talk explanation, according to the official ABC transcript, was: "Yes, it's fair because we didn't know what we were going to do until the fourth one. When we got to that stage, we were negotiating, then I signed him up, and with the price in the contract beforehand, it would not have been fair with him because what the price is, in today's market may be different in the future market."

Don King understood that every fighter who grew up poor was a sucker for a big pile of cash, that cash in fresh, green currency made more of an impression than a check for fifty times the amount. Tim Witherspoon, despite his high school diploma, was no exception.

Nine years later Tim's face still lit up when he described the feeling of importance and exhilaration of having that $1,500 in his pocket driving back to Philly. "I loved it. It made me feel big," Witherspoon said.

But for some chump change Don King had locked up Witherspoon body and soul. King held an exclusive contract as Tim's promoter. His stepson was taking 50 percent of Tim's earnings for nothing, and Don King was now Tim's de facto manager as well as his promoter. Witherspoon had no manager to get him the best deal. By signing Witherspoon, King now controlled nine of the top ten heavyweights in the world. The vulture on the ring post had another meal.

As always in the beginning of a relationship with a fighter, King was on his best behavior—attentive, enthusiastic, honorable.

Tim's first fight for the Kings was a shot at the heavyweight championship. King jumped Witherspoon over several more highly rated contenders and signed him to fight Larry Holmes in Las Vegas on May 20, 1983.

The fight with Holmes should have been the crowning achievement of his life, but instead it was the beginning of his disillusionment and his obsession to secure fair treatment from Don King.

Judging fights is a subjective, almost impressionistic, enterprise. But most people thought Witherspoon defeated Holmes that night and was cheated of the crown by the officials. Holmes was thirty-three and he suddenly got old walking up the steps to the ring. He didn't have the same mobility anymore.

Witherspoon was able to outjab the champion, and staggered him in the ninth round. Holmes sagged into the ropes and saved himself from a knockout by catching Witherspoon with a desperation punch and clinching. Even in his twilight, Holmes was most dangerous when he was hurt.

The television announcers thought Witherspoon had won. The crowd of sixteen thousand thought he'd won and booed the decision. But only one of the three officials gave Tim the decision.

Two days after the fight, Dave Anderson, with his typical grace and wit, wrote the truth in *The New York Times:*

> If the two boxers had fought in a street somewhere and now were on display, a latecomer would surely be able to identify the winner. One was unmarked and unafraid, his face glowing as he had said, "I had fun. I know I can beat him."
>
> The other was uncertain and unconvincing, his face glum and his right eye puffed as he said, "Maybe I'm going down a little bit, a couple of years ago he couldn't have worn my socks."
>
> But the fight had been in a ring, not a street. . . .
>
> Larry Holmes later talked about how, "the judges gave me the fight." One judge in particular, Chuck Hassett, imported from Anaheim, Calif., had the champion ahead, 118–111, awarding him nine rounds with one even—a scorecard that be-

longed in Disneyland in his hometown, not at ringside in the Dunes Hotel parking lot. . . .

On my scorecard Tim Witherspoon deserved to be the new champion, 115–113 in points, seven rounds to five.

After the fight Witherspoon got an ever bigger shock. He had been promised a payment of $150,000. His contract had been reported in all the newspapers. But instead he got a check from Carl King for only $52,750.

Carl had taken 50 percent, which was illegal in Nevada. The WBC sanction fee was deducted from Tim's purse and so was a $10,000 payment to the IRS.

A few months later Witherspoon learned that Scott Frank had been paid $350,000 when he was knocked out by Holmes. Frank was a stiff, a club fighter, but he had a manager who negotiated the best deal for him.

The nationally televised fight with Holmes made Witherspoon a popular figure. Strangers called him the real champ and told him he got swindled. In losing, he gained in stature and reputation.

But to get robbed twice—and to have no recourse—wounded his psyche and injected a bitter thread into his friendly comic nature.

About six weeks after the loss to Holmes, King told Witherspoon he would be fighting Quick Tillis in Richfield, Ohio. He also told him that he had to train at King's training camp in Orwell, Ohio.

"I want to train at Ali's camp in Deer Lake," Tim told King. "I love it there. Ali said I can use it."

King said absolutely not, that Ali was about to sell it, and the training location was not negotiable.

Witherspoon had a deep emotional attachment to Ali's camp, because of its association with Ali, because of all the good times he'd had there, because it was close to his home, and because it was free. King billed all of his fighters for the use of his facility in Ohio, including its use among the mysterious deductions from their purses.

By the time Witherspoon arrived for the Tillis fight, he was in open rebellion against King. He told reporters he had trained only five days for the fight "because I don't care anymore. . . . If I don't get paid the way I should, why should I care? I'm supposed to get $50,000 for this fight, but I know I'll only see about half that."

Witherspoon also told reporters that he was upset that Mark Stewart had sold his contract to Carl King the year before.

"It's like we're racehorses," *The New York Times* quoted Tim as saying. "They race us till we drop and then they shoot us. And if we win, they tie a blue ribbon around our neck."

Witherspoon knocked Tillis out at 2.16 of the first round, dropping him with a devastating right after a minute, and then with a short left hook a minute later.

He was paid only $22,500, just as he had predicted. Carl King took 50 percent—$25,000—for his share.

Despite Tim's outspoken complaints, Greg Page was even more of a malcontent than Tim. Page was complaining about King underpaying him to anyone who would listen, was threatening to sue King, and wasn't training, blowing up to about 260 pounds. So King matched his two frustrated fighters to meet for the vacant WBC title on March 9, 1984, in Las Vegas. The title had been vacated by Larry Holmes before King could have him stripped of the title. The fact that Carl King was the manager of both Witherspoon and Page did not trouble the Nevada commission, which sanctioned the fight, or HBO, which purchased the TV rights.

The match was a typical incestuous venture, with King getting paid three different ways and guaranteed to control the WBC title no matter who won. It was immaterial to King that both fighters despised him; his objective was profit and continuity of control.

"I would say that Don hated Greg even more than he hated

me before that fight," Witherspoon says. "I know that because before the fight Don told me that if I didn't get knocked out, he would make sure I won the decision. He said if I'm standing at the end, I'll win."

Like so many of King's alienated fighters, Page let his anger turn inward and become self-loathing. He sulked and barely trained, virtually going on strike at the gym. He overate, partied, and lost his motivation. It was a syndrome that would damage a whole generation of King's heavyweights, including Witherspoon, Dokes, Tubbs, and Tucker. The day of the fight Page looked blubbery and weighed in at 240 pounds, about 15 over his best weight.

Witherspoon trained only a little more strenuously; he came in about eight pounds over his best condition, looking merely puffy rather than blubbery.

Another sign that King wanted Witherspoon to win occurred twenty minutes before the fighters were due to enter the ring. One of King's bodyguards came into Witherspoon's dressing room with a piece of paper for him to sign.

"It's for the IRS, so you can get paid," the bodyguard told Tim.

In the dressing room was Tom Moran, a close friend who would later become Witherspoon's manager. He read the paper, and it had nothing to do with the IRS or Tim getting paid. It was a three-year extension of Tim's managerial contract. Angry at the deception, angry at the invasion of his privacy, Tim didn't sign the paper.

Walking toward the ring Witherspoon was confident he would win if King wanted him to, and that King controlled all the judges in Las Vegas. The combination of Witherspoon fighting just to go the distance, and Page being out of condition, made for one of the lousiest fights in years.

Page held, and slapped, and lay against the ropes. Witherspoon took no chances and accepted every clinch. It was a waltz between two demoralized, unprepared athletes.

Afterward Larry Holmes said, "I'd have seen a lot more action watching some old lady play the slot machines at the MGM Grand. At least she might have hit something once in a while."

Judge Chuck Minker scored the fight a draw, 114–114, perhaps implying neither one deserved to become champion. Judges Lou Tabat and Jerry Roth both scored it 117–111 for Witherspoon.

Witherspoon had boxed expertly against Holmes and lost. Now he performed slovenly against Page and became champion. That's boxing, but not much of a lesson to the young about rewarding hard work and pure desire.

After the fight Page was understandably bitter. "Ask the judges, ask Don King," he snarled at reporters in his dressing room. "I've been going through hell like this my whole career. This is my retirement. I've had enough of this bullshit."

Witherspoon's contract guaranteed him a purse of $250,000. But the net amount he was actually paid was $44,640.

Don King deducted from his purse: training expenses; tickets to the fight for his family; airplane tickets to Vegas for his friends and relatives; the cost of training equipment; the salaries of sparring partners; and "incidentals." Witherspoon never got the $100,000 in training expenses he should have under the contract. Instead he was billed $150 a day to train at a camp he didn't want to use.

Carl King again took 50 percent—$125,000. In its accounting report to the Nevada commission, Don King Productions claimed Carl King was paid only $83,000—33 percent. This was a false statement that should have cost King his license. But the commission never audits the financial records of promoters.

Financial records later obtained during Witherspoon's lawsuit against the Kings revealed that King tried to deduct every dime possible from both fighters. Three weeks after the fight, a memo from Celia Tuckman to Connie Harper and Marc Powell said: "When we receive additional billing from the Rivera Hotel on late checkouts, an additional amount may be due from Witherspoon."

A Celia Tuckman memo dated April 11, 1984, identified an additional $74.76 to be billed to Witherspoon for rooms rented by his trainer Aaron Snowell and Andrea Parks. This brought the hotel expenses deducted from Witherspoon's purse to $4,752— including his own hotel room and meals.

The April 11 memo added: "We withheld $5,000 from Witherspoon's purse for incidentals. Please check to see if any amount is due for airline tickets and ascertain if Tim owes us beyond the $5,000 which already has been deducted."

These documents show that King even deducted from Witherspoon's purse the cost of his protective cup ($98); his hand wraps ($5); his skip rope ($13); and the robe he wore into the ring ($54).

Three months later an unhappy Witherspoon was back in training at the Orwell, Ohio, facility for an August 31 title defense against Pinklon Thomas, who was also managed by Carl King.

"Oh, man, did I hate that training camp," Witherspoon reflected years later. "Being there was like being back in the ghetto. The mentality put most of the fighters back into a not caring situation. The fighters didn't have no money. There wasn't a hundred dollars between us. We knew Don was charging us for staying there. The morale was real low. There was drugs floating all around the camp. It was just like being back in Philly. . . .

"I had to eat pork bacon there even though I told them I didn't want it. When I mouthed off, Don said he would cancel the fight and I wouldn't fight at all. I wouldn't kiss his butt and he didn't like my attitude. I was too independent for him.

"I even tried to organize all the fighters there. Leon Spinks and Mitch Green cursed out Carl. Pinklon and Berbick left. But the conditions stayed the same. I would complain to Carl, and Carl would just say he had to ask his father.

"When I tried to organize the revolt, Don spoke to all of us and said the white man was trying to keep us all down. The next night Don had a big party in his house and it was all white people. None of us black fighters got invited.

"That camp messed us all up. That's where we became the lost generation of heavyweights, that's what I call us."

So it was in a depressed state of mind that Witherspoon arrived in Vegas for the fight. He was also not in the best condition, having participated in the pot smoking at the camp.

Witherspoon was also obsessing about being cheated out of so much money in the Page fight. Now that he was champion, he felt he was entitled to his own lawyer and hired March Risman of Las Vegas to make sure that this time Carl King took only 33 percent of his money instead of 50 percent.

Risman met with King, read the contracts, won an assurance that Carl would take only 33 percent this time. But King regarded the intervention of an attorney as treason by one of his chattel.

King got even by playing games with Witherspoon's head. This time he told Tim the reverse of what he had told him before the Page fight. This time King told Witherspoon he would lose the decision, and his title, if Thomas was standing at the final bell.

Witherspoon believed King could do anything he said. He had seen him manipulate the Cleveland commission to take away his license without due process, despite a legitimate ear infection. He believed King had influenced the judges to favor him in the judging of the Page fight. And now he believed he was about to be deprived of his title because he had tried to exercise his rights.

On the morning of the fight Witherspoon was in a state of panic and paranoia. Tim had an unusually vivid imagination, and King, the grand master of mind games, was exploiting this vulnerability.

To ease his nerves, Witherspoon drank a whole bottle of bee pollen about six hours before the fight, as part of his faith in vitamins. But the honeylike concoction only made him drowsy and dulled his mind and reflexes. Feeling he had made a mistake in drinking the bee pollen only served to escalate Witherspoon's anxiety.

Witherspoon's mental state was so crazed that he admits he

went into a urinal near his dressing room just before the fight and met with one of the officials for the fight. He says he offered the official $3,000 "to look out for me."

The fight itself was dull and Thomas was awarded a majority decision. Referee Richard Steele deducted one point from Witherspoon's total for "backhanding." Steele would later be accused of pro-King bias for stopping the 1990 Chavez–Meldrick Taylor fight with two seconds remaining and Taylor ahead.

The official contract King filed with the Nevada commission said Witherspoon's purse was $400,000, and claimed he had "no manager." It also said Tim was due to be paid $50,000 for "training expenses."

But after all the strange diversions and deductions, Witherspoon was paid only $116,000. Training expenses again were subtracted, not added. Carl took 50 percent after all. And Tim paid his trainer $30,000 out of his own shrunken share.

King subtracted from Witherspoon's purse: an $8,000 sanction fee, tickets to the fight valued at $5,900; a payment to the IRS of $50,000; plane tickets worth $3,400; and a $50 fine.

The flavor of King's penny-pinching is preserved in an internal prefight memo by Celia Tuckman. It read: "All fighters will be told in writing that they will receive $30 per day in the Cafe Roma only for food. It should be noted that the hotel is giving us $40 per day, and we are trying to keep the costs down. It should also be noted that both Pinklon Thomas and Tim Witherspoon are to be put in at $30 per day. Their actual arrangements, however, are for full food privileges."

Tim Witherspoon went home to Philadelphia a very bitter ex-champ. "I was all fucked up," remembers Witherspoon.

He tried to get some fights on his own, thinking he was marketable as the former champion, but King controlled all the other top heavyweights, and he wouldn't let any of them fight Witherspoon. Tim found himself blacklisted, frozen out, unemployed—despite his fame.

"I crawled back to Don," he says. "I had no choice. He told me to fire my lawyer, and I did it. He told me to sign a bunch of blank contracts, and I did it. They beat me. Carl was going to take fifty percent again. They wouldn't give me copies of anything I had signed. I was back into slavery."

Among the contracts Witherspoon signed in November 1984 was an exclusive three-year managerial contract with Carl King. This contract stipulated that Witherspoon would pay for: all trainer's salaries, all training expenses, room and board, all transportation to and from matches, all telephone calls, and all publicity expenses.

Witherspoon, now twenty-eight, aching for another chance at the title, decided to submit and make the best of a bad situation. Accepting that he would not get paid what he was worth, he engaged in a series of comeback fights to rebuild his reputation and confidence.

In April 1985, he knocked out 261-pound James Broad in two. In June he easily outpointed James "Bonecrusher" Smith. In September he knocked out an unknown named Larry Bielfus in Florida and was paid only $5,000. In October he knocked out Sammy Scaff in London, getting paid $4,000.

His record was now twenty-three wins and two loses, with sixteen knockouts. He had been able to mask his feelings and not criticize King to reporters, and King rewarded his "rehabilitation" with a title fight against WBA champion Tony Tubbs in Atlanta, on January 17, 1986. King billed the fight as a tribute to Martin Luther King, in King's birthplace, in celebration of the new national holiday honoring America's prince of nonviolence. The date was also Muhammad Ali's forty-fourth birthday, and King produced him at ringside for a generous fee.

But the whole evening turned out to be a grotesque farce, featuring almost all the self-destructive heavyweights of the lost generation. It was a seven-hour evening of dreadful performances by athletes who didn't train, didn't care, and knew most of their purses were getting attached by the IRS anyway. Before the fights even began, an IRS agent came into one dressing room with legal papers for all the waiting boxers, including David Bey, Mitch Green, and Witherspoon.

King put on seven fights with out-of-shape heavyweights who weighed an aggregate of 3,212 pounds. Every fight stank. The night began with about five thousand fans, but only about three hundred remained in the vast Omni arena when the last bout ended at 1:00 A.M.

Anyone whoever wanted to make a documentary about what's wrong with boxing should have had a few camera crews shooting this Animal House card, in a city that hadn't had a major fight in fifteen years, in a state where regulation was a joke.

In the opening fight, Eddie Gregg decisioned Walter Santemore in a fight so bad it helped convince the winner to retire. Mitch Green won a mismatch from 248-pound Percell Davis. Trevor Berbick looked awful in beating the much smaller Mike Perkins. Buster Douglas beat a disinterested Greg Page in a fight whose only artistic merit was in demonstrating to the public how Tubbs had been able to dethrone Page. David Bey won a decision from a 249-pound butterball named Wes Smith.

In the main event, Witherspoon regained the title with a fifteen-round verdict over Tubbs. Tubbs weighed 244 pounds and acted like he was trying to honor Dr. King by winning the Nobel Peace Prize in the ring.

Another farcical element was scoring: Witherspoon won twelve of the fifteen rounds, but one judge scored the match a draw.

During the course of the evening, the steadily vanishing audience sporadically chanted, "Ali, Ali," out of boredom and nostalgia, possibly trying to say that the sickly, retired hero could still beat all these blubbery whales.

Four days after the fight, the urine analysis came back from the laboratory with the news that Witherspoon had tested positive for marijuana in his system. He immediately admitted he had smoked "reefer," saying it was at a party a month before the fight.

King immediately began to position himself as a public crusader against drugs, while lobbying by telephone with the WBA officials not to change the result.

With typical hollow hyperbole, King declared, "I'm going to start my own drug abuse center with my fighters. I will do everything—preach—whatever, the disuse of drugs. We will take our own tests, and if we find a fighter is not drug-free, he'll not enter the ring. We must have some self-help in boxing, and my goal is to rid our sport of drugs."

King, of course, never set up any kind of drug abuse center or drug education for his fighters. He never even tried to ostracize the drug dealers who openly socialized with his fighters like Dokes, Tony Tucker, Tony Tubbs, Macho Camacho, and Mike Tyson.

As a result of King's backstage politicking, Witherspoon's victory was allowed to stand and he was ruled to be the legitimate champion. Witherspoon agreed to pay the Georgia boxing commission a $25,000 fine and to undergo drug treatment and counseling.

In the accounting for the Tubbs fight, Carl King took his 50 percent cut—$25,000—and $1,500 was deducted for training expenses. Witherspoon was paid $2,000 in cash and an $8,000 check was signed by Carl King from Monarch's bank account.

Tim Witherspoon was heavyweight champion again, but he still had no control over his own destiny. He was not allowed to have his own lawyer or accountant. He couldn't get copies of his own contracts or financial records. Carl was not really his manager but his father's employee and messenger. For all his intelligence and good intentions, Witherspoon was still just a powerless pawn in Don King's game, just as Holmes had been.

Witherspoon couldn't compete with King in the realms of numbers, contracts, psychology, politics, publicity, finance, or lawyers.

Tim was a fighter. And King had outnegotiated and outthought the CEOs of corporations, networks, casinos, the dictators of nations, and all the law enforcement authorities who had tried to convict him. Witherspoon didn't know to liberate himself from the spider's web. But he knew, better than any other fighter, that he was trapped.

And now that he was champion again, Don King was about to rape him more brazenly than he had ever been raped before. King had his compulsion to demonstrate control and dominance, and while he felt all fighters were interchangeable, he seemed to have a special urge to teach Tim a lesson for his sporadic revolts against his authority.

By the spring of 1986 the HBO heavyweight elimination tournament that King had sold to Seth Abraham was under way. Witherspoon was one fight away from a multimillion-dollar showdown with Mike Tyson.

One day Carl King told Witherspoon, "My father says you got a fight with Frank Bruno in London. If we're going over there, we're getting paid. I'm going to make sure of that."

"How much?" Witherspoon asked, knowing that if a champion travels to a challenger's home country, that is an unusual enough risk to assure a real payday.

"I'm going to ask my father what we're going to get," Carl replied.

Years later Witherspoon tried to capture his state of mind when he was informed he was going to defend against Bruno in his hometown.

"I knew I was going to get robbed," he says, "but I thought Don would be generous and give me maybe $600,000, $700,000."

The indisputable fact is that HBO paid Don King $1.7 million to deliver Witherspoon to the fight. King told his junior partner in the promotion, Butch Lewis, that he gave all $1.7 million to Witherspoon, and Lewis told this to reporters after the fight.

King not only misled his partner, he also tried to cheat him. Lewis says that during the promotion a check for $200,000 came into their partnership made out to the Dynamic Duo, Inc., and that King deposited it into the account of Don King Productions, through a friend at Chemical Bank. Only when Lewis confronted his partner did King say it was "a mistake."

Nobody represented Witherspoon in the complex prefight negotiations. For example, the challenger, Bruno, was given a percentage of the live gate and Witherspoon was not. Bruno's promoter, Mickey Duff, negotiated an exemption from British taxes for the challenger, but Witherspoon had to pay $75,000 in British taxes.

With the leverage of being champion, an independent manager should have gotten Witherspoon $1 million for this fight. The Associated Press reported his purse would be $900,000.

But Witherspoon had no clue how much he was getting paid. He can't even remember signing a contract for the Bruno match and assumes King just used the signature page of one of the many blank contracts he'd signed over the years. The official contract says Witherspoon would be paid $400,000 plus $100,000 for training expenses.

A few days before the fight, Witherspoon read in one of the London papers that his purse would be a certain number of pounds. He and his trainer tried to translate the pounds into dollars at the exchange rate and came up with $1 million.

"I'm gonna be a millionaire!" Tim shouted in his hotel room.

The crowd of forty-thousand at Wembley Stadium was in a Bruno frenzy. Bruno had won twenty-eight of his twenty-nine fights, twenty-seven by knockouts, and his fans believed he could become the first British citizen to win the heavyweight crown.

The fight itself was deadlocked and brutish going into the eleventh round. Witherspoon had been hurt several times and his face was swollen and his body ached. Bruno was motivated and in there to win. He was no Page, and no Tubbs, just going through the motions. But Witherspoon met the challenge.

In the eleventh round Witherspoon and Bruno landed rights at exactly the same instant. But Witherspoon's landed right on the chin and Bruno shook and fell backward into a corner. His eyeballs rolled like prunes on a Vegas slot machine.

Witherspoon hit him with two more rights and Bruno bent over. One more punch put him down on his haunches in a squatting position. Witherspoon hit him once again.

The count reached three when Bruno's corner tossed in the towel, ending the fight under British rules.

Witherspoon says that "was the best day of my life, the greatest moments of my life. I was the happiest man in the world."

Witherspoon celebrated with a small group of people he loved—his brothers, trainer, sparring partners, and his Irish neighbor and friend Tom Moran. The party began at King's lavish postfight party in a London hotel. But when they tried to take bottles of beer and champagne at the party, King personally stopped them.

This is how Tom Moran describes what happened next: "King's guy wouldn't even give us a beer. So a couple of us snuck in the back, got beer and champagne bottles and loaded up the bus. Tim was sitting in the back of the bus and I could tell he was in pain, because he was wearing sunglasses, and his eye was swollen, and his back was messed up.

"We had one cassette with three rap songs on it, and we kept playing the same three songs over and over and singing along. We drove all over London.

"We were singing, and telling stories, and laughing, and carousing, and drinking, and Tim was just sitting in the back, cracking a few jokes. He wasn't making a lot of noise, but he just had this big grin on his face. He had just conquered the world and he thought this was just too big an event for him not to walk away from it a rich man. He felt great that he was bringing the title home to America. We were all wearing red, white, and blue jackets and had felt very much in enemy territory. The fight made us all feel very American.

"After a while our bus started following a London newspaper truck. At each corner we would jump off and read the headline on the front page—WITHERSPOON STOPS BRUNO—and see the picture of Tim standing over Bruno. We would take some papers at each stop, and read it out loud on the bus.

"We were having so much fun I taped the bus ride, but the only thing you can really hear are the empty bottles banging around the floor. And the singing.

"I remember just before dawn we pulled up outside a park and there was a bunch of skinheads, and they were giving us the finger and screaming racist insults. They didn't like what Tim had done. He ruined their champion and their dreams. But we just laughed at them."

When Witherspoon returned to the hotel as the sun was coming up, he experienced an almost mystical epiphany. He ran into his idol, Muhammad Ali. Six years ago, he had been Ali's sparring partner, and tonight he wore Ali's old crown.

Ali did a little shuffle and hugged Witherspoon, who remembers Ali whispering into his ear, "I know you're not gonna get all your money."

Then Witherspoon went up and stretched out on his hotel-room bed. "I was so happy that even my soreness felt good," Witherspoon recalls. "It was good pain."

But three weeks later, when Tim was paid for his blood, he was given a check for $90,094. Frank Bruno, the loser, was paid $900,000.

Jimmy Binns, counsel to the WBA, says, "I know for a certain fact Don King made at least a two-million-dollar profit on the Witherspoon-Bruno fight."

Mickey Duff, Bruno's promoter says, "King grossed about five million on the fight and had a net profit of a couple of million dollars. He got revenue from HBO, British television, sponsorship from Miller Lite, and the live gate, which was two million."

According to the financial records of Don King Productions, Carl King took a $275,000 portion of Witherspoon's $500,000 purse—more than 50 percent.

King also deducted: $33,000 for cash advances, a $15,000 sanction fee, $75,000 for British income taxes, $25,000 for the WBC fine for flunking the urine test in Atlanta, $12,000 for "loans," and $1,400 for airfare.

The $12,000 in "loans" appears to at least partially be training-camp expenses, which the contract stipulated King would pay Witherspoon for, not the other way around. The financial records for the promotion show a $100,000 check made out to Carl King's company, Monarch, that says on the stub that the money is intended to cover "Witherspoon's training expenses."

But it seems clear Witherspoon never got this money from Carl King's company, which was located in the same Sixty-ninth Street office as Don King's company and had no independent existence, or financing, or corporate structure.

The problem was that all the money from HBO, British television, and other sources flowed into King's office in Manhattan, and then to Monarch. Nobody paid Witherspoon directly. His share of the proceeds was skimmed before it ever got to the fighter, whose talent made the whole revenue stream possible.

In his 1991 television interview with Sam Donaldson, King defended his accounting principles:

DONALDSON: Now, you promised him $550,000 for that fight.
KING: And I paid him that.
DONALDSON: You paid him $90,000.
KING: No, Sam. He borrows the money in advance. What he does is, he needs fifty for his mother, twenty-five for this, fifty for another thing, and when I advance this money to him, naturally, when the fight . . .

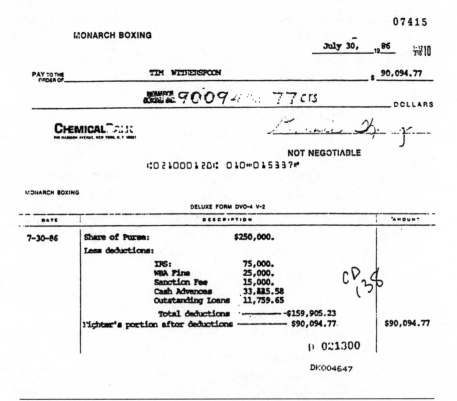

07415

MONARCH BOXING

July 30, 19 86 1-12/210 10

PAY TO THE
ORDER OF   TIM WITHERSPOON $ 90,094.77

MONARCH
BOXING INC. 9009.... 77 crs   DOLLARS

CHEMICAL BANK
940 MADISON AVENUE, NEW YORK, N.Y 10021

NOT NEGOTIABLE

021000120: 010─015337

MONARCH BOXING

DELUXE FORM DVO-4 V-2

DATE	DESCRIPTION	AMOUNT
7-30-86	Share of Purse: $250,000.	
	Less deductions:	
	IRS: 75,000.	
	WBA Fine 25,000.	
	Sanction Fee 15,000.	
	Cash Advances 33,145.58	
	Outstanding Loans 11,759.65	
	Total deductions ──── -$159,905.23	
	Fighter's portion after deductions ──── $90,094.77	$90,094.77

CP 138

0 021300

DK004647

Tim Witherspoon's $90,094 purse for beating Frank Bruno. Bruno, the
loser, was paid $900,000. But he had an independent manager, not Carl
King, who took more than 50 percent of Witherspoon's earnings for this
match.

DONALDSON: So, let me see if my math is right. You advanced him about $375,000?

KING: Yes, yes.

DONALDSON: Fifty dollars at a time?

KING: Whatever he got, he got his whole purse.

DONALDSON (voice over): If Don King advanced Witherspoon $50 a day, every day of the year, it would take more than 20 years to accumulate $375,000.

Donaldson did not ask King to explain the incredible 55 percent of Witherspoon's purse that went to his stepson Carl, who was essentially an employee of DKP.

To add insult to injury, Witherspoon later found out that King had flown most of the jurors who acquitted him in 1985 to be guests of the promotion, in ringside seats at this fight with Bruno.

Juror John Becker, a word processor for a Big Eight accounting firm, says King paid for his plane tickets, hotel rooms, and meals, as well as providing the ringside tickets. The fighter had to pay for his own protective cup, but the juror traveled first-class for free.

It's probably fair to say that Witherspoon never recovered from his morale-busting fleecing. The experience of making the fight of his life on foreign soil, and then getting robbed of his pay, just took something out of the fighter that was never restored.

"Tim's love for boxing as a sport just died after the Bruno fight," Tom Moran says. "Tim felt he had lost his manhood by staying with King for all those years."

Witherspoon joined Merritt, Dokes, Page, Tubbs, and the rest of the lost generation of warriors who had lost their self-esteem because of events outside the ring. He went on an unconscious strike against the cruelest sport.

For months after receiving the check for $90,000, Witherspoon seemed to be in a depression. He overate, he didn't train, he fell into the "don't care mentality" he associated with King's training camp.

In October 1986, Carl King told Witherspoon he was fighting a rematch with Tubbs at Madison Square Garden on December 12. Carl also had Witherspoon sign a separate contract to fight Mike Tyson for $1 million in March 1987, as part of the HBO tournament to unify the title.

But a few days before the fight, the zany, demoralized Tubbs withdrew, claiming he had a sore shoulder, although it is more likely he was just fed up with the Kings and was in no condition to fight.

At that point Don King made a deal with James "Bonecrusher" Smith. Bonecrusher agreed to drop his lawsuit against King and to retain Carl King as his new manager. In return, Don King named him the substitute title challenger against Witherspoon, without consulting Witherspoon. Carl King just signed Witherspoon's name to an amended contract, crossed out Tubbs's name, and wrote in Smith's name.

Witherspoon balked and said he would not go through with the fight. He had already beaten Smith. He didn't want to jeopardize the $1 million match with Tyson. He felt demeaned by the whole process, treated as a serving boy, like when he was setting up coffee and doughnuts for the surgeons in the Philadelphia hospital.

But once again King told him he would never fight again if he withdrew, and New York State Boxing Commission chair Jose Torres told him the same thing.

By the time he entered the ring, Witherspoon didn't care and wasn't even thinking about the fight. Tom Moran wasn't even allowed into his dressing room. All Tim wanted to do was get away from Don King and start his career over.

Bonecrusher, a strong puncher, knocked him out in the first round. Afterward, Tim said, "I didn't care. Losing meant Don was out of my life, and that was all I wanted."

After the fight, Joe Spinelli, the FBI agent who had probed boxing in the early 1980s, was asked to investigate the fight for New
York Governor Mario Cuomo. Spinelli was then the state's inspector general.

Spinelli discovered that Carl King managed both fighters—and
didn't even have a valid New York license.

Bonecrusher—a college graduate—told Spinelli he didn't want
to employ Carl King to be his manager and had been managing
himself, but Carl had told him that his father wouldn't let him
into the HBO tournament if he didn't sign with Carl as well as
Don. Bonecrusher told Spinelli he had to hire Carl but felt it was
"a total injustice that a fighter had to give up one third of his
purses before he could get a championship fight."

Once again, Witherspoon's purse was skimmed and shrunk by
the Kings. Training expenses were subtracted instead of added.
The itemized deductions for training expenses came to $75,594.

Incredibly, King deducted $28,000 for using his Ohio training
camp, charging Witherspoon *$1,000 a day* instead of the more
usual *$100 a day*. He even billed Witherspoon $38 for a "drug
test" in Atlanta.

So instead of $400,000, Witherspoon was given a check for
$129,000. Most of that was quickly taken by the IRS, and he
gave $30,000 to his trainer, Slim Robinson, who should have
been paid by King.

Two days after the fight it was announced that Witherspoon
had again tested positive for marijuana. He was threatened with
another $25,000 fine and a one-year suspension as a two-time
offender.

But it was a mistake. The New York State Athletic Commission
had mishandled the urine test. Witherspoon's sample had not
come back positive. But the humiliating story had been printed
around the world. The correction, a week later, barely received
any coverage.

Urine samples taken after a fight are given a coded number. A

WITHERSPOON EXPENSES

SPARRING SALARIES	14,113.89
FOOD-MIAMI	2,950.00
MR. EARLY - CHEF	3,642.00
TRAINER EXPENSES (MIAMI SLIM)	500.00
ADVANCE TO WITHERSPOON	1,000.00
MIAMI OTHERS	115.52
CAR RENTAL 10/27 thur 11/30/86	2,108.99
MARRIOTT ATLANTA (DRUG TEST RM)	836.26
BUDGET CAR RENTAL 11/7 thur 11/9/86	113.68
TRAINING CAMP 28 DAYS @ 100.00	28,000.00
CAMACHO CAMP 10/26 thur 10/29	4,000.00
TIRES FOR TIM'S CAR	251.30
EDEN HOTEL PARKING CHGR 36 DAYS	252.00
DRUG TEST (ATLANTA 11/8/86)	38.00
EDEN ROC HOTEL 10/29 thur 11/30/86	13,881.93
MANHATTAN LIMO NY TO PENNA	75.00
TRAVEL EXPENSES FOR PRESS CONF	3,514.50
FED EXPRESS CHGR SHIPPING CHGR PAYROLL SPARRING , ETC 10/30,11/6,13,21,27,12/4/86	201.20
TOTAL DEDUCTIONS	**75,594.27**

Don King's deductions from Tim Witherspoon's purse for his 1986 match with Bonecrusher Smith. Note miscalculated deduction of $28,000 for 28 days of training at King's camp for $100 a day. Also, the contract called for the promoter to pay for training expenses, not the fighter.

boxing commission staff member had misread the number on the urine sample. It had been the sample from a preliminary fighter that had come back from the laboratory with the positive result for marijuana.

Two weeks after the fight I interviewed Witherspoon at his home in Fairless Hills, outside of Philadelphia, in an apartment complex. He was totally broke. His phone had been shut off. His car had been repossessed. He was facing eviction for nonpayment of his $500 rent. It was Christmas week and he had not been able to buy presents for his family or pregnant girlfriend He was at rock bottom.

"You know," Witherspoon said, "I was thinking how both times I lost my title, I tried to fight Don King the week of the fight, as well as my opponent. I just couldn't do it. It just destroyed my focus."

After a long pause he added: "I wonder how Joe Montana would play in the Super Bowl if every season he knew in advance he was going to get robbed and be given less than half his pay for the game."

Early in 1987 Tim Witherspoon filed a $25 million lawsuit against Don and Carl King, accusing them of fraud and conflict of interest. Lawsuits are part of boxing and usually they are dropped after a few months when the publicity dries up.

More than one hundred lawsuits have been filed against Don King since 1978. Two fighters won settlements. One was Randall "Tex" Cobb, who was cheated out of money when he fought Larry Holmes. That case took five years before King paid about $300,000. King also paid a Texas heavyweight named Tony Perea, and his promoter, Tom Prendergast, $1.4 million, for contract interference. King also paid promoter Butch Lewis a settlement for stealing Greg Page in 1981.

But all the other lawsuits withered and vanished without money to sustain them. Few expected Witherspoon would stick with it. But he did. He went through four different lawyers, rejected small settlement offers from King, and even handled death threats and messages from the mob to settle.

Part of what kept Witherspoon going was Tom Moran, who became his manager after the loss to Bonecrusher. Moran had his own career, working as the director of programming for a cable TV company, and was just Witherspoon's friend and sports buddy who didn't want anything—except to see his friend turn his life around and rescue the remnant of his career.

"I was not the most qualified person to be Tim's manager," Moran says, "but I was the guy who was always telling him to organize his life, get copies of his contracts, and become a free agent. For years I just went to his fights and celebrated afterward with Tim.

"Then I agreed to become his manager, even though I never dreamed I would ever be in the boxing business. I know video and music. I thought boxing was a low and dirty business. I had been in London for the Bruno fight and saw what happened. Don kept me out of Tim's dressing room before the Bonecrusher fight. I lived in the same housing development as Tim and saw how depressed he was. So as a friend I felt I had to intervene and try and help the guy. Even if he didn't listen to me all the time."

In 1989 there was a big meeting in King's office to try to settle the lawsuit. Don and Carl and several of their cohorts were there. So was Witherspoon, his brother Steve (whom King had paid to set up the meeting), and Moran, who was the only white person in the room, which was often his circumstance.

King offered Witherspoon $30,000 to settle a vague offer of a few fights.

"This won't even pay our legal bills," Moran responded.

King leaped up, slapped Moran's hand, hard, and shouted, "Shut up! You don't know what you're talking about. You're ignorant. You don't know anything about boxing."

Witherspoon's brother said, "Yeah, Tom, shut up."

But then Witherspoon said to King, "You shut up! You don't even know who you're talking to. You don't know anything about my people. And you will never know anything about my people until we see you in court."

For the next two years Witherspoon kept winning small fights on cable TV shows promoted by Bob Arum, but no heavyweight controlled by King would fight him, which meant no substantial income.

Meanwhile, the lawsuit progressed through depositions. Mickey Duff provided a supportive deposition on the way Witherspoon was paid for the Bruno fight. DKP had to turn over all its financial records on all of Witherspoon's fights, documenting that Carl King was taking an improper 50 percent of his earnings. A federal judge, Thomas Grisea, then ruled that Witherspoon's lawyers could get access to the tax returns and financial records of Monarch, which showed how much it was a subsidiary of DKP. The lawyers also got cartons of internal memos from DKP, which showed Carl functioning as an employee, working at his stepfather's direction.

King had to know Witherspoon had a very strong case. By the autumn of 1990 Witherspoon started to get threats and ominous messages. Witherspoon called me up in October and said his former trainer, Slim Robinson, had visited his house and reported that Blinky Palermo, the old Philadelphia mobster and fight fixer, wanted to see him about dropping his lawsuit against the Kings.

A few days earlier, Robinson, and an ex-fighter named Lightning Bob Smith, had asked Witherspoon to accompany them to Atlantic City to meet with King directly about ending the lawsuit. Smith had once been Tim's best friend, but he had lately developed a drug problem.

Witherspoon told his two old friends, "Tell Don I'll see him in court."

Jimmy Binns, the WBA counsel, based in Philadelphia, supports Witherspoon's account. Binns told me: "King's lawyer, Charles

Lomax, told me that King was using Blinky as an emissary to Tim. King himself told me he knew Blinky was still part of the Scarfo gang. King told me he knew Scarfo was about to get out of prison. Don had ties to Palermo. I told both Don and Lomax that it was inappropriate for them to be dealing with Palermo."

In May 1991 Witherspoon still did not have a working phone in his apartment. His close friends who wanted to reach him knew to call a woman neighbor who took care of his three children.

In mid-May this woman got a call from a man identifying himself as "Kareen Sadat." He told her, "You tell Tim that if he doesn't settle his lawsuit by Friday, he won't be breathing by Sunday."

Witherspoon was so frightened by this call that he immediately went out and "I got a gun to protect myself." He also moved out of his apartment and asked a cousin, who was also armed, to stay with him. Moran thinks Witherspoon "may have overreacted, but that was Tim's mental state. His conflict with King was an obsession. It had taken over his whole life."

But by October 1992, King began to feel more pressure to settle the lawsuit. Judge Grisea was now demanding a firm trial date be set, since the suit was almost six years old. Grisea also ordered that King be deposed for a second time, and now Witherspoon's lawyers had even more ammunition, more documents on the financing of the Bruno fight to ask him about, and a copy of a contract that Witherspoon had signed under duress awarding Carl King 50 percent of his earnings.

Even more threatening to King was a new federal investigation into his business practices being conducted by the FBI and the U.S. attorney in the Southern District of New York. King was paranoid that questions he was asked under oath in the Witherspoon civil deposition would be used against him in the federal criminal investigation. He felt he had to get out of his deposition at almost any cost.

King knew that the new federal investigation had been triggered by the information provided by his former chief financial officer, Joe Maffia, and he was worried that Maffia would become a witness for Witherspoon in the civil suit. So over a two-week period in October, King's lawyers and Witherspoon's new attorney, Richard Emery, engaged in intense negotiations to try to finally settle the lawsuit. King's cash offer kept going up in each bargaining session. He seemed almost desperate to avoid a trial and his sworn deposition.

In one of the final sessions, both King and Witherspoon were in the room at the same time, and King launched one of his vicious rants against the fighter.

"Timmy, you are a good-for-nothing, low-life nobody," King said. "You are dope addict trash." But Witherspoon, in a jovial mood, now could laugh at King.

Finally, after negotiating nonstop through a weekend, King agreed to pay Witherspoon what he wanted. Although the agreement was sealed, it is known that King agreed to pay Witherspoon more than $1 million in three installments over a twelve-month period—and King did make all the payments on time.

The final part of the negotiation consisted of King insisting that the language of the press release disclosing the settlement contain nothing adverse about him. Witherspoon didn't care what kind of face King put on the deal in a press release, while King seemed more concerned about saving face than saving money.

In the end, the settlement was the biggest payday of Tim Witherspoon's boxing career.

Unfortunately, after a year of big spending, all Witherspoon had to show for the more than $1 million was a new house and a car. The rest he gave to Tom Moran, or handed out to friends with problems, or spent on partying, or was conned out of by leeches. Some of the money seems to have been extorted from him by a faction of Muslims.

At the end of the year, Witherspoon was back in the situation of not having a phone in his new house, after riding around with a cellular phone for the year he was flush.

Tim Witherspoon is now thirty-seven and still fighting. But in October 1994 he disappointed his friends, and broke Tom Moran's heart, by signing a contract with Mark Stewart, now an ex-con, the same early manager who had led Tim into Don King's web without fully explaining what was happening.

"You'll always be my friend, but I'm finished with trying to help your boxing career," Moran told him.

Witherspoon will never be thought of as one of the great fighters of the contemporary era like Ali, Leonard, Duran, Whitaker, Hearns, Chavez, Hagler, Sanchez, or Mike Tyson in the comet of his prime.

He was not a heroic figure larger than his sport like Curt Flood, Jackie Robinson, or Ali. He didn't have their mental strength, or the sense of commitment to a destiny greater than himself.

In some ways Witherspoon is more of a tragic hero. His personal flaws subverted his effectiveness—his escapism from responsibility, his streak of self-destructiveness that led him to dabble with drugs and re-sign with Mark Stewart.

But in the end, in his own wobbly way, Witherspoon stood up to King, and the whole boxing system, more courageously than any other fighter. He stuck to his lawsuit for almost six years so that young fighters in the future can have some measure of independence, some measure of dignity and honest accounting, some freedom of choice in a manager.

Witherspoon was too flawed to become the Spartacus of the gym, to lead the slave revolt. But he gave it his best shot so that other fighters would not be as exploited and demoralized as he was.

Tim Witherspoon has earned the last word in this chapter, as emblematic of King's lost generation. This is how he summed up his thoughts about Don King in February 1991—four years into his lawsuit, almost two years before it was finally settled.

"Don's specialty is black-on-black crime. I'm black and he robbed me, so I know this is true," he said.

"Don's problem is that he would rather put a dishonest quarter into his pocket than an honest dollar. You know, that's just the way he is. It's a feeling he gets. He gets that big old knot in his pocket. And he's rubbing it. He loves money. And they say money is the root of all evil. And that's what he is, an evil man.

"Don King just destroyed everything that I tried to be. And there's nothing else I can say about it."

The Hostile Takeover of Mike Tyson

It was about 6:00 A.M. on Thursday, March 24, 1988. The phone was ringing in the bedroom of Jose Torres in his middle-income apartment in Independence Plaza in lower Manhattan. Torres was in a deep sleep and he picked up the phone on the third or fourth ring.

"It's Don," the familiar fire-engine voice said. "What time are they going to LA? What airline? What airport? What flight number?"

Jim Jacobs, Mike Tyson's co-manager, had died the day before, and Don King was crashing the funeral party.

Even in his semi-alert state Torres realized what King was up to. He was trying to insinuate himself into the heavyweight champion's life at this moment of grief, even before Jim Jacobs's body was placed under the earth.

But Torres didn't like conflict, even though he was a former champion. And he was still friendly on the surface with King, so he gave King all the details of the flight that would carry Tyson and Jacobs's widow and closest friends to Los Angeles for a funeral ceremony the next morning.

Jimmy Jacobs's death was traumatic for Tyson. His whole life had been a quest for a father figure—and an identity—after never knowing his biological father as he grew up wild on the streets of Bed-Stuy and Brownsville.

Cus D'Amato, who had rescued him from a juvenile prison at thirteen, had been his first father substitute, slowing earning Tyson's trust, and then love, and finally becoming Tyson's legal guardian. But D'Amato, who had trained Torres, died in November 1985, when Tyson was just eighteen and a pro for just eight months.

Jacobs had replaced D'Amato, developing a warm personal bond with the moody Tyson, helping him out of a few jams with the law, guiding him to one version of the heavyweight title when he was twenty, fulfilling D'Amato's prophecy that Tyson would become the youngest heavyweight champion in history.

Jose Torres had become Tyson's surrogate big brother: both spiritual children of Cus; both champions shaped by Cus's system of head-moving technique and psychology of will; both children of poverty and proud men of color.

Tyson now had lost his second father substitute in three years, and was feeling abandoned and betrayed again by a harsh world.

The night before King's cunning wake-up call, Torres and a bereft Tyson had walked through the darkened Manhattan streets near Jacobs's apartment on East Fortieth Street. The heavyweight champion of the world sank his head in Torres's chest and shoulders and cried like a baby.

"People think I'm tough, but that's bullshit," Tyson said when he regained his composure. "I'm a fucking coward. You know something? I feel like taking my own life. But I don't have the fucking guts to do it, you know what I mean? When Cus died, I felt the same way."

Torres, grieving himself and moved by Tyson's intimacy, replied: "My friend, you had a commitment when Cus died that was fulfilled. You have a commitment now, and I see no obstacle to preventing its execution. You must keep winning until you want the championship no more. You and only you must make that decision. Both Cus and Jimmy will be happier wherever they are."

"I could trust Cus and Jimmy," Tyson said after a silence. "You know, trust and love are two different things. I love Robin, but I don't trust her."

Robin was his wife of five weeks, actress Robin Givens. His remark was a window into the solitude and confusion of a millionaire young champion, not yet twenty-two years old and feeling overwhelmed by the experience of public fame and private loneliness.

The next morning, as Don King called his travel agent to get him on the flight, Tyson was reading the obituary for his manager in *The New York Times,* written by Phil Berger. The obit said that Jacobs "had suffered from lymphocytic leukemia for nine years."

This came as a shock to Tyson. He never knew his manager was sick with a terminal disease. He had been told the day before that Jacobs had died of pneumonia. Suddenly he was even less sure of whom he could trust in this world. He didn't trust his bride. And now none of his closest boxing friends had told him the truth about his own manager's medical condition. His surviving co-manager, Bill Cayton, who handled the business side, and whom Tyson didn't know well at all, had told everyone, including the Associated Press, that Jacobs had died of pneumonia. The leukemia had been kept secret and covered up with well-intentioned lies for years.

King showed up at the American Airlines terminal at JFK Airport in time, and joined the funeral party on the cross-country flight. On the plane were Tyson; Jacobs's widow, Lorraine; Bill and Doris Cayton; Steve Lott, the assistant trainer and Jacobs's

Mike Tyson and Don King in November 1990 LOUIS LIOTTA

Muhammad Ali (*left*) and Jeremiah Shabazz. In 1982, Ali sued King for shortchanging him by $1 million for the Larry Holmes fight. Jeremiah then delivered $50,000 in cash to Ali from King, and Ali dropped the lawsuit. Jeremiah now regrets acting as King's bagman.
HOWARD BINGHAM

Joe Spinelli investigated boxing—and King—for four years as an FBI agent.

Carl King (*left*) with his stepfather in 1978. As a manager, Carl took an unethical 50 percent of the earnings of many of his fighters, including Tim Witherspoon and David Bey. In two of Saoul Mamby's title defenses, Carl King managed both Mamby and his opponent. When Mamby won the championship in South Korea, Carl King didn't even go with him to the fight. But Carl took 33 percent of his purse when he got home, and Don took 20 percent. JAMES HAMILTON

Heavyweight Jeff Merritt, Don King's first fighter, scores a knockout early in his career. In 1991, Merritt was a homeless crack addict ranting about Don King in the lobby of the Mirage Hotel. He was begging money from the fight crowd. *BOXING ILLUSTRATED*

Mob Godfather John Gotti (seen in 1972 mug shot) met with King in 1982. King swore to reporters he'd never met Gotti. But when the U.S. Senate asked King under oath if he'd met Gotti, King took the Fifth Amendment.

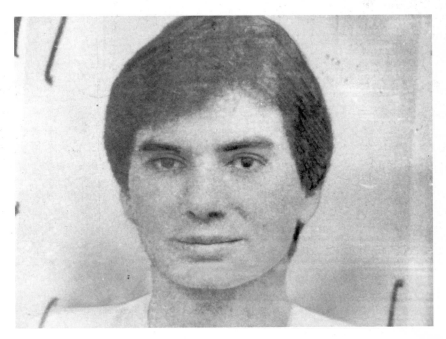

Columbo family capo Michael Franzese arranged the meeting in which King agreed to do a co-promotion with an FBI undercover agent posing as a drug dealer seeking to launder cash.

When manager Jimmy Jacobs (*left*) died in March 1988, Mike Tyson was inconsolable. King crashed the funeral, and a few months later he took over Tyson's career. *BIG FIGHTS*

King posed with Larry Holmes and Earnie Shavers before th[e]
title fight. King was both the promoter and manager of bo[th]
Holmes says that he received only about 45 percent of hi[s]
over the course of his career with King, and that King
of his purse for the Shavers fight. Shavers says that in s
he got only a few thousand dollars of his promised ear[nings]

NEW YORK POST

Joe Maffia and Don King at a luncheon in 1987. Maffia was King's chief financial officer who released the affidavits describing how King siphoned millions of dollars out of Mike Tyson's accounts to pay for his own overhead and enrich his own family members. His information led to King's indictment in 1994.

ter" Douglas
on King after
ike Tyson
ed him,
mpton
ying to
ave Act

W YORK

protégé; Kevin Rooney, Tyson's trainer; Jacobs's doctor, Gene Brody; and his friends Matty Decatur and Sal Rappa.

Tyson sat alone during the entire flight, seeming in a trance of sorrow and loss. Neither Cayton nor anyone else made any effort to comfort Tyson, or try to talk to him about the pain he was so visibly feeling.

King also kept to himself, not really being part of this group of mourners, and not having been a friend of Jacobs. They had negotiated a few deals but never socialized. Jacobs had, in fact, echoed Cus D'Amato's warnings to Tyson to beware of Don King's practices, even before he turned pro. D'Amato had even told Bobby Stewart, the staff member of Tryon Reformatory who first noticed Tyson, that one reason he wanted to legally become his guardian at sixteen was to prevent "promoters like Don King and Bob Arum" from stealing him away.

King had coveted Tyson for years. You didn't have to be a gym rat, or attend every amateur tournament, to know about Tyson. CBS network had profiled Tyson before the 1984 Olympics. His defeat in the Olympic trials was on national television. Boxing people had been talking about Tyson since 1982, when he was sixteen.

King's relationship to young boxing talent is a little like Alan Freed's and Morris Levy's relationships to young music talent in the 1950s. Like them, King is a hip exploiter. He knew enough to know whom to rip off. Freed and Levy stole songwriting credits and performing royalties. King stole fighters. Like Freed and Levy, King was a predator who was not patronizing. He was smart enough to take over the best. Like Freed and Levy, he was a knowing flesh peddler.

King sensed Tyson was emotionally open to a strong father figure like himself, that Tyson was someone who would be impressed by King telling him he had killed two men in his lifetime, because when Tyson was a teenage mugger, he looked up to people like King on the streets of Brooklyn.

King began to make his moves as soon as the plane landed in Los Angeles. He saw that Tyson was standing at the curb, outside the American Airlines terminal, with no limo or car there to pick him up and take him to the Beverly Hilton Hotel.

"These people don't know how to deal with this kid," King said to Torres, loud enough for Tyson to hear. "There should be a couple of limos waiting for the champ, before you people got here," King commented. "I'll tell you something, Muhammad Ali never had to wait this long at an airport. Never!"

Although an uninvited mourner, King was already planting seeds of doubt in Tyson's mind about whether Cayton had the proper respect and competence to now guide Tyson's future, with Jacobs gone.

King had arranged in advance for a limo to pick him up, and he gave a ride to Tyson and Torres, to show how a champion should always travel in the style of royalty. King was already demonstrating to Tyson how he could take care of him, solve his little problems, like a father.

While Don King started to make his first moves for Mike Tyson's body, Robin Givens and her mother, Ruth Roper, started making their first moves for Mike Tyson's money. One hour after Jim Jacobs was pronounced dead on March 23, Givens and Roper showed up, without an appointment, at the offices of Merrill Lynch vice president James Brady, in the Pan Am building at 200 Park Avenue.

They told Brady to shift $1.9 million from Tyson's stock account in order to make a down payment on buying a $4.2 million mansion in New Jersey. Brady, although taken aback by the coldness of the move, followed instructions and transferred the money to a joint account Givens and Tyson had at Citibank.

The next day, as Tyson was arriving in Los Angeles, Givens and Roper showed up again unannounced at Merrill Lynch. They handed Brady—a personal friend of Jacobs—a letter from Tyson giving his new wife power of attorney for the house purchase.

Roper had gotten Tyson to sign the letter just before he left for the funeral.

Givens now told Brady to transfer the $1.9 million from their joint account at Citibank to an account solely in her name at the European-American Bank. But European-American would not accept the transfer because it came from an account in two names to a proposed new account only in the name of Robin Givens.

Givens threw a fit.

"I want my money," she shouted. "Where is my motherfucking money, you motherfucker?"

Givens finally reached Tyson by phone in Los Angeles and he instructed Brady to do whatever his wife wanted. Even after Brady agreed to complete the transfer, Givens was still angry, telling him, "You're one of Cayton's boys. We're going to take our money out of here."

Two months later she did, transferring the $10 million account to the United States Trust Co.

Brady was only trying to be prudent and follow the instructions that Jacobs had given him. Jacobs had set up a $2 million annuity for Tyson in 1987 and tried to guard his money. He had told Brady never to let Tyson withdraw any cash without waiting for twenty-four hours and notifying him or Cayton. He thought this would protect Tyson from being fleeced by hustlers, and from his own shopping binges for cars and jewelry.

Brady later told me, "Robin didn't seem to care at all about Jim's death. She wanted the money and wouldn't wait one day. I was surprised she wasn't attending the funeral and even asked her about it. She ran through about one million of Mike's money in the first sixty days of their marriage."

Meanwhile, back in Los Angeles, Don King was openly making a play for Mike Tyson during the funeral, in front of Cayton and Jacobs's closest compadres.

Before the services, King told Jose Torres that he should become Tyson's manager and work with him as Tyson's promoter.

Torres was then the chairman of the New York State Athletic Commission and could not become anyone's manager without creating the appearance of a conflict of interest.

King spoke directly to Tyson and proposed that he take four or five "easy fights" before he met Michael Spinks to unify the title, a bout already scheduled for June 27. King was not the promoter of Tyson-Spinks and was getting only a set fee of $3 million for his subordinate role to Butch Lewis, Spinks's promoter. King's role was to make the undercard matches.

John Martin, the president of Ohlmeyer Communications, was one of Jim Jacobs's pallbearers and eulogists at the funeral. He recalls: "I saw it all happen right in front of me at Jim's funeral. At one point I spoke to Mike, who was inconsolable and crying. I told him to be careful, that all these forces will try to take over now that Jim is gone.

"I said that to Mike because I could see King maneuvering right in front of the open casket in the private family room. Don was working on Mike right next to the casket. Don has the guts of a burglar. The room was watching. Don was leaning all over Mike. He wouldn't let him get away from him. Mike was weeping and Don was hitting on him."

Gene Kilroy, Muhammad Ali's camp facilitator, was one of the mourners who watched King start his play for Tyson. He went to Tyson and told him, "You can trust Bill Cayton. He's honest and a good businessman."

A few days later Kilroy urged Cayton to "bring a black guy into Tyson's camp, as a trainer, or lawyer, or accountant," to help fend off the race card when King played it. But Cayton ignored Kilroy's perceptive counsel.

By the end of the funeral Tyson was like a lost child, not knowing which way to turn, or whom to trust. Robin had told him she was pregnant, but he didn't know if he completely believed her. He didn't really know the seventy-year-old Cayton, who was honest, but condescending and egocentric. He had always been warned about King by D'Amato and Jacobs, but he was charmed by King's funky charisma, and he felt he could control King, telling a friend, "I can handle a snake if I keep the light on."

King, the uninvited guest, had ended up one of the pallbearers.

Tyson was so upset by the funeral that he asked Torres to accompany him back to New York on a red-eye flight and not wait for the next morning, when most of the funeral party was flying back.

On the plane Tyson noticed Dr. Gene Brody in a nearby seat. Tyson sat down next to him and asked about Jacobs having leukemia—if it was true, why nobody had ever told him, and did Jimmy know he was dying?

Brody told Tyson he didn't want to discuss it on the plane, and that he should call him at his office in New York. Tyson was reaching out for information, for an anchor, at a moment he felt he was drowning. It wasn't his custom to defer gratification and make an appointment a week later. He never called Dr. Brody.

At the start of 1988 it seemed that Mike Tyson's rise to the unified heavyweight championship would cause the eclipse of Don King as boxing's dominant promoter.

King did not have a piece of Tyson. Tyson was loyal to Jacobs and Cayton. They had managed Tyson into being an authentic free agent—like Ali and Ray Leonard—avoiding exclusive entanglements with any promoter, putting each fight up for the highest, free-market bid. At twenty-one, Tyson looked like an invincible superman who would remain champion for years.

King had watched with envy and frustration as Tyson defeated all his heavyweights during his march to the unified title: Trevor Berbick, Bonecrusher Smith, Tony Tucker, and Tony Tubbs. All these King's men were intimidated and vanquished by Tyson.

Although still able to tell a bank his net worth was between $20 and $25 million, King had lost $3 million in the October 1987 stock market crash, as a result of margin calls he couldn't meet. The loss irritated King, but still not as much as his loss of control over the heavyweight title.

But then King saw his opening with the sudden death of Jimmy Jacobs, and Tyson's equally sudden marriage to actress Robin Givens. King saw a vacuum and he saw chaos and he took advantage. He didn't make one false step in a six-month campaign to capture control over Tyson's future and fortune.

At first King had to compete with both Bill Cayton and "the women" for Tyson's loyalty. His strategy was to lie back, poison Robin's mind against Cayton, and let Robin turn Tyson against his surviving manager, while he just befriended and flattered Tyson with no strings seemingly attached.

King also had to maneuver with Jose Torres, an important influence on Tyson in this period, as the living link back to Cus. Torres says King during this time made "anti-Semitic remarks" to him about both Jacobs and Cayton, and assumes that he was making the same points to Tyson in private.*

Givens and Roper were also trying to win Torres over to their side in the triangular tug-of-war. They suggested they could get him a job with Donald Trump if he advised Tyson to let them control his career.

Torres had also been close to Jacobs and knew that Jacobs and Cayton had not cheated Tyson out of any money, although King was saying this almost daily.

Torres knew that Jacobs and Cayton had gotten Tyson a seven-fight contract with HBO worth $26 million. He knew they had gotten Tyson commercial endorsement contracts worth over $2 million from Diet Pepsi, Nintendo, and Toyota. And he knew they

---

*Torres quoted King's comment to him that "the Jews want to control Tyson" in his book, *Fire and Fear*, page 192. Torres also heard King refer to Cayton, Jacobs, and Shelly Finkel as "Jews in suits." King also made an anti-Semitic remark to Bob Arum when they were grappling with each other after the Hagler-Leonard fight. In July 1988, when King appeared on Bill Mazer's New York television show, he admitted he couldn't say he "never" made an anti-Semitic remark. When Katz quoted the "Jews in suits" line in a column, and wrote that Tyson was "beginning to sound like Don King," King went on Mazer's show and called Katz a racist.

had set up a $2 million annuity for Tyson on his twenty-first birthday that would mature when he was thirty.

(In October 1989, Price Waterhouse would complete a confidential audit of all of Tyson's fights and contracts under Cayton and Jacobs. The bottom line was: "Mr. Tyson actually received approximately $168,000 more than that required under the existing contracts.")

While Torres felt loyal to Cayton, he also could see that Cayton had trouble communicating with Tyson and was acting defensive and embattled when Roper and her lawyer asked him financial questions, even though he had nothing to hide. Age, ego, and rigidity made Cayton a poor infighter in the arena of charlatans.

Torres urged Cayton to make peace with Robin and Ruth and form a united front with them against King, but Cayton couldn't even try. Torres also advised Cayton—as had Gene Kilroy—to bring some people of color into Tyson's circle, to make Tyson feel more comfortable and to counter King's black solidarity song.

But King vs. Cayton was a mismatch from the start. Cayton had no interpersonal skills. He even alienated Joe Spinelli, who had become perhaps King's most profound critic after investigating him for the FBI.

Shortly after Jacobs's funeral, Cayton came to see Spinelli at his New York State Inspector General's office.

Cayton came with a pad and told Spinelli that Jacobs had made eight phone calls the last week before he went into the hospital, and two of them were to Spinelli.

"What were they about?" Cayton asked.

Spinelli was offended by the question.

"It's none of your business," he told Cayton. "It was between me and Jimmy. If he wanted you to know, he would have told you."

Spinelli had actually done a favor for Jacobs, getting Los Angeles lawyer David West to successfully represent Tyson in a civil case growing out of Tyson's slapping a parking-lot attendant. Tyson had slapped the attendant after he had objected to Tyson's harassment of a woman.

But if Cayton's imperious manner turned off a law enforcement official who should have been his biggest ally, he had no chance to communicate with the twenty-one-year-old ghettocentric Tyson.

King, meanwhile, continued to play the wolf in sheep's clothing. He hung out with Tyson in Los Angeles, making him feel like he was making decisions, giving him advice, being his friend, talking boxing, making up lies about Cayton.

In early May King bought Tyson two luxury cars. One was a Rolls-Royce convertible with a sticker price of $183,000. The other was a black Rolls-Royce limousine with a sticker price of $198,000. He paid for them with checks drawn on Don King Productions and had them registered to Tyson personally.

King purchased the minimum amount of liability insurance for the cars—$15,000 on each. When Cayton found out, he told reporters King didn't know what he was doing, that the liability was too low for a poor driver like Tyson. Cayton increased the insurance on each car to $6 million.

And the cars weren't really gifts. On June 8, King admitted during a TV interview with Greg Gumble that the cars were "a bridge loan . . . he'll pay me back."

On the same show, Gumble asked, "Do you deny that you're trying to take control of Tyson?"

King's reply was: "Categorically. Why would I need it? I'm the promoter. That's all I really want. I don't want nothing but to solidify my position. I don't want his [Cayton's] position. But he seemingly don't want me around at all. I don't know why. I'm really shocked and extremely disappointed."

The struggle to control Tyson's future had its daily ebbs and flows, and King was not always confident of the outcome.

On June 15, two weeks before the fight with Spinks, King picked up Jose Torres in his customized Cadillac and took him to a soul-food restaurant. King was furious that Torres had advised Tyson not to sign an exclusive promotional contract with King before the Spinks fight.

"We lost the chance of our lives," King said. "We had Tyson and because of you we lost him."

"You mean *you* lost him," Torres replied.

The environment around Tyson leading up to the Spinks fight was total anarchy, but somehow Tyson was able to convert chaos into controlled rage.

His wife's always mysterious pregnancy ended in an alleged miscarriage at an Atlantic City hospital on June 3, although a private detective hired by Cayton, who gained access to hospital records, says there never was a pregnancy.

Ruth Roper decided to sue Cayton over a February 12 contract extension Tyson signed, making Cayton Tyson's manager should Jacobs become deceased. Cayton was then the assignee on the contract on file with the athletic commission. The new contract also made Jacobs's wife, Lorraine, the new assignee, should Jacobs die.

The timing of the contract extension till February of 1992 became suspicious in retrospect—six weeks before Jacobs's death. But the contract amendment does seem legal and valid.

It was signed by Tyson and by Jacobs and Cayton and their wives, and witnessed by Torres and commission staff member Peter Della. Some of the signatures were actually signed during Tyson's wedding party at the Helmsley Palace hotel. The papers were prepared by Carl DeSantis, the commission lawyer, and notarized.

About ten days before the fight, Tyson was being interviewed by Jerry Izenberg of the *Newark Star Ledger,* one of the best writers in the business. Tyson was saying, "They died [meaning Cus and Jimmy] and then everything became money, money, money. Now, I don't have anyone to talk to."

Suddenly Tyson stopped speaking, buried his head against Izenberg's chest, and cried for several minutes.

"He was in hysteria," Izenberg later told filmmaker Barbara Kopple. "He cried so much that I had to change my shirt."

Eight days before the fight, Wally Matthews published a long article in *Newsday,* reporting that Tyson had punched his wife in the head with a closed fist and had engaged in violent rages while drinking heavily.

Givens went on live television and told local NBC-TV anchor Sue Simmons that $20 million of her husband's money was "missing" (not true), and that she was frightened because her mother was being followed by a private detective (true). Givens also aired the false story—fed to her by King—that Cayton had bribed the Chicago priest who married her.

The next day King dropped his nice guy pose and called Cayton "Satan in disguise."

Three days before the fight, Michael Winston, the lawyer for Givens and Roper, sent Cayton a letter by certified mail in behalf of Tyson. It began: "Starting now, you are to take no action in my behalf as a boxing manager." It directed Cayton to send all money held, or due from the Spinks fight, to Winston's office. This triggered three years of litigation.

In the midst of this madness, Mike Tyson went out and destroyed unbeaten Michael Spinks in ninety-one seconds, ending his career with two punches, one of them to the body. When Spinks was counted out, Tyson was still in a rage, his pent-up anger unspent. He looked like he wanted to keep punching somebody. He seemed robbed of his release. He seemed somehow frustrated and disappointed in his moment of vindication.

During the summer of 1988, Don King bided his time and waited, as Mike Tyson's life spun out of control into a tabloid soap opera. The champion's marriage was falling apart in a public way. King was positioning himself to be Tyson's father figure at the end, after having used Robin Givens to weaken Tyson emotionally and drive the emotional wedge between him and Bill Cayton. It was strategic thinking worthy of the three-dimensional chess master. King's patient plan was to be there when the plane crashed and to inherit the wreckage.

On August 23 Tyson got into a street fight with boxer Mitch Green at 5:00 A.M. outside a Harlem all-night clothing store. Tyson broke Green's nose, but fractured a bone in his right hand with the punch.

On September 7, *Daily News* columnist Mike McAlary wrote a page 1 story saying that Tyson had tried to commit suicide three days earlier by crashing his silver BMW into a tree. He also reported Tyson was being treated by a psychiatrist for manic depression.

On September 20, while on a trip to Russia, Tyson assaulted his wife and threatened suicide by drinking lithium that had been prescribed for his alleged bipolar illness. Tyson, drunk on vodka, chased Givens through the hotel and then hung from a hotel balcony for ten minutes, threatening to kill himself.

On September 30, the ABC-TV network show *20/20* aired an unforgettable hourlong interview with Tyson and Givens, conducted by Barbara Walters. The champion said, "I'm not a psychopath or a maniac. . . . I've seen some doctors and I have a very slight illness that I had all my life, just being extremely hyper. . . . I'm a moody person by nature." Tyson also said, "I never struck my wife."

Later in the show, in a segment taped separately, Tyson and Givens sat next to each other on a couch. Tyson was heavily medicated and seemed dopey. He did not voice any dissent as Givens contradicted him, and demeaned him.

"He gets out of control," Givens said, "throwing, screaming, he shakes, he pushes, he swings . . . and just recently I've become afraid, very much afraid. . . . Michael is manic-depressive. He is. That's just a fact." Givens also said, "He's got a side to him that's scary. It's been torture, pure hell. It's worse than anything I could possibly imagine . . . every day has been some kind of battle."

As soon as the interview went off the air, Tyson started getting a deluge of phone calls from his friends telling him he looked like a chump, a fool, a dummy, sitting there in docile silence while his wife trashed the Baddest Man on the Planet, as millions watched.

On Sunday, October 2, still seething from his humiliation on national television, Tyson went berserk in his New Jersey mansion. He threw a sugar bowl at his wife's head. He threw a chair through a window, sending glass all over his lawn. Givens and her mother ran out of the house to a pay phone and called their friend Henry McCurtis, a sports psychiatrist, who had diagnosed Tyson as manic-depressive.

McCurtis told Givens her husband should be hospitalized for psychiatric examination. The women then called the police, who in turn called Dr. McCurtis. McCurtis told the police the women were in serious physical danger if they remained in the house any longer with Tyson.

This episode was the end of Tyson's marriage. Before the police arrived he drove to New York City. He was at his emotional rock bottom. Strangely, Don King was not the first person he turned to for help.

Tyson called his old friend from Bed-Stuy, boxer Mark Breland. Breland was four years older than Tyson and had been a five-time New York City Golden Gloves champion when Tyson was boxing in smokers at sixteen. Breland had won an Olympic gold medal in 1984, then won and lost the welterweight championship, and was training for a comeback fight that week, when a distraught and needy Tyson called him.

Breland dropped what he was doing and went to pick Tyson up on Columbus Avenue and hugged his old friend. As they talked, Breland suggested they go immediately to Bill Cayton's office on East Fortieth Street and attempt a reconciliation.

"Go back to the people who got you here, your old boxing family," Breland advised. "I don't know Cayton that well, but I do know that King has cheated all the heavyweights he has had."

"I'm embarrassed. I've said too many bad things about Cayton," Tyson replied.

"Just forget the past and look to the future," Breland rebutted.

Tyson agreed and Breland called Cayton to say he was bringing the estranged champion to his office in the next half hour. Breland chauffeured Tyson to Cayton's office in his Mercedes 380. They walked through the door at 11:00 A.M.

The first person Tyson saw was assistant trainer Steve Lott, in whose apartment he had often slept when he was fourteen and fifteen, and who was in his corner in every fight. They hugged and Lott started to cry for joy.

Tyson then walked up a flight of stairs to Cayton's office and the two men embraced a little stiffly.

"I'm glad to be back," Tyson said. "Sorry 'bout the things I said. I wanna work with you."

Cayton told Tyson the first thing he wanted to do was remove the "manic-depressive stigma that has been attached to you" by the Barbara Walters TV show.

Cayton asked Tyson to come back the next day, Tuesday, October 4, and be examined by a psychiatrist, Dr. Abraham Halpern of the United Hospital Medical Center of Port Chester, New York. Tyson agreed and left, although there was some apprehension in the room that he would not return the next day. In advance of the session with Tyson, Dr. Halpern called some of Tyson's closest friends to solicit their perceptions, including Jose Torres, Tyson's sister Denise, and Camille Ewald, his adoptive mother, who had lived with D'Amato in the Catskills for years.

Tyson did show up on time the next day and was interviewed by Dr. Halpern for an hour in a room in Cayton's duplex office, filled with twenty thousand boxing tapes, and old boxing photographs. After the examination, Dr. Halpern declared, "Mike is definitely not manic-depressive."

"I'll call the press and make an official announcement" was Cayton's first reaction. But Dr. Halpern first wanted to call Dr.

McCurtis, who had made the formal diagnosis that had been publicized around the world.

McCurtis occupied a little-known position in the psychiatric profession, while Halpern was widely respected. In their conversation, McCurtis quickly surrendered, claiming he never had really diagnosed Tyson, or even examined him. He said his information about Tyson had all been anecdotal from Givens and Roper. McCurtis told Halpern that he had actually thought Tyson was suffering from "atypical pugilistic disorder," a condition Halpern had never heard of. McCurtis did admit that he had prescribed lithium for Tyson to take as the medication for this nonexistent condition.

Halpern then told Tyson he was not a manic-depressive, that he should not be taking lithium, and that in his opinion, the best therapeutic treatment for his mood swings was to get back into "the discipline of regular training and frequent fights."

Tyson then went into Cayton's office and Cayton sketched a schedule of six fights for Tyson that would earn him more than $50 million. The schedule was international, and included fights in England, Brazil, and Italy. None of them would be promoted by Don King.

Tyson seemed receptive, and then he and Breland left Cayton's office and encountered dozens of reporters and camera crews outside on the sidewalk.

"I'm coming back," Tyson said. "I'm happy when I'm in the gym. I'm going back to the way I was before, but better."

He then drove off with Breland. He told Breland he would fly to Detroit and be in his corner on Friday to see his old buddy from Do-or-Die Bed-Stuy fight. It was the least Tyson could do for his friend, who had interrupted his own training to spent these two eventful days with Tyson.

But Tyson never went to Detroit. Two days later, on Thursday, October 6, he was with Don King.

King later testified at a court hearing that Tyson called him on his own initiative and asked if he could come directly to his house for help. But both friends of Tyson, and former employees of King, say that King paid several people to find Tyson and bring him to his home. These sources say that Tyson was located at a rap concert and was driven to see King for a late-night meeting. King certainly had read the newspaper accounts of the King-Cayton reunion, which all the tabloids ran in the front of the paper, not back in the sports pages.

Once Tyson was in his clutches, King was smart and decisive as usual. He took command and made all the right moves to protect Tyson's interests. King didn't bring in a psychiatrist, or lay out a plan for future fights. He got into a limo with Tyson and drove around Manhattan to secure Tyson's assets, before Givens could grab any of Tyson's money. King's activist reactions were *street*. He sensed Givens and Roper were small-time hustlers, and he was the best hustler in the world. He knew how they would think.

On Thursday, October 6, King, with Tyson in tow, visited all of the fighter's bank and brokerage accounts. All the accounts were switched into Tyson's name. Givens could not make any more withdrawals. King also showed Tyson how to cancel all their joint credit cards and get new ones in his own name.

King and Tyson also went to the offices of Mike Tyson Enterprises, which was really only a phone and a desk in Roper's office in the Lincoln Building. The door was locked and Roper had the key, and she was already in Los Angeles with Robin.

By dusk on Thursday, King had used his marvelous business skills to protect all of Tyson's assets, which were about $35 million, including the $12.3 million that had been his net for the June fight with Spinks.

It proved to be a brilliant move. As soon as she arrived in Los Angeles on October 3, Givens had written a check to Robin Givens Productions for $581,812.60. It was check number 1312 from the checkbook of Mike Tyson Enterprises, which was Mike Tyson's money. In her own hand, Givens had written on the check, "Reimbursement for expenses."

But the check bounced, thanks to King's changing all of Tyson's joint accounts to his own name. King had frozen the Mike Tyson Enterprises account. When rumors about the $581,000 check began to circulate among reporters, who were now in a feeding frenzy over the impending divorce, Givens claimed, "The check was never written."

That's when King leaked a copy of the check to *New York Post* boxing writer Mike Marley. The *Post* published a blown-up copy of the check across five columns, at the top of page 3.

After Givens filed for divorce in Los Angeles on October 7, King hired one of the best lawyers in the country to represent Tyson, Howard Weitzman of Los Angeles. It was another adroit move that only King had the national contacts and experience to make.

For the next six weeks King hardly let Tyson out of his sight. Tyson moved into King's mansion in Orwell, Ohio. King took Tyson with him to the WBC convention in Venezuela and the WBC convention in Mexico City. The fifty-seven-year-old King accompanied the twenty-four-year-old Tyson to discos and rap concerts. On those rare occasions when King couldn't be with Tyson, Tyson's two friends John Horne and Rory Holloway went with him. Since both of them were on King's payroll, they served as baby-sitters and spies for King.

King cut Tyson off from his old friends. Torres, Rooney, Lott, Breland, Brian Hamill, and others couldn't get through to Tyson. It was as if Tyson had been kidnapped into a cult and was being brainwashed. When he emerged into public view, he was spouting ideas and phrases King had used in the past. He even accused Cayton of stealing from him.

While staying in King's home, the promoter gave Tyson a book to read called *Countering the Conspiracy to Destroy Black Boys*. King had two dozen copies of the book in his library and had given out copies to other fighters and associates. The book is filled with anti-white conspiracy theories.

When Tyson seemed bored, King supplied him with prostitutes from Cleveland. They were high-class, and sometimes John Horne picked them up in Cleveland and drove them back when Tyson was finished with them.

When they were alone, King talked his philosophy to Tyson, the way Cus had. King's philosophy was the brotherhood of black outlaws, two survivors of the ghetto and jail, at the top of the world. They had to trust each other because the white world was out to destroy them, especially the media.

Tyson loved rap and hip-hop music, especially Public Enemy, and King kept telling Tyson the two of them were the two biggest public enemies in America. King, the great salesman, gave Tyson a heroic outlaw self-image that made Tyson feel part of history and destiny.

In November, Tyson took time out from his debauchery to be baptized in the Holy Trinity Baptist Church in Cleveland, with King on the pulpit and TV news crews present to record the religious ritual. For a few weeks afterward Tyson was saying he was "born again."

The ironic truth is that Tyson may have been inadvertently programmed for brainwashing by his savior, Cus D'Amato. Although a great trainer and original thinker, D'Amato expected all his fighters to think like him, and he subjected them to long orations about fear, will, loyalty, and character.

Tyson sounded like Cus before Cus died. Tyson, needing love and seeking a strong father figure, was susceptible to this kind of influence.

I first met Tyson when he was fourteen years old, when Jose Torres took me to see him work out in Catskill. You didn't have to be an expert to see he was a natural prodigy with extraordinary punching power and hand speed. For me it was like the first time I ever saw Willie Mays play the outfield, or Bob Dylan sing in a folk club. It was like watching the new standard at creation.

In December 1985, after D'Amato's funeral, I wrote a long profile of Tyson for *The Village Voice* that was called "Cus' Unfinished Masterpiece." Tyson was then nineteen and I spent a fair amount of time with him.

Between 1986 and 1988 I saw him sporadically and watched him try on different personalities. I heard him say things he thought others wanted to hear. I saw both his guile and his lack of a strong core identity. I saw that he could be manipulated by someone who knew how to penetrate his wall of defenses and booby traps.

Tyson was smarter than most people gave him credit for, but he was not as smart as he thought he was. He could be conned by a powerful personality. He was ripe for Don King.

In October, Don King had rescued Tyson from a bad situation by saving and freezing his assets, just as Cus had rescued him from a bad situation when he took Tyson into his home when he was paroled from juvenile jail. King would give him a whole new worldview, just as Cus did.

What's amazing is that Tyson was willing to buy into an anti-white worldview, since all his own life experiences with whites in boxing had been positive—Bobby Stewart, Cus D'Amato, Camille Ewald, Teddy Atlas, Jim Jacobs, Steve Lott, and Kevin Rooney had all befriended him. None of them had betrayed him except Cus and Jimmy by the act of dying.

But as soon as Tyson moved into King's home, he started sounding like a King echo, not like himself. In mid-October Tyson let a reporter from the Chicago *Sun-Times* interview him at King's Ohio house. Tyson told him that Givens and Roper "don't like black people." Tyson went on to say, "They want to be white so bad. The way they talk about black people, you'd think you were living with the Ku Klux Klan. She and her mother want so much to be white, it's a shame. And they were trying to take me away from the people I grew up with and throw me into their kind of high-class world."

Tyson couldn't see that his words—spoken in a high-class mansion with a swimming pool, a sunken bar that could seat twenty people, a pool table, a beautiful skylight—could also apply to him, to King, and to his original friends, who fed him, sheltered him, taught him his craft, and made him a millionaire.

On October 7, HBO's Seth Abraham tried to make a truce between King and Cayton, so his cable subscription network could put on a Tyson–Frank Bruno fight. Cayton was still Tyson's manager, with a contract valid till February 12, 1992. Tyson was living with King, and again angry with Catyon, but Cayton still had a legal right to approve Tyson's opponents. King didn't want the Bruno fight because he was not Bruno's promoter. But he went to the meeting at the HBO office on Sixth Avenue to buy time and gain information.

King apologized for calling Cayton "Satan," and Cayton complimented King for protecting Tyson's bank accounts.

Afterward, he and King met privately in Cayton's office. Cayton says King told him: "Of course I have poisoned Mike's mind against you. But if you give me a four-year, exclusive promotional contract with Mike, I will unpoison his mind."

Cayton said he would think about it.

The next day King called him and said Tyson had injured his right hand again, and that he would mail him X-ray photos to prove the injury was legitimate.

But King had already invited his old love-hate partner, Richard Giachetti, to his home, to meet Tyson and become his new trainer, replacing Kevin Rooney.

The short period of pretend truce ended on October 21, when Tyson signed a four-year exclusive contract with King. The terms of the contract were all favorable to King, and obliterated all distinctions between the roles of promoter and manager.

King would pay Tyson $1 million per fight, plus $200,000 in training expenses, plus 66½ percent of all "net receipts" after "out-of-pocket expenses" and all applicable taxes.

With King's gift of flexible accounting and manipulating the "net," and inflating his own expenses, the contract was not in Tyson's interests. As undisputed, undefeated heavyweight champion, he should not have a monopolistic contract with any single promoter but should make all promoters bid competitively for his services.

Seth Abraham asked for one last meeting to negotiate a truce and avoid protracted litigation, and it was held in Las Vegas on October 29. King and Cayton actually agreed to a compromise under which the Hilton Hotel would promote the Tyson-Bruno fight in Las Vegas, Cayton would select Tyson's future opponents and remain Tyson's manager till 1992, and King would be Tyson's exclusive promoter for the four title defenses after Bruno. The deal included Cayton getting 20 percent as manager.

But eight hours later, King told everyone that Tyson had vetoed the deal. Cayton was certain that was a ploy, and that it was King himself who killed the compromise. Seth Abraham believed King, since King would have made $10 million for minimal work under the proposed detente.

A source at HBO says the truth is somewhere in the middle. He says that when Howard Weitzman explained the deal to Tyson, the fighter objected to one detail, and then King, still anxious to impress and please Tyson, overreacted, and started screaming how he had been pressured in the room to accept the deal when he didn't really want to. Another source told author Montieth Illingworth, "Don was covering his ass. If Mike had just sat there and nodded, there would have been a truce."

Nevertheless, King had essentially won his hostile takeover of Mike Tyson. Cayton would get paid his 20 percent, but King was the promoter, and he had Tyson's loyalty. Soon Rooney was fired and Giachetti was Tyson's new trainer. King was in control of the heavyweight championship again, making more than $10 million a year off Tyson.

In a coda to this part of the drama, Robin Givens called Bill Cayton on November 9.

"I want to apologize for all the vicious things I said about you,"

Robin said. "I'm really sorry. Now I know they aren't true."

"So why did you say them?" Cayton asked.

"Because King told me they were true," Robin answered.

Mega-fame is hard to handle. It has killed or damaged the biggest stars—Elvis, Marilyn Monroe, Scott Fitzgerald, Jim Morrison, Janis Joplin, Marlon Brando, Michael Jackson, Pete Rose, Jerry Lee Lewis, Doc Gooden, Charlie Parker, Kurt Cobain. Fame can be a mind-altering narcotic.

So it is not fair to blame all of what happened to Mike Tyson on Don King. Tyson always had his internal demons, was always a time bomb. There were incidents with women, incidents of violence, when Cus and Jimmy were alive, incidents papered over with cash settlements. And once Tyson became champion at twenty, temptation and trouble came looking for him.

But, on balance, the better angels of Tyson's nature were nourished and reinforced by Tyson's first boxing family. Bobby Stewart, the aide in Tryon Reformatory, told him he would teach him how to box only if he learned how to read. Teddy Atlas gave him discipline and a code of honor. Cus gave him love and technique. So did Kevin Rooney. Jacobs, Lott, and Cayton tried to give him humane values and a sense of personal responsibility.

But once Tyson went with King in October 1988, almost all positive reinforcement vanished from his life. The more lawless and antisocial side of his nature went back into the ascendancy. He began to hang out with criminals and grifters. He began to work in the gym with the outlaw trainer Panama Lewis, who had gone to prison for removing the padding from the gloves of a fighter before a match.

Tyson began to travel with bodyguards Anthony Pitts and Dale Edwards, who were paid $1,000 a week by King and kept Tyson's old friends away from him. He also began to travel with Rudy Gonzales, who was paid to be a driver and gofer but also helped screen women for Tyson.

And in this fast lane of mega-fame, Tyson became more and

more aggressive with women—an interpersonal imperialist.

Cus D'Amato's philosophy was based on the mastering of emotionalism inside the ring. But Tyson never learned to discipline his emotions outside the ring.

After aligning himself with King, Tyson slapped a parking-lot attendant in Los Angeles. He fathered at least two children with different women. He was arrested for drag racing in Albany—with a friend who was later arrested for dealing cocaine. Police began to notice him hanging out with major drug traffickers. Erin Cosby, the daughter of comedian Bill Cosby, accused him of attempted rape. Two women (Sandra Miller and Lori Davis) sued Tyson for grabbing their buttocks in a Manhattan disco. The two incidents happened on the same night.

Neil Leifer, the great *Sports Illustrated* photographer (who took the classic shot of Ali standing over Liston), was scheduled to photograph Tyson at King's home in Ohio. Tyson stood him up for two straight days, making dates and then not showing up, staying in Cleveland. When Leifer finally asked him about his broken promises, Tyson replied, "I guess my word is no fucking good."

King arranged for Tyson to get an honorary doctorate degree at a college in Ohio. With degree in hand, Tyson said from the stage, "I don't know what kind of doctor I am, but with all these fine young foxes here, I hope I'm a gynecologist."

Tyson's public image began to change, from the Cus-and-the-Kid Fairy Tale, the uplifting story of ghetto redemption, of black-white, young-old cooperation, to an antisocial rap lyric. "Welcome to the Terrordome" seemed to become his motto. He began to act like a gangsta rapper, instead of Joe Louis.

By the summer of 1989, *Boxing Illustrated* published a cover story called: IS MIKE TYSON BECOMING THE MOST UNPOPULAR HEAVYWEIGHT CHAMPION IN HISTORY?

After June 1988, Tyson received no commercial endorsement contracts from major corporations. (He had gotten three lucrative ones under Jacobs and Cayton.) His image was turning too negative.

Phil Berger wrote in *The New York Times:* "With Tyson, things happen, and the more they happen, deeper grows the feeling that whatever bad endings await Mike Tyson, the chances are they will happen outside the ring."

Mike Katz wrote in the *Daily News:* "Mike Tyson's character seems to be developing along wrong lines. He is a bully. He is disloyal. He is arrogant. . . . Obviously, Cus did not have enough time."

As Tyson's decline became a story line, I thought back to the night he obliterated Spinks, and that look of frustration in his eyes. It was as if he had climbed the highest mountain, kicked in a door, and discovered the room was empty. The look seemed to ask: *Is this all there is?*

As a teenager Tyson would hug reporters like me, gently tend to his pigeons, and talk about how he didn't care about fame and wealth, just success in boxing. He once nodded in agreement when Cus repeated the old aphorism, "The only thing money is good for is throwing off the back of trains to strangers."

But now Tyson was a different person. He bought dozens of luxury cars and gold jewelry, and was into a routine of rough sex with women he picked up in clubs, a lifestyle he called "tramping."

He was cut off from his old boxing family. Now his two best friends—John Horne and Rory Holloway—were on King's payroll. Tyson had complained to Jerry Izenberg that it was all about money now, but then, in his confusion, he embraced what he had lamented.

Tyson began to resemble a Greek tragedy searching for a stage. Like Marilyn Monroe, or Brando, or Kurt Cobain, he had both fame and wealth, but he also seemed lonely, and to secretly lack self-esteem. All Tyson knew were strangers and leeches.

Once Tyson reached the mountaintop he lost some of his desire, his hunger to be the best for its own sake.

Because of all the old black-and-white fight films that Jacobs had given him, ever since he was a teenager, Tyson had developed a reverence for certain ancestral champions who personified purity and pride. Tyson loved Rocky Marciano, Sam Langford, Gene Fullmer, Tony Zale, Carmen Basilio, Mickey Walker, Ray Robinson, and Henry Armstrong, who was Cus's favorite fighter.

Tyson loved them for their unbreakable will, their basic toughness, and their work ethic, preparation, passion, and longevity. But Tyson seemed to be losing these qualities in himself. He seemed to be hemorrhaging his own pride, will, and work ethic.

Once he fell under King's domination, Tyson seemed to think he was so good he could rule the sport indefinitely on autopilot, without giving his absolute best each time out. There was nobody in his orbit who could tell him no, who would tell him he was stagnating at an age when most great fighters had not yet reached their physical peak.

Sometime in 1988, at the age of twenty-two, Tyson stopped advancing as a fighter, stopped learning new things in the gym.

Teddy Atlas, Tyson's first amateur trainer under Cus, once told me Tyson might be destined to be "a comet, not a star." Atlas had a theory that Tyson had some small, hidden defect in his character. He thought it had something to do with a lack of firmer disciplining when he was a teenager, his streak of furtive lawlessness, and a tiny speck of fear, and how Tyson tried to cover it up with jailhouse jive intimidation.

Once, in an amateur fight, Tyson wanted to quit after the second round, and Atlas had to talk him into coming out for the third round. Before another amateur fight—in an incident captured on video for a documentary—Tyson cried on Atlas's shoulder, sobbing that no one would like him anymore if he were to lose.

Even before some championship fights, Tyson's hair fell out because of nerves, and he bolted from camp and disappeared for a few days to get himself back together.

The combination of these hidden, and unresolved, vulnerabilities made Atlas think Tyson might burn himself up after a short, bright arc in the heavens. Atlas said this when Tyson was twenty-one and everyone else was already comparing him to Ali and Liston.

The deterioration of Tyson's character was accompanied by the deterioration of his boxing skills. The erosion of his ring mechanics was more subtle, but it was unmistakable.

When he fought Frank Bruno, he won in five, but didn't look like the same Tyson who beat Spinks. He fought only in spurts, and lacked the intensity that was the essence of his style. He accepted clinches in a way he never did before. He moved his head much less, and was easier to hit. He stopped using particular combinations, like the left to the body, followed by another left to the head.

Head movement was one of the things Kevin Rooney used to stress in repetition drills, but Kevin was no longer in Tyson's corner. Or in the gym. Or in his face at 6:00 A.M., nagging him to run five miles when no one else was watching.

Tyson signed to fight Razor Ruddock in Edmonton, Canada, in November 1989, but he hardly trained for the fight. He was getting beaten up in the gym by Greg Page, the aging former champ, now his sparring partner. Three weeks before the fight, Tyson pulled out. Tyson claimed he had pleurisy—a lung infection—but he wouldn't let the Edmonton promoter give him any tests in the local hospital. Canadian reporters on the scene said Tyson had only a minor cold. Three days after the fight was canceled, Tyson was seen having a drink in Sharks, a Las Vegas club, by boxing writer Wally Matthews.

The pre-King Tyson never pulled out of a fight on a flimsy excuse. That Tyson was a warrior like Jack Johnson and Dempsey. The consensus was that he just wasn't in any shape, and feared he might lose, so he pulled out as a precaution.

There was nobody in the Tyson camp who could tell him things he didn't want to hear. He had no one who loved him, the way Cus, Jimmy, Lott, Rooney, Breland, and Torres loved him. His only friends were on King's payroll, and afraid to offend him with responsibilities.

Don King, so brilliant at business, so sensational at strategy, didn't seem to see that Tyson was on a path of self-destruction as a human being. Most boxing writers could see it, but not the only person Tyson looked up to. Not the only person who might be able to alter Tyson's conduct, and values, and save him from himself. King's passivity during this period remains a mystery.

Then again, he let the same thing happen to his earlier heavyweights, Jeff Merritt and Michael Dokes, both of whom squandered their gifts and became drug addicts. Or Tim Witherspoon, Tony Tubbs, and Greg Page, who became overweight, demoralized examples of wasted talent. There was just some basic, caring humanity that was absent from King's relationship with his fighters, and from the environment he created around his fighters.

In February 1990, Don King promoted a fight in Tokyo between Mike Tyson and Buster Douglas. On paper it was a gross mismatch. Tyson was the undefeated twenty four-year-old champion, and Douglas was a mediocre journeyman. He had lost four of his thirty-five fights, quitting in the tenth round of a title opportunity against Tony Tucker. He had been knocked out by David Bey and Mike White. Even King went around saying Douglas was "a dog with no heart." On the fight contract, King crossed out "25" and wrote in "zero" for Douglas's allotment of free tickets.

To King the fight was just programming for HBO, activity for the idle Tyson, and a moderate payday for himself of about $2 million. In Las Vegas most bookies wouldn't take bets on the fight, although the book at the Mirage made Douglas a 42 to 1 underdog.

Tyson didn't train rigorously for the fight. His mechanics continued to erode—no head movement, less stamina, less intensity, fewer jabs, less body punching.

King took Tyson to business meetings in Japan when he should have been in the gym, including meetings to see to the foreign rights. King even took Tyson to meetings to discuss a "match" with wrestler Hulk Hogan, on pay-per-view. Vince McMahon, the president of the World Wrestling Federation, flew to Tokyo two weeks before the fight and held two days of meetings with King and Tyson, trying to find Japanese investors for this grotesque farce.

"It would be a matchup of superheroes," King crooned to reporters. "If Vince can come up with a hundred million, we'll do it." King, letting his P. T. Barnum instincts get out of control, was trying to imitate the 1976 charade in Tokyo, when Muhammad Ali entered the ring against Japanese wrestler Antonio Inoki.

The negotiation never went anywhere, but it was a further distraction for the already disengaged Tyson. King dragged him to the meetings as a trophy of his control.

Ten days before the fight Tyson was sparring with Greg Page. He was slow, lethargic, and overweight, and Page knocked him down with a right hand. It was a real knockdown with padded gloves and headgear. It should have been a wake-up call to King and Tyson. But it did not cure their overconfidence, or focus their discipline on the fight at hand.

King seemed in denial about what was going on. Afraid to alienate the surly Tyson, he continued to pamper the champ, letting him run when he felt like it, spar when the spirit moved him. Tyson didn't even look at any videos of Douglas's past fights, sticking exclusively to his collection of martial-arts films. Tyson missed the fierce and fearless prodding of Kevin Rooney, a disciplinarian who knew—and cared—when Tyson was faking his preparation.

Tyson's only lesson from the knockdown was to stop eating so that he would lose weight and appear to be in shape. This superficial self-deception, however, probably only served to weaken him. He came in at 220 pounds but wasn't really fit or strong. Larry Merchant recalls that at the weigh-in Greg Page told him, "Mike could definitely lose this fight."

Although what happened after the fight was one of the lowest moments in boxing history, the fight itself was one of the redeeming glories of the sport. It was the real-life Rocky, it was a night of common-man courage, a shining hour of pure drama.

Walking to the ring, waiting through the introduction, Tyson did not seem to be there mentally. He wasn't the caged-up, pacing beast he was before Spinks and Berbick. He seemed almost bored.

On the other hand, Buster Douglas was inspired to be better than he was, a Born Again believer on a mission for God.

The mother of his eleven-year-old son was dying of a terminal disease. His wife had left him. And just twenty-three days before the fight his beloved mother, Lula Pearl, had died of a stroke. Douglas fought like he had nothing more to lose.

As the Kris Kristofferson song "Me and Bobby McGee" says, "Freedom's just another word for nothing left to lose."

Freedom made Douglas fearless, relaxed, and determined. He jabbed hard, and moved, and won the early rounds. Tyson had no intensity, no fire, no focus. He was like a sleepwalker, and soon his left eye began to puff, and swell, and then begin to shut into a slit.

During the fight King sat next to Donald Trump, who was his guest in Tokyo. During the early rounds King assured Trump that Tyson would soon warm up and knock out Douglas. King was openly rooting for Tyson, and could be heard shouting, "Come on, Mike."

But as Tyson fell behind in the fight, and seemed to be weakening, King began to renegotiate a rematch deal and site fee with Trump as the fight entered the fifth round. They agreed that the rematch would be at Trump's hotel-casino in Atlantic City.

At one point Trump said to King, "You have options on both guys. You can't lose."

"That's right, I can't lose tonight," King replied.

After seven rounds Douglas had thrown a total of 272 punches, and 50 percent of them had landed. Tyson had stopped moving his head side to side, neglecting Cus's cornerstone credo of "elusive aggressive." Tyson had thrown only 132 punches, less than half of the Douglas output.

Tyson's corner was completely unprepared for crisis. Aaron Snowell and Jay Bright were an inadequate substitute for Rooney. They offered no tactical adjustments to Tyson. And, incredibly, they had no Enswell in the corner to treat his closing left eye. Enswell is a fundamental. Trainers in six-round fights keep it in their pockets to stop an eye from closing. It is a flat, chilled iron bar that can reduce swelling with pressure. Instead, Snowell and Bright had a soft old icebag—that looked like Dizzy Gillespie's hat—that they applied with no effectiveness.

Behind for the first time in thirty-eight fights, all Tyson heard from Snowell after round seven was "You gotta relax. You're down."

Late in the eighth round Tyson ducked a jab and landed a right uppercut that knocked Douglas down. But Douglas was not badly hurt. At the count of "two" he pounded the canvas with his right glove in a gesture of self-disgust for getting careless. Douglas followed the referee's count closely and was up at nine, just before the bell rang.

Between rounds, Don King went berserk. He screamed at Jose Sulaiman, "Look what you've done! What kind of fucking referee did you bring me from Mexico? Stop the fight! The fight's over. Your referee is getting my fighter beat."

As referee Octavio Meyran walked over to hand the scorecards for the round to Sulaiman, King screamed at him, "What the fuck were you looking at? You should have known the man was out. You should have counted him out."

The first minute of the ninth round was the turning point of the fight. The old Tyson would have rushed out of his corner to finish off a wounded challenger who had just been knocked down.

He knew Douglas had quit against Tucker when he was ahead, and had a reputation for wilting in adversity. But it was Buster Douglas who had the inspired will on this night.

Douglas rushed from his corner and won exchange after exchange with Tyson. He regained command of the fight, and it was the champion who looked like his will was ebbing. With a minute left in the round Tyson almost went down along the ropes. The crowd was now screaming for Douglas, and the reporters at ringside began composing Cinderella leads in their heads, describing a miracle, as the round ended.

In the tenth round Douglas knocked Tyson out with a monster three-punch combination that started with a picture-perfect right uppercut.

Tyson's head banged off the canvas and his mouthpiece fell out. Tyson fumbled for it with his glove, trying to put it back in, but it fell out on the canvas.

He finally retrieved his mouthpiece, which was the transitional object of his scrambled brain. He stuffed it backward into his mouth, where it dangled oddly.

He got up just a fraction after the count of ten, but he was in no condition to continue, lurching into the referee, who saved him from falling again and then signaled the fight was over. Tyson left the ring without giving Larry Merchant an interview. When Merchant got to the delirious new champion, Douglas stammered, "My mother. Mother. Mother. God bless her heart." Then he broke down in tears.

As soon as the fight ended, Muhammad Ali, who was home in Los Angeles, telephoned his biographer, Tom Hauser, who was in New York.

"Do you think folks will now stop asking if I could have beaten Tyson in my prime?" Ali asked.

An hour after the fight, King got the officials of the WBC and the WBA into a room and convinced them to withhold recognition of Douglas as the new champion. King pleaded that the referee had missed four seconds when he picked up the count from the timekeeper when Douglas was down in the eighth round.

King's logic violated all boxing rules that say a fighter who is knocked down must follow the count conducted by the referee in the ring, and rise before the referee says ten. The timekeeper is irrelevant. Douglas had no obligation to pay any attention to the timekeeper. There was a four-second discrepancy between the referee and the timekeeper—which occurs often—but the discrepancy had no legal meaning.

Sam Donnellon, the boxing writer for the now defunct *National,* happened to see King come out of the secret meeting with the international regulating bodies. Donnellon's tape recorder memorialized Don King's intense, emotional words: "Here's the facts. Mike Tyson knocked out Buster Douglas. The man knocked the man out officially in the ring. And the count went to thirteen. I issued a protest to Mr. Mendoza and Mr. Sulaiman. . . . It's a grave misjustice here. It's a grave misjustice here if the decision holds that Mike Tyson is knocked out. . . . The fact is Buster Douglas got knocked out first, and if that knockout had been officially recorded, it would have been a second knockout of Mike Tyson. That's what I'm saying."

A reporter interrupted to ask, "Do you expect it to be overturned?"

King answered, "I expect them to do justice. If they do justice that's what they're here for."

Jose Sulaiman then said, in support of King: "There was a violation of the rules."

A few minutes later, King told reporters, who were still filing their copy: "The first knockout obliterated the second knockout. . . . Tyson won."

King then met privately all afternoon (the fight was held at 9:00 A.M. Tokyo time) with the WBC and WBA officials, arguing that Tyson should be declared the winner. He browbeat Sulaiman so much that Sulaiman went out at 6:30 P.M. and told the stunned press corps: "At the moment I am suspending the recognition of anybody as champion."

Gilbert Mendoza, the WBA president, nodded in agreement. (In his famous quip, Arum once called Mendoza and Sulaiman "two little Noriegas.")

Sulaiman said that a decision on who won the fight would be made at a WBC meeting in ten days. Since every boxing writer Regarded Sulaiman as King's puppet, the result was sure to deprive Douglas of what he had won fair and square, with the performance of a lifetime.

Later that evening Tyson and King appeared before several hundred angry boxing writers, who were feeling they were witnessing a crime on the scale of Watergate. Tyson said, "I feel I am the champion."

After several hostile questions were shouted out to King, Mike Marley of the *Post* asked Sulaiman: "Shouldn't it be declared that Mike Tyson is still the heavyweight champion of the world?"

The other reporters groaned and laughed so loudly that Sulaiman never answered.

The next day the newspapers around the world began to report what King was trying to do. *The New York Times* published a front-page story under the headline: BOXING OFFICIALS COULD OVERTURN DEFEAT OF TYSON.

Mike Lupica wrote in *The National* the next day:

So it figures that the first reaction to Buster Douglas would be for Don King and Mike Tyson, and the WBC and the WBA, to think about stealing the night. They can't help themselves. These are people you wouldn't trust around silverware. . . .

Douglas beat up Tyson and finally knocked him out. No one knows better than Tyson. Still Tyson tries to steal the night. Maybe he is nothing more than a common thug after all. Maybe he should look out, because whatever Don King has, you can catch.

If the WBC and the WBA take away the title the world saw Buster Douglas win, if they take that night and try to leave it in a junk heap, then King has bought them. . . .

Don King, of course, has become such a complete slob as a promoter, he cannot see how bad Tyson looks trying to win a fight in a hearing room or a courtroom, when he didn't have the game to win it in a ring. . . .

King and Tyson, true to their instincts, immediately look to take the other fighter's wallet.

In the *San Jose Mercury News,* the marvelous Pete Dexter wrote:

Sitting at the same table, of course, is one Donald King, who owns promotional rights to Tyson for the next 100 years, and probably the rights to all his children.

For 15 cents King will put his boys in the ring, and the girls on the street. He is easiest to imagine as a disease. . . .

Mike Tyson, beaten up and knocked out in the ring, sitting in sunglasses, complaining he lost on a technicality.

One by one he has sold out his friends for Don King—sold out even the memory of Jimmy Jacobs, who loved him and took care of him a long time before Tyson was worth anything—and now he has sold himself.

Sold the last integrity he had left—his physical integrity—for Don King.

And that is how for a short time this week—until the world-wide public censure finally finds its way even into the dark holes where the governing bodies of boxing do business, and Don King is prompted to say his attempt to overturn what happened in the ring was "misinterpreted"—the greatest warrior of our time is transformed into a crybaby.

The disease is Don King and Mike Tyson rots in front of our eyes.

And Joe Gergen wrote in *Newsday:*

> The man [Tyson] declined to discuss the bout immediately afterward, and when he did appear at a news conference a few hours later, he mouthed the King party line: "I knocked him out before he knocked me out." . . .
>
> So much for truth, justice, and the American way, virtues King trumpets loudly and incessantly, even whilst in Japan. If either Jose Sulaiman of the WBC, or Gilberto Mendoza of the WBA, dismisses Douglas' apparent victory, it would be the equivalent of Peter Uberroth voiding the results of the 1985 World Series because umpire Don Denkinger missed a call at first base in Game 6.
>
> Not since Jack Dempsey's manager/promoter Doc Kearns set out to relieve the good citizens of Shelby, Montana, of their hard-earned money in a 1923 title fight, has a boxing man attempted such a bold scam.
>
> And if King were to succeed, Tyson might well become an unwitting victim. How pathetic a sight it would be then, this macho champion propped up by the transparent rulings of overfed bureaucrats beholden to King.

It's hard to imagine what King was thinking. The fight had been witnessed by millions of people on HBO, and the ending replayed on television newscasts. Boxing writers from all over the world had filled the working-press rows and had written second-day stories about scandal and the shame of boxing.

King can make words dance and violins cry, but he couldn't convince the world it hadn't seen what it had plainly seen.

On Tuesday, February 13, King held a press conference in Manhattan and ended his attempt to change the outcome or withhold recognition of Douglas as the champion. He not only conceded Tyson lost, *he denied he had ever tried to change the result.*

"There's never been a question from my side," King said, "as to who the heavyweight champion was. No one had designs to overturn the decision."

King also said, slyly, that he had only been trying to stir up some controversy to help sell the rematch. King was only ratifying the obvious. The day before he spoke, Sulaiman had announced the WBC would recognize Douglas. The WBA and the IBF had also confirmed what happened in the ring.

It was, in part, a victory for the profession of sportswriting. The columnists and reporters (except for Mike Marley, who later became a King employee) had all brought honor to their craft by screaming, "Stop, thief!" in their copy.

Dave Anderson, Jerry Izenberg, Pete Dexter, Wally Matthews, Mike Katz, Ron Borges, George Kimball, Ira Berkow, Phil Berger, Vic Ziegel, Mike Lupica, Joe Gergen, Ed Schuyler—and many others—reported a burglary in progress. They ignited a fan firestorm that not even Don King could contain with his rap-opera filibuster. Jose Sulaiman may be a puppet, but he is not a dummy.

A few weeks after the fight Tyson admitted in an interview that he had not been in shape to fight Douglas.

"I abused myself," he said, "abused my body. Like when you reach a status at that young age, you know what I mean. Being twenty and being the heavyweight champion of the world, you know, you're really too young."

Nine months after his loss to Douglas, Mike Tyson was in a courtroom in Manhattan. He had been found guilty by a civil jury of fondling a woman in a Manhattan disco in December 1988, and there was a hearing to assess damages. As part of the hearing Tyson had to supply a complete statement of his finances and testify before the jury.

In the course of testifying Tyson had to admit the records showed that Don King still owed him $2,097,000 from the losing fight with Douglas. Normally fighters are paid within a month of a major fight. It was highly unusual to still be owed such a large portion of the contracted purse so long after a fight, especially a fight that had been broadcast on HBO, rather than pay-per-view. HBO had paid King in March.

This was the first public sign that King was ripping Tyson off. In every fight for Jacobs and Cayton, Tyson had not only gotten his full share quickly, but the Price Waterhouse audit had documented that Tyson had been *overpaid* $168,000 by Jacobs and Cayton.

When Tyson was asked if he had received any of his money for the Douglas fight, he responded, "I don't know. It's been a long time since Tokyo."

In 1992 Mike Tyson went on trial for rape in Indianapolis. And for the first time Don King's strategic genius seemed to leave him.

King selected—and Tyson paid—Vince Fuller to represent him. Fuller had won King his acquittal on tax charges in 1985, but he had no experience in rape cases, and he was over the hill by 1992. Tyson would have been much better off with a local lawyer from Indianapolis.

Fuller let Tyson testify before the grand jury—an error even a legal-aid novice wouldn't make. Then he let Tyson contradict his grand jury testimony during his trial testimony, a blunder the prosecution effectively exploited.

Fuller also mounted a defense that was demeaning to Tyson. His basic excuse was that the world knew Mike Tyson was an animal, a predator with women, and that the victim, Desiree Washington, should have known about Tyson's awful reputation.

The Indiana Court of Appeals actually criticized Fuller's competence in its decision affirming Tyson's conviction. It said Fuller failed to raise proper objections to defend Tyson's rights.

On the eve of the trial, King imported the anti-white hatemonger Louis Farrakhan to speak at a pro-Tyson rally in Indianapolis.

This was suicidal in such a predominantly white and conservative city. It could not have made a helpful impression on the Tyson jury pool.

King also picked Alan Dershowitz to represent Tyson on appeal, another blunder, since Dershowitz kept attacking the integrity of the prosecutor and the fairness of the Indiana court system. He even condemned the popular local prosecutor in an article published in the May 1993 issue of *Penthouse* magazine. This only created more enemies for Tyson in conservative Indiana.

All of Dershowitz's motions and appeals were rejected by Indiana judges, and Dershowitz and Fuller together cost Tyson millions in legal fees, leaving him with little of the $77 million he had earned during his career.

During nineteen months as champion, when Cayton and Jacobs controlled his career, Tyson earned $48.5 million, and was undefeated in eight fights from November 1986, till June 1988. He received endorsement contracts from Toyota, Diet Pepsi, and Nintendo.

In October 1988, Tyson rejected the six-bout, $50 million plan Cayton proposed to him—fights Tyson probably would have won if he had retained Kevin Rooney as his tough-love trainer.

Under Don King, from 1989 to 1991, Tyson also had eight fights, earning $29 million on paper. He received no commercial endorsement contracts.

Under Don King's tutelage, Mike Tyson lost his crown, lost his money, and lost his freedom.

On March 25, 1995, Mike Tyson was paroled from prison. He emerged wearing a traditional Muslim skullcap and went directly to a mosque to pray.

For a few days the boxing world—and news pages—were filled with reports that Tyson was about to take a Muslim name and drop King as his exclusive promoter.

But on March 30, Tyson read a prepared statement that took

less time than his ninety-one-second knockout of Michael Spinks. He affirmed that King would remain his promoter, that Showtime would be his cable network, and that the MGM Grand would be the site of his comeback fights.

"Don is the greatest promoter in the world, as we know," Tyson read, in an echo of King's signature self-description.

The night before, in one of his greatest rap-opera diva solos, King had begged, wept, and conned Tyson into retaining him as his exclusive promoter.

King had come to this meeting fortified with a $36 million, six-fight deal with the MGM Grand—and a $20 million advance from the casino, controlled by Kirk Kerkorian.

Tyson did not wait to hear any other offers, although HBO would have certainly topped the Showtime deal since it is owned by Time Warner, which has much greater financial resources.

Tyson also did not listen to the offers from other promoters, including Butch Lewis, Madison Square Garden, Harold Smith, Bob Arum, and Akbar Muhammad and Bilal Muhammad, both of whom came to Tyson's press conference expecting him to convert to Islam and entertain their offer.

But just before Tyson took the podium, Bilal, Akbar, and former champion Matthew Saad Muhammad were ordered to leave the room by Tyson's bodyguard, Anthony Pitts.

"He couldn't face me," Saad, who was once a hero to Tyson, said to boxing writer Wally Matthews.

Tyson could have revolutionized the feudal economics of boxing by declaring himself a free agent, as Ali and Sugar Ray Leonard had done. He could have put his services up for the highest bid, in the free market, on a fight-by-fight basis.

Tyson could have announced he didn't need any exclusive promoter. Or that any promoter had to work for him, not the other way around.

Tyson could have acted like a star, not a serf. All he really needed was an accountant and a lawyer. All the offers were ready to flow to him because, somehow, during his exile in prison, he had become an even bigger attraction than before he had gone away in public disgrace, and in boxing stagnation, if not decline.

But the tricks of memory, the alchemy of absence, and the dearth of a new heavyweight star to displace him, all conspired to make Tyson bigger than ever upon his release.

Don King was still the best in the world at what he does. And Tyson, although now twenty-nine years old, remained a follower, a sad case of arrested development, unable, for all his jailhouse talk, to think independently and take responsibility for his life. He still needed a father figure to take care of everything for him.

As Lou DiBella, HBO's vice president in charge of boxing, said, "Mike was playing poker with a full house. And then he switched and decided to play solitaire."

"I'm coming back to kick your ass"

Ten days after Don King had attempted to steal the championship of the world from Buster Douglas, he tried to become Buster Douglas's promoter.

On February 21, 1990, King and his son Carl came to the $750 per night bungalow at the Mirage Hotel occupied by Douglas's manager, John Johnson, an intense former assistant to former coach Woody Hayes at Ohio State.

King arrived as the angry, aggrieved party, feeling no shame for what he had tried to do in Tokyo. He had forced Douglas into signing a contract that gave King options on all his title defenses should he upset Tyson. King was acting like he now owned Douglas and he could command Douglas to give Mike Tyson an immediate rematch.

John Johnson thought this was crazy, and was in the final stages of negotiating a two-fight, $50 million contract for Mirage owner Steve Wynn to promote Douglas's first two defenses. Johnson felt that he and Douglas had been coerced into signing the exclusive option contract with King, and that King had breached the contract by not acting in Douglas's best interests by attempting to reverse his victory.

"You can't deal me out, John, you *can't* deal me out," King began, belligerent and not deterred by the presence of two reporters in the bungalow.*

"This is where I make my bonanza," King continued. "The sad thing is we've got this turkey sitting here ready to eat, and we can't slice it up."

Johnson told King he would pay him $3 million to step aside from Douglas's first defense, if he would let Steve Wynn promote a Douglas–Evander Holyfield match. Wynn wanted to become a promoter like King, not just be a host and pay a site fee like Donald Trump.

King acted hurt by the offer of $3 million.

"I've got an office full of people I have to support," King said. "This is my business. You give me back the money I put into it for five and a half years? I put in three million, getting nothing back, subsidizing you for five and a half years, and then I'm supposed to get back what I put into it, and nothing more? That's a good business deal?"

"Not two weeks ago," Johnson answered, "you convinced the governing bodies to withhold recognition of Buster as champion of the world. If you could have spent those five or six hours in the hotel with us, agonizing over whether he was going to get those championships, that those championships are going to be taken away from him, after what he did."

King claimed he had no power over the governing bodies, and that he was only trying to promote interest in a rematch.

"I've got a deal," Johnson told King, "that's gonna pay James

*The account of this meeting is based on two weeks of testimony during a King-Douglas civil trial in July 1990, and on an excellent article by Ian Thomsen that appeared in the October 18, 1990, issue of *The National*.

Douglas twenty-five million to fight Holyfield, and you offered him ten million to fight Mike Tyson again."

"That's bullshit, bullshit," King shouted. "No such offer was made."

"You won't take the money from James Douglas, that's for sure," Johnson replied, getting more emotional himself in response to King's raising his voice and lying about what he knew to be the truth. "He's making more money than anybody else, and that's the way it should be."

"He's not making more. He's making *all* of it," King roared.

"That's the way it should be," Johnson, the football romantic, answered.

"That's *not* the way it should be," countered King. "There's enough money for everybody. Buster just shouldn't make it. Everybody should make it. It's not just for the fighter. You go from [earning] fifty thousand to one point three million [for Tyson], to twenty-five million, and he should keep all of it?"

Johnson smiled and nodded vigorously in the affirmative.

"John, you are a stupid motherfucker," King repeated twice. Each time he said "motherfucker" he slammed the palm of his hand down on the table.

King then warned Johnson that he had control over Holyfield, which was not true, and Johnson knew it was not true.

"You're in way over your head," King shouted, now in the kind of rage I had experienced myself in the Mirage Hotel.

"You'll find out. I'm coming back to kick your ass," King warned.

Johnson calmly responded, "You can make you own deal with Steve Wynn, but James Douglas isn't taking any less money."

With the argument at an impasse, King then turned away from Johnson and started to engage Buster's trainer and uncle, J. D. McCauley.

"It isn't Buster who wants to fight Holyfield, it's Johnson," King said, trying a little divide and conquer between the white manager and the black trainer of the new champion.

"Buster told me he doesn't care who he fights next," King claimed. "It's not Buster, it's Johnson who wants to fight Holyfield. John Johnson is the boss, not the fighter."

That was too much for Johnson.

"If you want to start trying to divide us," Johnson said, "you can just go to hell. That divisionist shit! Fuck you! Fuck you!"

Johnson went into another room to dial Steve Wynn and tell him what King was up to, and that he'd better come right over.

Left alone with McCauley, King immediately tried to play the race card, boasting how much every black fighter owed him, how if it wasn't for him, there would be no one to give black fighters a chance, how you can never trust white promoters.

"I completely subsidized Buster," King claimed. "He couldn't draw flies to a dump."

McCauley tried to speak, but King just rode over his words with his own steamroller of louder words, one of his signature tactics. What McCauley wanted to say was that he knew King had not treated Buster well during those years Buster was fighting preliminaries for King, and that he himself had tried to convince Johnson that he should take Buster away from the yoke of King's empire.

"You stupid motherfucker," King told the black trainer and former fighter. King launched into one of his stock monologues on race and boxing, changing history and rearranging facts as he went along. McCauley tried to speak, but King wouldn't let him.

Finally Steve Wynn arrived in response to John Johnson's phone call.

"I'm going to own this fucking hotel," King declared. "Six hundred and fifty million dollars and I'm going to own it."

Steve Wynn sat down right in front of King and told him, "You are a no-good, lying, thieving cocksucker. . . . You are extinct, like dinosaurs."

That concluded the meeting. Within a few weeks Douglas sued

King in Nevada to get out of his option contract, and King sued Douglas and Steve Wynn in New York to force Douglas to fight for him.

Murray Kempton would call King's suit against Douglas the first attempt in the twentieth century to enforce the Fugitive Slave Statute.

The third week in March Don King moved into the Radisson Hotel in Columbus, Ohio, to keep his pledge to come back and kick John Johnson's ass.

King was now an overweight fifty-eight-year-old with high blood pressure. But he was still a vagabond workaholic who could wear down any foe with his supply of words, life-force, ideas, and money.

Columbus was where Buster Douglas and John Johnson lived. King had studied and probed for weaknesses, and now he knew what they were, and he came like an old gunfighter to drive the new sheriff into hiding.

King knew that Douglas was estranged in a painful way from his father, Billy "Dynamite" Douglas, a tough main-event fighter from the 1950s, who once nearly beat the much-feared Bennie Briscoe in Briscoe's hometown of Philadelphia. The father, a hot-tempered disciplinarian, had managed Douglas until his son just quit against Tony Tucker, and then the father walked away in disgust. King knew that Billy Douglas and John Johnson disliked each other and had differed over the son's training habits and choice of opponents.

So the first thing Don did after he settled into Columbus was give the father a "gift" of $10,000. Then he threw an extravagant fiftieth birthday party for Dynamite Douglas that became the buzz of Columbus. And soon Dynamite Douglas was saying what Don King wanted him to say about Buster's future, and who Buster should be fighting for. Billy Douglas needed no extra incentive to trash Johnny Johnson as the wrong man to be guiding his son's career.

On March 24, King crashed a Buster Douglas press conference at the Parke Hotel in downtown Columbus.

"Just like it used to be," King shouted at fire-engine decibels. "We're gonna make it happen again." He smiled and forced an embrace with Douglas and John Johnson, who seemed to be cringing.

While Johnson told reporters he had no interest in doing business with King, J. D. McCauley let his emotions go. With King standing a few feet away, he told *Columbus Dispatch* sportswriter Bob Baptist: "Don King is a dirty, sneaking, lowdown leech. I've been around King for five and a half years now. I watched what this man did. He talks about the black fighters he's helped, and it's bull. The fighters he helped, I can name them, and they're all digging ditches right now. Tim Witherspoon, David Bey, Dwight Braxton. None of them have a quarter to their name on account of Don King.

"All those guys made money. Who's got the money? Where's the money at? Tell me about Don King and what he's done for black fighters. He ain't done nothing. And he's not going to do it to my nephew. I'll die and go to hell first."

At the end of the news conference, King screamed at John Johnson: "You're so brainwashed, you don't understand. You are sick. You need help."

King also started turning up on radio station WCKX, which has a mostly black audience, and attacking Buster Douglas for choosing a white man over his own father to be his manager, for betraying Don King after all King had done for him.

King got Benjamin Hooks, the director of the NAACP, to come to Columbus and endorse what King was saying, which had a significant impact on black public opinion. Don King Productions also made a $12,500 payment to Hook's wife, Frances, for no apparent work, and a $12,500 donation to the NAACP. Both checks were written on May 5, 1990.

King's propaganda campaign was effective. It did shift public opinion in the black community against its native son, who had just gotten off the floor to knock out Superman.

Like many fighters, Douglas was essentially private, introverted, and hometown. He thought he would have a few quiet months to savor his accomplishment. Instead, in his own neighborhood, people he knew personally were taking King's side, telling him he should dump Johnson and Wynn and "fight for a brother."

"I couldn't believe people were coming out and siding with this man," Douglas told *The National*'s Ian Thomsen. "He [King] dug so deep to find the people who came out against me. It was like people were coming forward and saying: 'I gave him a dollar, and he didn't give me the dollar back.'"

Douglas and Johnson were not used to this kind of media blitz of personalized venom. Douglas was deeply hurt that King would use his own father against him, and that Columbus could so easily be turned against its heroic native son. Whatever innocence Buster Douglas had left, he lost in March 1990.

He began to ask himself: *Why am I fighting? Who am I fighting for? Who are my fans?*

Tensions got so high that John Johnson began to carry a gun in his briefcase, just as Tim Witherspoon felt he needed a gun to protect himself. Just as Richie Giachetti had feared for his life in 1981. Johnson was a tough guy, but he feared King's associations and felt violence was not out of the question with millions of dollars at stake.

"I thought somebody might come after John," Douglas said, "that somebody would be sent out to get him."

Douglas admits he became a little paranoid himself. The heavyweight champion of the world, driving at 5:00 A.M. in his hometown, noticed a car behind him that seemed to be following him. He said he was so scared that he sped through an intersection to escape, fearing the driver might have a gun and be out to assassinate him.

Six weeks after achieving the heavyweight upset of the century, the joy was going out of boxing for Buster Douglas. His mind was playing tricks on him. There wasn't much pleasure or recreation. Don King's pressure, the lawsuits, the new demands of fame, the unkind words from old friends, the racial tensions—they were all starting to spoil the great prize of Buster's life.

It was a little like the Hemingway short story "The Old Man and the Sea." Buster caught his prize fish, and before he could get it to port, the hungry fish in the sea of boxing saw the blood on the water and were stripping his prize down to the bone, even before he could show it off and enjoy it.

But Don King was more single-minded, with a stronger ego, than any competitor, or Buster Douglas. King's will to power, his instinct to control, are gargantuan. That's why he is such a survivor.

Buster Douglas had vanquished Superman inside the ring in Tokyo. But he was no match for Don King in the more ruthless pit of the boxing business, where there is no referee, and almost no rules.

Don King's lawsuit against Buster Douglas and Steve Wynn went on trial on July 2, 1990, in the same Manhattan federal courthouse where King was acquitted in 1985. King was seeking between $24 and $27 million in damages. His claim was that Douglas was trying to break a valid contract with him by choosing to fight for another promoter, and that Wynn, as chief executive officer of the Mirage casino, was wrongfully interfering in his contract with Douglas.

The trial was the best-ever seminar on how boxing really works, what its moral assumptions are, how routine its double-crosses are, the lack of scruples among its biggest names, and the lack of dignity accorded the fighters who generate all the wealth.

At about 3:00 P.M. on July 3, Donald Trump took the stand as a witness for King, to bolster King's claim he was only trying to generate interest in a rematch with all his screaming during and after the Douglas-Tyson fight. Trump was under oath, although Alair Townsend, a former deputy mayor of New York, once said, "I wouldn't believe Donald Trump if his tongue was notarized."

Trump described how he and King sat next to each other in ringside seats and negotiated the terms of a Douglas-Tyson rematch while their first fight was still in progress. Trump told the six jurors, "I was of the opinion that Don King had the right to commit Douglas. I thought he could choose the site and the amount for Douglas."

This was the kind of testimony that made this civil trial such an inadvertently spectacular educational experience on boxing morals and practices. This kind of negotiating would never occur in the normal corporate world. It would never occur in any other sport. It would never occur in the entertainment industry. No movie, or concert tour, or TV pilot would ever be negotiated like this, with the talent not consulted, or even notified.

Here you have Buster Douglas in the middle of a brutal fight with Mike Tyson, a fight for which Don King has deprived Douglas of even the customary twenty-five complimentary tickets for family and close friends. And while Douglas is still in the ring, King is telling Donald Trump who Douglas will fight next, and where he will fight next. And it is just accepted as routine by the two millionaire Donalds that Douglas has no say in the matter. The two Donalds are making their deal, assuming Douglas has no mind of his own and has no independent manager who will negotiate for his rights.

King and Trump were carving up Buster Douglas as if the fighter were Poland and they were Hitler and Stalin in 1939.

"At the end of the fight," Trump told the jury, "King and I shook hands on a rematch for twelve point five million."

This was a reference to the site fee Trump would pay King to deliver the fight to Trump's Atlantic City hotel-casino.

King and Trump shook hands on the rematch even though such immediate rematches are prohibited by the rules of the WBC and WBA, and even though there was no rematch clause in the Tyson-

Douglas contract, something King was certainly aware of.

And King had first gained control of the heavyweight title by convincing the WBC that immediate title rematches were morally wrong, and that they should strip Leon Spinks of the title because he gave Muhammad Ali an immediate rematch. King then steered Larry Holmes into the vacated title.

On cross-examination, Douglas's lawyer, Stan Hunterton of Las Vegas, pressed Trump on whether King had rooted openly for Tyson—something several other people in adjacent seats had plainly heard.

"I don't recall," Trump said. "He might have done it, but I don't remember."

Trump, who had done business with King on many fights, including Tyson-Spinks, was trying to tailor his testimony to help his once and future partner, whose fights would increase the "drop" in his casinos.

Trump was also a rival of Steve Wynn and the Mirage, since part of boxing politics is based on the competition between Atlantic City and Las Vegas for the biggest fights. Big fights attract gamblers and high rollers to the casinos, which is why Atlantic City and Las Vegas bid competitively to host all the major matches. It is also why boxing regulation is so lax in both New Jersey and Nevada: Each state is afraid aggressive regulation will drive boxing into the arms of the rival gambling state. This is also the reason the only possible reform of boxing would be the naming of a *national* commissioner—as in all the other major sports.

The only light moment during Trump's testimony came when John Sharer, the attorney for the Mirage, mistakenly called Trump "Mr. King."

"I'd like to be Mr. King," Trump shot back.

When WBC president Jose Sulaiman testified, Douglas's lawyer played the jury videotapes shot in Tokyo that showed Sulaiman saying he was suspending recognition of Douglas as the new champion.

Confronted by that irrefutable evidence, the sport's most powerful regulator said plaintively, "In the bottom of my heart I did not withdraw recognition. My embarrassment to the people of the world was in not having the courage and intelligence to say it openly."

Sulaiman also testified that the only person he heard call for the fight to be stopped after the eighth round was Tyson's friend John Horne. But Hunterton played an audiotape on which Sulaiman said, "The protest originally came from the promoter," meaning King.

Another who testified on King's behalf was his archenemy, Bob Arum.

Arum and King hated each other. They had called each other anti-Semite and racist. They had a physical confrontation after the Leonard-Hagler fight when Arum tore King's jacket and a gun fell out of King's pocket. They had sued each other dozens of times.

But in July 1990 Arum's anger at Steve Wynn was fresh and fanatical. Arum and Steve Wynn had also looked at Buster Douglas and seen Poland. They originally had a handshake understanding to together promote all Douglas's fights while he was champion.

Arum is a graduate of Harvard Law School and former federal prosecutor, and he had given Wynn a shrewd tactical plan on how to win the rights to Douglas from King by filing a lawsuit first, in the Nevada state courts, where Wynn and Arum had vast influence, before King could file his lawsuit in the federal court in New York. But when Wynn filed his suit, he had dropped Arum as co-plaintiff.

Before he took the stand Arum stood in the hallway outside Room 443 and told me, "Steve Wynn stabbed me in the back and now I am about to get even. He double-crossed me and made his own deal with Douglas. He froze me out. Everything I ever said to you about King is still true, but I'm going to go in there, swear to tell the truth, and kick the shit out of Wynn and help Don win this case. Wynn is a greedy, stupid fuck. He and I could have shared control of Douglas, and of the heavyweight championship, and King would have been out in the cold. But Wynn got greedy. He wanted to hog it all for himself. He filed the Vegas suit too late, and without my name on it. That's why King's case went first in New York. I was forum-shopping, handing Wynn the home-court advantage before a state judge in Las Vegas. He blew it because he is a dumb schmuck. And that's why I am here today, as King's witness."

Arum told the jury how Wynn had eased him out of the deal after milking him for his advice and legal knowledge. Arum justified what King did in Tokyo, saying, "In the heat of combat we all say things we are not accountable for. . . . A protest is the correct procedure. You yell your head off, otherwise nobody pays attention."

Wynn's lawyer asked Arum why he shook hands with Wynn on a $2 million fee to promote a Douglas-Holyfield fight, which violated King's contractual rights to Douglas.

Arum, in an unusually relaxed mood on the stand, smiled and said with an impish grin, "I threw caution to the wind and did a bad thing."

The courtroom, filled with boxing writers and insiders, broke up in laughter, and even Judge Robert Sweet grinned.

Wynn's lawyer expressed sarcastic shock at Arum's sudden alliance with King, given their long history of rancor and acrimony.

"This is relative peace," Arum quipped. "We only have one lawsuit pending."

Arum added, "Don and I have done dastardly things to each other."

Perhaps thinking of some of these past treacheries, Arum began to smile, and then laughed out loud in the witness box.

Several times during his four hours of testimony Arum drove home his main legal point to help King: Based on his own deal with Wynn, and their private conversations, Wynn knew he was violating King's contractual rights, but was confident he could buy King out of the contract once he had Douglas under contract himself.

Arum quoted Wynn as telling him, "We'll buy King off, give him a piece of pie, and let him take a walk."

And Arum described how Wynn's two lawyers—Bruce Levin and Steve Enz—had advised Wynn against signing any contract with Douglas because it might interfere with King's contract with Douglas.

Arum testified, "Bruce Levin said, 'Steve, I'm against this, you shouldn't do this,' but Wynn was kicking Levin under the table."

On cross, Mirage lawyer John Sharer confronted Arum with perhaps his most repeated quotation—"Yesterday I was lying. Today I am telling the truth."

Arum winced as Sharer recited it, and tried to preempt any embarrassing questions about all the occasions he'd used that line. Arum volunteered an anecdote about the first time he said it.

"One night I was drinking with some boxing writers," Arum explained, "including Bob Waters [the wonderful, deceased boxing writer for *Newsday*] and I was bombed out of my mind. I told them fighter 'A' was better than fighter 'B.'

"The next night I was out with them again and we were all drunk. I told them fighter 'B' was better than fighter 'A.' Bob Waters reminded me what I had said the previous night. So that's when I first said, 'Yesterday I was lying, but today I'm telling the truth.' "

Sharer then tried to press Arum on the moral lessons of lying, to taint Arum's credibility with the jury.

But Arum interrupted the half-formed question to say, "Look, the only thing that taught me was never to go drinking with sportswriters."

Don King was on the stand for three days and was at his bril-

liant best.* He was selling a mostly false story that was contradicted by video- and audiotapes, yet he was funny, likable, and
even believable.

King used his invented words like "trickeration" and
"insinuendo." He imitated a Japanese accent. He filibustered,
used hyperbole, told stories like an old actor. He kept smiling and
looked directly at the jury. He was doing what he does best—
promoting and selling. And this time he was selling and promoting himself.

King swore his goal in Tokyo was only a rematch, not a
changed result.

"I'm stirring the pot, I'm instigating," he said. "I'm promotin'.
I'm selling. I was trying to box them in."

Revealing his self-knowledge of his own methods, King said,
"If you have both fighters there, you have an opportunity to blow
everything out of proportion. The internal combustion was there
and I could play on it. It's like a big mushroom."

King complained that John Johnson wasn't cooperating in his
stirring the pot for a rematch. "He should have been as happy as
a sissy in a girls' school," King said, looking right at the perplexed
jury.

King's story was that the referee "panicked" when Douglas was
knocked down, but that he was not responsible for the withhold-
ing of recognition of Douglas as champion. But he was pleased
that someone else had lodged a protest, allowing him to start
"stirring the pot."

"I was happy," King said on direct testimony. "Under normal
circumstances you can't have a rematch. But a protest puts a taint
on Buster's victory. You have a valid argument for a rematch. It
can be mandated. You don't have to go to the commissioners for
approval. My agenda was to get a rematch. I had the opportunity

*Well-known attorney Thomas Puccio told me, "Don King is by far the smartest person I ever cross-
examined, in a trial or a deposition. And I questioned Ivan Boesky."

to do something big, extraordinary. It would have been the biggest payday in the history of boxing."

But almost in the next breath, King was demeaning Douglas, unable to suppress his hostility to the champion who became his fugitive slave.

"Buster was a boring, lazy fighter," King said. "He was the kind of fighter people would throw hot dogs and beer cans at. When Buster came on, everybody went to buy hot dogs. Nobody wanted to see Buster. I moved him up in the rankings through attrition, without him having to fight anybody. . . . I had to take Buster to Japan because I couldn't sell him in America. I told the Japanese how great Buster was. I kept selling, selling, selling."

Even on cross-examination King remained appealing in his rascality. He managed to maintain his jaunty poise, even as the Mirage's lawyers scored some solid points against his credibility.

John Sharer pointed out that Trump had testified he and King had made "an oral contract" for Douglas-Tyson II at the end of the fight in Tokyo, but the day after the fight King had told reporters, "We don't have a rematch right now."

"I don't lie to the press," King explained. "I just withhold some of the truth because I'm trying to make something happen. I don't consider it lying when I don't tell them everything. . . . I wasn't under oath with the press."

King insisted he had never tried to change the result, or withhold recognition, even after Wynn's attorneys played the video- and audiotapes from Tokyo. King sat on the stand, impassive, as his own voice filled the courtroom:

"Here's the facts. Mike Tyson knocked out James Douglas. . . . Douglas was knocked out and the referee did not do his job. . . . If the rules is kept, the first knockout automatically obliterates the second knockout. There would never had been a second knockout. . . . All I can do is voice a protest. . . . It will be a grave injustice here if it holds that Mike Tyson was knocked out. . . . I issued a protest to Mr. Mendoza and Mr. Jose Sulaiman.

The six-four King, with his graying, spiked hair, towered over everyone else in the Tokyo ringside section, especially the shorter Japanese. And with his supersonic voice, it was impossible not to see and hear him between rounds. But King concocted a fictional detail to deny what dozens of people witnessed.

King swore he never spoke with Meyran after the eighth round, "because the referee didn't speak English. How was I going to speak to him, in sign language?"

But Wynn's lawyer reminded King that he had sat right next to Meyran during the postfight press conference, and ᵗhat the referee "spoke the English language."

"I guess so," King admitted, in one of his few flustered moments in three days. King also had to admit that he never actually spoke the word "rematch" in Tokyo, in all his hours of raving with the press.

John Sharer asked King if he had ever been sued by boxing promoters other than Arum. King took a deep breath, closed his eyes, tilted his head back as if in a pensive trance, and said, "I don't remember."

It was a great act, but King surely could remember being sued by Tom Prendergast, to whom he paid $1.4 million; and by Butch Lewis, whom he paid over $200,000 to settle a trial over Greg Page; and by Murad Muhammad, who sued him over Razor Ruddock; and by Sam Glass, who sued him over Gerry Cooney. Or that he paid Cedric Kushner $150,000 over the theft of Gerrie Coetzee.

In response to another question on cross, King did admit that he "didn't want Douglas to get up" when he was floored by Tyson.

But these admissions and inconsistencies may have been neutralized in the minds of the jurors later that day when the attorney for the Mirage, Bruce Levin, took the witness stand.

Levin testified that the court should void King's contract with Douglas on the basis of a Nevada commission regulation that prohibits exclusive promotional contracts. But under questioning from King's lawyer, Bob Hirth, Levin had to admit the Mirage itself had exactly the same exclusive contract with middleweight champion Michael Nunn.

"At the time we wrote the contract," Levin explained, "I was not aware that exclusive promotional contracts were invalid in Nevada."

"Have you since ripped up the Nunn contract?" Hirth asked.

"No, we have not," the Mirage's attorney replied.

In boxing there are no good guys or white hats among the promoters. There is no reform faction to root for among the casino interests. Steve Wynn, Donald Trump, and Bob Arum did not come across any better than Don King during this trial. They all seemed rapacious, they all seemed cynical, they all disrespected the craft and dignity of the fighter.

Arum was there for revenge. Trump was there to gain leverage for future deals with King. Wynn had double-crossed Arum, and wanted to do exactly what King had done with monopoly control. And King had rewritten history.

Right after the trial ended, Vic Ziegel wrote in the *Daily News:* "Take it from someone who was in Tokyo, who listened to King plead Tyson's case, long and hard, immediately after the fight. He wanted to change the verdict."

Putting contracts and legalities aside, it is emotionally impossible to fault Douglas for not wanting to work for the promoter who tried to rob him of his crown, said he was so lazy that fans tossed beer cans at him, deprived his family of tickets to the biggest fight of his life, admitted he was rooting for him not to get up when he was knocked down, and poisoned his hometown neighbors against him.

On Friday, July 17, the lawyers began serious settlement talks. The talks lasted through the weekend, and continued on Monday, as Judge Sweet recessed the trial to give the lawyers more time.

One factor tipping Douglas toward a settlement was that his

estranged father, Billy Douglas, was on King's list of witnesses. Billy Douglas was even at the courthouse, wearing a Panama hat, sitting with King's faction, letting the son know what was coming, putting psychic pressure on the son to settle.

The issue became the cross-examination of Billy Douglas. Buster was told his father would be humiliated and exposed for taking money from King, for letting King pay for his birthday bash in Columbus. But Buster was reluctant to see his father crushed on cross, even though his father was prepared to testify against him.

A friend of Douglas's told me, "Buster is torn up. He's having imaginary conversations with his dead mother, about whether it is worth the effort to expose his father on the stand. Buster is just a soft-hearted guy. He had too much dignity to offer his old man more money than King paid him."

On Saturday, July 18, Steve Wynn flew from Vegas to New York, and that night he and King bargained face-to-face at the Waldorf Towers in Wynn's suite. The broad outlines of deal were agreed to.

Judge Sweet recessed the trial for Monday, and the parties negotiated all night at Hirth's law office. By midnight, all the principals were there in separate rooms—King, Douglas, Wynn, Johnson. They were in touch with Trump by phone. At 2:00 A.M. a deal was finalized and everyone shook hands and joked with one another. It was announced the next morning in Judge Sweet's courtroom.

The settlement gave Douglas his freedom to fight Holyfield for Steve Wynn and be paid $24 million for his purse.

King and Trump got $7 million from the Mirage for their rights, with King getting $4.5 million.

King agreed to pay Douglas a promised $100,000 bonus for beating Tyson that he had reneged on when the litigation started.

King would have the opportunity to promote a Douglas-Tyson

rematch after the Holyfield defense. He needed this to keep Tyson in line.

Douglas would be free of all obligations to King, except for the Tyson rematch.

John Johnson was thrilled, telling reporters, "We did what we set out to do—get rid of Don King and get James the greatest deal in sports history."

In the hallway outside Room 443, the jurors gave interviews to reporters. It turned out three of the six jurors were leaning toward King and three others sounded neutral, waiting for Wynn and Johnson to testify.

Juror Carol Solanto, a junior high school teacher in the Bronx, was impressed by King's testimony but said, "They're all being greedy. It's just a whole underworld."

Juror Gabrielle Mellet, a fund-raiser for the ACLU, said, "You couldn't believe what anybody said about anything."

Juror Erica Franklin, a health magazine reporter, said, "I didn't believe anybody. King was an effective witness, but you have to take everything he said with a grain of salt."

King then showed up, in an ebullient mood, and shook hands with all the jurors. He invited them all to attend Tyson's next fight—an echo of his flying the jurors who acquitted him of tax crimes to London to see the Witherspoon-Bruno fight.

King also promised one juror—Daniel Kahn, a graduate student—a Team Tyson jacket. A press assistant gave King's business card to each juror.

"This is what makes America so great," King proclaimed. "The ability to put away animosity and hostility, and sit down at the table of brotherhood and understanding."

On October 25, 1990, Douglas made his first title defense against Evander Holyfield at the Mirage. Steve Wynn had invested more than $40 million in this fight: $24 million for Douglas, $8.1 million for Holyfield, $7 million paid to King and Trump to settle the lawsuits, $4 million in legal fees, $2 million in advertising costs. But Wynn believed the event would propel him into the dominant position in boxing, displacing King.

As has happened so often in the recent past, a new heavyweight champion beat himself before the bell rang. Buster's motivation was destroyed by fame, money, his conflict with his father, divisions within his own camp, King's attacks on him, the attainment of the title, and the absence of any new goal to inspire a work ethic.

Douglas weighed in at an obese 246 pounds, 15 pounds more than he weighed in Tokyo. In the hours between the weigh-in and the fight, the odds moved from even money to 8 to 5 in favor of Holyfield.

In the fight Buster was lackadaisical in the first round, gasping for oxygen at the close of the second round, despite the lack of exertion. In the third round Douglas missed a lazy, looping, long-range uppercut. Holyfield stepped in and countered with a sharp right cross, and all of Steve Wynn's boxing dreams evaporated on his canvas, pitched on his property called the Mirage.

Douglas took the ten count on his back with his eyes open. He rubbed his nose three times with the thumb of his glove. He looked like a beached whale.

Referee Mills Lane told reporters afterward, "Buster was not unconscious. His eyes were open. I thought he was gonna get up. He made no attempt to get up. That's the truth."

Eddie Futch, the grand old trainer of Joe Frazier and Larry Holmes, told the press: "Buster Douglas was disgraceful tonight. He allowed himself to come in in such poor condition. He had no snap. He showed me that he could get up, but he didn't, for his own reasons."

Mike Trainer, Steve Wynn's boxing consultant, said, "What a piece of junk! He was a dog! It's embarrassing. I don't want to say he was a disgrace, but what he did was wrong."

"He quit again," cackled King.

But King's promotional rights to a Tyson-Douglas rematch were now meaningless. King had lost something too, although he still controlled Tyson, and Tyson gave him leverage with the casinos and the Showtime cable network.

After this fiasco, Steve Wynn pulled back from the boxing business, letting the MGM Grand casino, Caesars, and Trump bid for the big fights. He had lost about $20 million on his attempt to topple King. But King had proved he was far from the extinct dinosaur that Wynn had called him back in February at the Mirage cottage of John Johnson.

Although only thirty years old, Buster Douglas never had another fight. By May 1994 he had ballooned up to over 350 pounds. He talked about a comeback, and visited a gym occasionally, but he never stuck with it. In July he fell into a diabetic coma and nearly died.

Once again Don King was the winner and survivor. Douglas had money and was better off than Jeff Merritt or Michael Dokes. But King had made his brief, eight-month reign as champion a painful experience that left a bad taste in his mouth.

Buster Douglas ended up as the Fugitive Slave who got rich in one fight for Steve Wynn. But he never realized his full potential. He beat the mighty Tyson, but he couldn't beat the system—or Don King.

"He underestimated me because I'm so quiet"

In June 1986 Joe Maffia needed a job. He was working for Paramount pictures as an accountant, but his office was soon moving to California.

He went to a headhunter, who happened to know Don King's director of operations, Celia Tuckman, and that's how Maffia got an interview with lawyer Charles Lomax, and then King himself.

This was two days before King was promoting a Hector Camacho–Edwin Rosario fight at Madison Square Garden, and when Maffia showed up at King's offices, TV camera crews were coming and going, and the prefight publicity was in high gear.

Maffia was interviewed for an hour by Lomax, and for five minutes by King. The first thing King said to him was "Don't believe what you read about me in the newspapers."

A few minutes later King told Maffia he would hire him to be the assistant to the controller.

"You do right by me and I'll do right by you," King told Maffia, then twenty-seven years old. Maffia said he would begin in a month after giving proper notice to his supervisor at Paramount. He started with King at the comparatively low salary of $30,000 a year.

Despite the sound of his name, Joe Maffia is not an Italian American. His father was of mixed German and Spanish heritage, and his mother was a black from the Caribbean. He has thought of himself as black all through his adult life, although he looks white. His father was adopted by an Italian family when he was a child, and Maffia was the name of this adoptive family.*

Maffia's ex-wife is Jewish, and he says, "I don't know how to describe the ethnicity of my children in less than a minute." He is quiet, conventional, and private—the opposite of King is almost all ways.

By the time Maffia reported for work at Don King Productions in mid-July of 1986, the controller had apparently absconded with about $100,000, and Maffia assumed the functions of controller of the company from his first day on the job. He was given the formal title after about a year.

Most of Don King's relationships start out well, and so did his association with Maffia. Maffia received several raises and bonuses his first year on the job. King also gave him a $25,000 interest-free loan to buy a co-op apartment.

Maffia saw King pay $5,100 for the funeral of Ali's trainer and spiritual inspiration, Drew Brown, when no one else stepped forward and the body was lying in a funeral home. As a favor to Maffia, King flew back from California to speak at a luncheon of CPAs and dazzled them without any preparation.

As controller of DKP, Joe Maffia saw every check that went out. As a cautious stickler for the letter of the law, Maffia soon

---

*Maffia's sister, Roma Maffia, is a talented actress who had a lead role in the film *Disclosure* with Michael Douglas and Demi Moore. She has also appeared in several TV series.

realized King operated in his own secretive style that was a little different from a public corporation like Gulf + Western, which owned Paramount. And when Maffia started, King's financial records were not even computerized.

In October 1987, Maffia says, King was "freaked out" by his loss of about $3 million in the stock market crash. He had it in blue-chip stocks, on margin. The losses created havoc with King's cash flow, and when the day came that King needed to write a check for $350,000 to the IRS for his federal taxes, the money was not available from the normal DKP accounts.

"I remember," Maffia recalls, "being shocked when Don suddenly produced $350,000 in cash that had been wrapped in plastic and sealed with heat, and had been stamped by the Caesars Palace casino. It was dated five years earlier, in 1982, around the time of the Holmes-Cooney fight at Caesars. I deposited the cash at the bank and wrote out a check to the IRS. This was a pretty unusual transaction."

Gradually Maffia began to notice quite a few unusual transactions.

King always carried what he called "flash cash," a roll of $5,000 or $10,000 he kept in his pocket. King kept bank accounts in Puerto Rico, Jamaica, and Panama, and safe-deposit boxes in Puerto Rico and at the Lincoln Savings Bank in Manhattan, near his office.

He was always dealing in cash. Maffia says it was not unusual for him to cut checks of $100,000 or $200,000 made out to cash.

"Don would make out checks to cash all the time," Maffia says, "and he would write 'Project Zoro' on the stub. When I would ask him what 'Project Zoro' was, he would get angry and not tell me.

"When I would tell him I needed to know because of the 1099 accounting and reporting requirements, he started calling me a '1099 motherfucker.' "

King often asked Maffia to cut checks to a wide variety of

people whose function it was to generate political support for King in the black community.

Sylvester Leaks* would get "expenses" and "consultant fees" when he wrote favorable articles about King in the *Amsterdam News*. The Reverend Al Sharpton got expenses reimbursed for as long as he kept defending King's practices. The Reverend Franklin Richardson of Mt. Vernon collected $10,000 in 1989. The Reverend T. J. Jemison, president of the National Baptist Ministers Association, got at least $25,000. Yamil Chade, a manager and friend of Jose Sulaiman, was given $10,000. The wife of Benjamin Hooks received $12,500.

All these payments were taken out of Mike Tyson's accounts.

In 1989, Maffia accidentally sent Reverend Richardson a 1099 form for his payment. King got angry and told his chief financial officer, "You are the most 1099 motherfucker I have ever known."

Once King directed Maffia to write a check for $325,000, and to write on the stub "to open offices in Latin America."

"Is it a lease?" Maffia asked. "Are we buying a building?"

King wouldn't say.

On another occasion Maffia was instructed to give Yamil Chade four checks made out to a Panamanian company, and to record the purpose as "public relations offices in Latin America." The next day the money came back by wire transfers.

Maffia wasn't sure what was going on.

On another occasion King asked Maffia to falsify some records that had been subpoenaed as part of Tim Witherspoon's civil lawsuit.

"Don wanted me to add some fake expenses that would make it look like he made a smaller profit than he actually did on the Witherspoon-Bruno fight. But I never did it," Maffia said.

---

*Leaks wrote two puff pieces for the *Amsterdam News* in December 1994 about King's visit to Ecuador. That same month Leaks was removed for mismanagement as president of Community School Board 17 in Brooklyn.

The job was exciting, and King kept paying him bonuses, so Maffia was able to rationalize for a while what was going on right under his nose. He certainly found some of the people coming into the office for money highly suspicious, and he was troubled by some of the transactions, but he felt all he could do was keep the books as honestly as he could and make sure King paid his taxes.

A saint might have quit right away, but there are no saints in the boxing business.

"The first two years I really liked Don," Maffia says. "We were friends. He asked about my children. If I worked eighteen hours a day, he worked twenty-four. He had his faults, but on balance, I have to say I liked him."

Maffia dates the beginning of his disenchantment to the way King took advantage of Mike Tyson, when Tyson became the crown jewel of King's empire in October 1988.

"He began to have me bill part of everything to Tyson," Maffia recalled. "Mike started absorbing all of Don's overhead without really knowing it.

"Don showed the spread sheets [detailed worksheet accountings] really fast to Mike, and he had Mike, and me, and Rory Holloway sign them to cover himself. But nobody really analyzed them for Mike, and Mike couldn't understand them. Don had me keep the originals in a fireproof safe and told me never to let them out of the building, never to let Mike be able to show them to anyone outside the building.

"I suppose, at some level, Mike knew and didn't care. But no one really explained anything to him, where his money was going. Don gave Mike what he wanted—cars, cash, women. And Mike let Don control his money, which was in the multimillions. Don kept telling me to write checks reimbursing DKP from Mike's accounts."

King developed a shorthand code with Maffia.

"OTP" was King's code for "off the top." Whenever King said

"OTP," it meant he wanted Maffia to deduct some expenses off the top of a Tyson promotion, before Tyson's specific percentage was allocated.

"This began to bother me emotionally," Maffia says. "My own bonus was billed to Mike. The salary for Don's bodyguards was billed to Mike. Don billed his own maid services in his Las Vegas and Los Angeles condos to Mike. Mike was paying one thousand a week, plus bonuses, to Don's daughter, Debby, to be the president of the Mike Tyson fan club. And I could see that thousands of fan letters to Mike were sitting unopened in cartons in the basement of King's office. The fan club had the license to market Mike Tyson jackets and T-shirts. It should have been a profit-making venture. But Don was just using it to pay his family with Mike's money."

By the spring of 1991, Maffia's relationship with King had become irrevocably poisoned. One factor was that Maffia and King were both involved with the same woman. (Maffia would not discuss the tensions and emotions caused by this triangle except to acknowledge its existence.)

Second, King became uncomfortable with all the questions Maffia kept asking. He became paranoid about the possibility that Maffia was an FBI informant.

Maffia asked him so many insistent questions about disbursements to people who did no visible work, and about all the checks generating cash, that King came to doubt Maffia's motives and loyalty.

Maffia was not an informant. He kept asking King about the large checks made out to cash only because he had to file an "8300 form" with the bank each time it was done.

In April 1991, King blew up and accused Maffia of stealing money from him. The occasion was a meeting where King was to pay his first-quarter taxes (about $1.8 million) and pay off the mortgage on the townhouse where his office was located. A vice president of Peat Marwick was present, and so was lawyer

Charles Lomax and Maffia's assistant, George Taira.

King, as usual, was in a rush because he was flying to Europe that night with Tyson. When Maffia said there was a cash-flow problem, and there wasn't enough money in the active accounts to both pay the taxes and pay off the mortgage, King shouted at Maffia, "You must be stealin'."

It took a while for Maffia to explain how most of the pay-per-view revenue from the Tyson-Ruddock fight in March hadn't come in yet, and how the foreign sales revenue hadn't come in yet, and that King was confused about which accounts this money would go into.

After King calmed down, he didn't apologize to Maffia but said, "You should have explained it better."

But the accusation of theft hurt and made Maffia realize his days at DKP were now numbered.

It will always be a mystery why someone as street-smart as King would make an enemy out of his chief financial officer, by first accusing him of being an FBI informant and then accusing him of being an embezzler.

King, meanwhile, had a cash-flow problem, mostly because he had no interest in promoting regular, local nonchampionship fights on the USA or ESPN cable networks, the way Bob Arum did, which generated a small, steady revenue stream for Arum. More and more King was interested only in extravaganza fights, or the pay-per-view shows where he could promote four title fights in one night.

The steady flow of midlevel fights required an attention to detail, patience, and discipline that King didn't have, possibly because they didn't give him a large stage and national publicity.

In August, King demanded that Maffia sign a confidentiality agreement, promising not to divulge any secrets he learned while in King's employment. Maffia showed it to an attorney, who told him the document was valid only for the future, not for the past five years.

So Maffia signed it reluctantly and was forced to resign from King's company, effective September 28, 1991.

Maffia says that as of 1990, King's net worth was about $25 million, depending on how the value of the tape library and video rights to his fights were appraised.

This estimate does not include the $15 million in profit King made from the two Tyson-Ruddock pay-per-view bouts in 1991. It also excludes accounts in his wife Henrietta's name, maintained in Ohio. And Maffia didn't know how much cash King kept in his safe-deposit boxes, or in his homes, which were well guarded with high-technology surveillance cameras.

Since King had produced $350,000 in cash on an hour's notice—bills shrink-wrapped in Vegas five years earlier—to pay his federal taxes, it is likely that he keeps significant cash reserves.

"Cash is king with Don," Maffia says. "He thinks you are only as good as the amount of money in your pocket. He never outgrew that mentality from the numbers business. Don always needed that cash in his pocket to bolster his ego, even though he knew his net worth with the bank was twenty-five million."

Joe Maffia was angry, hurt, and he knew things. But alone in the world he was no danger to Don King. He had no strategy of revenge.

Maffia did not run to the FBI or prosecutors with his knowledge. He did not go to the boxing writers he knew. The most he did was get in touch with a literary agent named Knox Burger to explore the possibility of a book, but that never went very far.

In March 1992 Maffia was working as an accountant for David Rosenzweig's company and dabbling on the fringes of boxing when he received a subpoena from the United States Senate, the permanent subcommittee on investigations, chaired by Republican William Roth of Delaware. This invitation would prove to be the catalyst that put into motion a chain of events that would lead to Don King's indictment more than two years later.

Senator Roth had begun an investigation into boxing after a

Delaware constituent—a fighter named David Tiberi—lost a bad decision to James Toney in a nationally televised fight. Roth's staff began to poke around the toxic dump of boxing and easily began to find the material for public hearings and remedial legislation.

When Maffia received the subpoena, he retained Tom Hauser for $1,000 to advise and represent him in his contacts with the Senate committee. Hauser would end up representing him for two years pro bono.

Tom Hauser disliked Don King as intensely as anyone interviewed for this book. Hauser once said to me, "I like fighters and I hate injustice. I like fighters like Ali, Witherspoon, and Mamby. I don't like what Don King did to them. They are decent people. We are on earth for a short time and we have to do good."

Tom Hauser was Ali's avenger. *Muhammad Ali: His Life and Times* was one of sixteen books Hauser has published. He also wrote *The Execution of Charles Horman,* which was nominated for the National Book Award and served as the basis for the Academy Award–winning film *Missing* that starred Jack Lemmon and Sissy Spacek.

Hauser was also a fine lawyer, having clerked for a federal judge and been a Wall Street litigator for the firm of Cravath, Swaine & Moore until he began to write in 1977.

When Joe Maffia called him in March 1992, Hauser was a "legal consultant" to Bill Cayton on his civil lawsuit with Tyson, and knew as much about Don King's dealings as anyone involved in the cruelest sport.

He had written about King in his 1985 boxing book, *The Black Lights,* and in his biography of Ali he had described how King had cheated Ali out of $1 million after the Holmes bout and described the tragic damage that fight inflicted on Ali's health, and why that match should never have been sanctioned or promoted.

When Maffia called him, Hauser asked Maffia one question. "Will you tell the whole truth?" When Maffia said yes, Hauser agreed to represent him in a meeting with the Senate committee staff.

Two years later Hauser would tell me, "I didn't know how much Joe knew. But, yes, the thought did cross my mind during our first conversation that Joe could bring Don down."

A few weeks later, the Senate committee lawyers, Daniel Rinzel and W. Leighton Lord, came to New York and interviewed Maffia for several hours.

One of them asked, "Is Don King tied to organized crime?"

"You don't understand," Hauser said. "Don King is organized crime."

In preparing Joe Maffia for this interview and listening to him during the session, Hauser realized just how penetrating and detailed Maffia's knowledge was. He had the accountant's memory for numbers.

The Senate committee never did much with Maffia's information, and King took the Fifth Amendment when he testified in executive session a few months later. But the committee served the purpose of bringing Hauser and Maffia together.

In April 1992 Tom Hauser conceived what he calls "the strategy of the subpoena."

His client Bill Cayton was bogged down in breach-of-contract litigation with Tyson. Hauser and Cayton wanted King to pay a price for this draining process. Hauser knew that Maffia had been forced to sign the confidentiality agreement with King just before he left.

So he figured out a way around the confidentiality letter. He got Cayton's main lawyer, David Branson, to send Maffia a notice of deposition in the civil case against Tyson. Branson then sent Maffia a subpoena to compel his testimony. That was the device around the confidentiality agreement. The subpoena waived and superseded any promise of confidentiality.

Hauser then orchestrated an exchange of letters between Maffia and Branson, in which Maffia said he was busy and would prefer to answer specific questions in the form of an affidavit rather than sit through a time-consuming deposition. By mid-April Branson had submitted a series of written questions that Hauser was eager to answer and Maffia was willing to answer.

Writing and signing the affidavit—and then going public—was a crossing of the Rubicon for Maffia. When asked about it more than two years later, he said, "It never occurred to me not to respond to the subpoena as honestly as I could. I didn't want to go out of my way to hurt Don. But I didn't want to go out of my way not to hurt him, either. I just did what I thought was right. But I wasn't as emotionally committed to exposing Don as Tom was."

For three nights Hauser and Maffia worked till after midnight over the word processor in Hauser's apartment. The affidavit went through many drafts, with some elements added and others deleted. Maffia thought he was mainly helping Cayton win his lawsuit and that at most, there would be a small story about what he had done back in the sports section of the newspaper.

When it was finished—nine pages packed with financial details about how King fleeced Tyson out of millions of dollars—Hauser leaked it to Mike Katz of the *Daily News,* who had been writing columns critical of King for years. He read the affidavit and immediately knew he had a groundbreaking scoop. On Saturday, May 2, Katz reached King in West Palm Beach, Florida, to get his response to the sworn statement accusing him of the financial rape of Tyson, who was then in prison for sexual rape.

"You are a racist motherfucker," King screamed at Katz over the phone. "You used to be a good guy, but you've been out to get me for years."

In response to another question, King shouted, "You're just out to get me and Tyson. You're just like the cops who brutalized Rodney King. I'm another Rodney King. . . . Why don't you write about Desiree Washington [Tyson's rape victim]? She's black on the outside and white on the inside. Her father molested her. Put that in the paper."

"What about your daughter Debby getting fifty-two thousand

a year as president of Mike's fan club?" Katz asked.

"Print what you want," King yelled. "It's all bullshit."

Then King abruptly changed his tune. He began to sweet-talk Katz, who was immune to flattery or gratuity.

"We can work together on this," King said. "You and I should be partners. You'd be stronger as an ally than as an enemy. You can be pernicious."

Katz thought King meant to say tenacious, but didn't interrupt.

"Writers are under control, you know," King said.

Katz thought that may have been an implied offer to pay him money not to write the story, but he ignored it.

"Let's have dinner," King continued, in his seduction mode. "I'll give you an exclusive, all the papers exposing Cayton as a thief."

The conversation lasted about fifteen minutes. Each time Katz tried to ask a specific question about a fact alleged in the affidavit, King cut him off with a filibuster, or just shouted over his words.

The next day, Sunday, May 3, Katz's story ran on page 3 of the *Daily News* under the five-column headline: WAS TYSON SUCK-ERED? EX-AIDE: KING SIPHONED OFF MILLIONS.

"It was ten times bigger than I anticipated," Maffia said later. "I never thought it would be a big story in the front of the paper."

Katz's story reported that Maffia's affidavit described how "King charged Tyson for the promoter's personal security, travel bills, and renovations to King's house in Las Vegas and his E. 69th Street brownstone. . . . Debby King, the promoter's daughter, got $52,000 a year as president of the Mike Tyson fan club. Debby King's husband, Greg Lee, received about $15,000 per fight, for several fights, as a 'consultant.' Carl and Eric King, the promoter's sons, were paid about $50,000 a fight."

Katz's story also quoted from a deposition from Tyson's King-appointed accountant, Mohammad Khan, reporting that Tyson had no liquid assets left. Kahn had testified that Tyson had bor-rowed against the $2 million life insurance annuity that Cayton and Jacobs had set up for him, in order to pay his legal bills.

(Tyson had to pay Vince Fuller about $5 million, and was starting to get bills from Alan Dershowitz, his appellate lawyer, when Maffia's affidavit was submitted.)

The Katz story also summarized the affidavit's revelation that Tyson was charged for a $2 million fee King paid to Razor Ruddock's promoter, Murad Muhammad, in exchange for which King received future promotional rights to Ruddock.

The story also cited King's gambit of billing Tyson for King's inflated purses to fighters on Tyson undercards who were managed by Carl King, naming specifically Julian Jackson and Azumah Nelson. Tyson also paid for Simon Brown's purse at a time King was trying to get Brown to sign a long-term contract with him.

Maffia's affidavit also disclosed:

After the first Tyson-Ruddock fight, Don King told me that he had received a letter from Vincent Fuller [counsel of record for Mike Tyson in this litigation] in which Fuller stated that, due to improper deductions, Tyson had not received his fair share of revenue from the fight. According to King, the letter also stated that King was exploiting Tyson financially in other areas and had hired King controlled "puppets" to represent Tyson in various financial matters relating to King.

King expressed outrage that Fuller, who he had chosen as Tyson's attorney, would make a claim against King's own interest. He then spoke to Fuller by phone in my presence, and told Fuller "You can't do this to me," and demanded that Fuller retract that letter. Immediately after this telephone conversation ended, King told me that Fuller was "just covering his ass," and said that Fuller had agreed to retract the letter.

The Maffia affidavit recounted (in a section Katz had room to mention only briefly):

On several occasions, Don King advised me that Mike Tyson was a "50-50" partner in all business conducted by DKP. As the controller of DKP, I had physical possession of the corporate record book which included the corporate stock transfer ledger. I an unaware of any stock being issued to Mike Tyson, or any income from non-Tyson fights being paid to Tyson, but it is possible that such payments were made. I do know that Tyson bore many DKP expenses.

Tyson paid substantial legal fees and disbursements to finance DKP's litigation against Buster Douglas. . . .

Among expenses charged to Mike Tyson after Tyson received his purses were: all of the travel expenses incurred by Don King and his travel companions whenever King was traveling to or from meetings with Mike Tyson; the cost of security personnel for Don King as well as the salaries of several other DKP employees; two-thirds the cost of several automobiles owned by DKP; the partial cost of the construction renovations at DKP corporate headquarters in New York, and house owned by DKP in Las Vegas.

One section of the affidavit actually dealt with the Cayton-Tyson litigation and was supportive of Cayton's claims. It said:

I believe that there were numerous instances where expenses reported to Cayton were overstated and the amount overstated was shared between DKP and Mike Tyson.

For example, for several Tyson fights, a ten percent "trainer's fee" was deducted from the total income reported to Cayton. [Cayton was due 20 percent of Tyson's purses as his manager till February 1992.] However, that fee was never paid in full. Tyson's trainers received only a small percentage of that amount, and the unpaid portion was divided between Tyson and DKP.

The June 16, 1990, Tyson-Tillman fight was typical of this arrangement. With regard to that bout, trainer's fees in excess

of $460,000 were reported to Cayton. But in reality, Aaron
Snowell, Jay Bright, and Richie Giachetti were paid a total of
$150,000. This resulted in roughly $300,000 in income to Tyson above that which was reported to Cayton, and Tyson gave
DKP half of that amount.

In other words, had Cayton been paid a 20 percent managerial share, the $300,000 would have been divided $240,000
to Tyson and $60,000 to Cayton. Instead, it was divided
$150,000 to Tyson and $150,000 to DKP.

The next day the other New York tabloids picked up the story,
and a day later, *The New York Times* ran a story. The *Times*
story quoted King's press spokesman John Solberg as saying, "I'm
not going to dignify these charges. There's nothing to comment
on. It sounds like a disgruntled ex-employee."

But disdainful spin control could not smother this story. By
Tuesday, papers all over the world were picking it up. Maffia got
calls from London newspapers and an invitation to be a guest on
NBC's *Today* show, and dozens of messages from radio call-in
shows as far away as California. He turned down every request.

King did give a series of interviews to boxing writers, but he
had no answers. Wally Matthews wrote in *Newsday:*

> While there was plenty of fire in King's 30-minute telephone
> diatribe, it was largely a smokescreen. The promoter refused to
> provide specific answers to troubling questions about the con-
> dition of Tyson's finances. . . . When asked specifically about
> the charges, King retreated to the ropes.
>
> "It ain't about no deductions," he said. "I would rather not
> say anything other than what's in the release."

King's office had put out a press release saying the affidavit
was "filled with lies, fabrications, and half-truths about me, my
business, and my family."

On May 7, Katz published a follow-up column on King. He wrote:

> Used to be, I could tolerate King. There was a *joie de vivre,* and an energy level there, despite the old scandals, like the ABC tournament in 1977. But he has grown more than tiresome. He has grown mean.
>
> He is boxing's Citizen Kane. He wants love.
>
> He campaigned hard for several years to get the Boxing Writers' Association to honor him with the James Walker Award for "long and meritorious service." He was worse than rebuffed.
>
> Obviously the boxing writers are read by the boxing fans because there is not an arena in this country where his introduction does not cause widespread booing.
>
> He has long wanted his picture on the cover of *Time* and *Newsweek* as a black entrepreneur who made it. I'm sure that a lot of white businessmen who have been so honored are no more moral or ethical than King. But that does not give King any license.
>
> Many years ago, the late Jimmy Cannon wrote of Joe Louis, "He's a credit to his race—the human race."
>
> King is a discredit to his race.
>
> Our race.

The next week Maffia and Hauser released two more affidavits. One was leaked to me at the *New York Post* and the other to Jerry Izenberg at the *Newark Star Ledger.* Together, they disclosed:

• In 1990, Don King charged Mike Tyson two thirds of his own legal bills of $1.3 million from the Chicago law firm of Sidley & Austin. The firm represented King in his lawsuit against Buster Douglas, but did no work for Tyson during 1990. The firm won a $4 million civil settlement, but King did not share

this with Tyson. Tyson paid the bills, and King kept the spoils.
• Tyson overpaid Jose Sulaiman's WBC $209,000 in sanction-
ing fees for his title fights against Frank Bruno, Carl Williams,
and Buster Douglas.
• King directed that Tyson pay the WBC a $100,000 sanction-
ing fee for his 1991 fight with Razor Ruddock, even though the
match required no sanctioning fee because it was not for any
WBC championship.
• King billed Tyson for the cost of maintaining a corporate
apartment rented by DKP at 420 East Fifty-fourth Street in
Manhattan, a house owned by DKP at 968 Pinehurst Road in
Las Vegas, and a duplex apartment rented by DKP at 19590
Wilshire Boulevard in Los Angeles.

Among the bills Tyson paid was one for maid service on all
three DKP apartments, $3,595 monthly rent on the New York
apartment, cable TV charges for all three apartments, $5,295
for installing a new phone system in King's Las Vegas home,
and swimming-pool maintenance and neighborhood association
dues for the Las Vegas corporate apartment.
• Carl King illegally took 50 percent of the earnings of boxers
he managed, and false declarations were filed with the Nevada
State Athletic Commission by Don King on the amount he paid
his fighters. Nevada rules stipulate that a manager cannot deduct more than a 33 percent share of a boxer's earnings.

Maffia swore that Carl's company—Monarch Boxing—"was
financed and controlled by Don King, and the bulk of the
money received by Monarch was paid in turn to Don King Productions as a 'loan repayment.' "

For years fighters like Tim Witherspoon, David Bey, and
Saoul Mamby had complained that Carl King improperly took
50 percent of their earnings.

All three Maffia affidavits were sent by Hauser to federal and state
prosecutors in Manhattan, and to the state boxing commissions
of Nevada and New Jersey.

But the first official government response came from John Ryan of the Internal Revenue Service. He read Katz's story in the *News* and called Maffia, and then Hauser. A meeting was arranged at the United States Attorney's office for the Southern District of New York. Present at this first meeting were FBI agent Warren Flagg, IRS agent John Ryan, federal prosecutor Sarah Chapman, and her supervisor, David Lawrence, who would soon depart the office and leave the case to Chapman.

During this first meeting Hauser and Maffia both said it was within King's character to shred documents and destroy evidence as soon as he learned there was a new federal investigation brewing.

It was in this first meeting that Maffia mentioned the possibility that King had defrauded Lloyd's of London, the clearinghouse for insurance underwriting syndicates. Maffia was fairly certain that King had submitted a false contingency insurance claim for the postponed fight between Tyson and Alex Stewart in 1990, and thought he might have repeated the scam after the canceled fight between Julio Cesar Chavez and Harold Brazier in June 1991.

King purchased contingency insurance to cover expenses in case a fight is canceled. On the Tyson-Stewart fight, Maffia believed a $400,000 claim was paid to DKP, and that $200,000 in checks had been made out to Tyson, and that none of these checks was actually endorsed by Tyson. On the Chavez-Brazier fight, Maffia remembered that he had sent a fax to the Gagliardi Brothers Insurance Company of San Jose, California, in July 1991, containing official notification of the cancellation, and sending the official report from the Nevada boxing commission doctor saying Chavez had injured his nose in training seven days before the fight.

The fax to the broker also said that receipts to support a claim were being compiled.

Maffia had no knowledge of what happened after he left DKP, but thought it was likely a false claim was also paid on this fight.

The meeting convinced the feds that they had to act fast, and that Maffia was a credible witness.

Under pressure from Maffia's affidavits, Don King had a paranoid episode on Friday, May 8.

David Branson, Cayton's attorney, sent a process server to King's home on East Sixty-second Street to hand him a subpoena to give a deposition in the civil suit filed by Cayton against Tyson. A deposition in a civil suit is usually as routine as combing his hair for King.

But on this Friday evening, at about 8:45, King started to act irrationally. He called the police of the 19th Precinct and said an assassination squad was outside his home trying to kill him with machine guns. He called his friend the Reverend Al Sharpton to come to his house immediately to help protect him from the assassins.

King also called UPI boxing writer Dave Raffo.

"They've come to kill me," King said. "They've broken the security cameras outside my house. It's just like Rodney King. When they want to kill the black man, everyone looks the other way."

Raffo said, "King sounded scared and desperate," as he rambled on.

"There's three of them," King said. "One of them has a suitcase with a change of clothes for a getaway. They've been sent by Seth Abraham, Michael Fuchs, Bill Cayton, and Jose Torres."

Raffo then called the police at the 19th Precinct and could not confirm what King was telling him.

Meanwhile, King called Flo Kennedy of the *New York Post*.

"There's three men and a woman outside my house trying to assassinate me," King said. "They're dressed in combat fatigues. There's a conspiracy to destroy Don King and kill Mike Tyson." He kept Kennedy on the phone for an hour.

King also called EPSN television reporter Chris Myers with the same story of an assassination attempt in progress against him.

"He sounded real scared," Myers said the next day.

When the police arrived at King's townhouse they found only the process server and a lawyer, Dean Purchick, who was affiliated with Branson's law firm. The cops called Branson in Maryland, and Branson confirmed he had authorized the serving of papers for a civil deposition.

The cautious police then frisked the process server and searched his car for concealed weapons. They even called his wife to confirm his identity.

Finally, at about 1:15 A.M., the process server was allowed into King's home and handed him the subpoena while cops from the 19th Precinct served as witnesses and peacekeepers.

The next morning, King and Reverend Sharpton spoke at a rally in Harlem, at a school on West 135th Street. King repeated his story that a team of professional assassins had come to his home the night before to kill him. "Me and Mike Tyson are targets for murder," King said.

As is sometimes his style, Reverend Sharpton was trying to please both sides in the conflict. The same day he appeared at King's side at the Harlem rally, Sharpton gave me a quote that I published in the *New York Post*. He said: "Joe Maffia is a guy with total integrity and sincerity. He has credibility with me. These charges are very serious because they come from Joe."

Sharpton also left this message on Maffia's answering machine: "We both know what Don does. I'm in your corner."

(In December 1994, Sharpton visited Tyson in prison and gave him copies of Maffia's affidavits. Sharpton told me that Tyson had never read them before, and that he encouraged Tyson to be "an independent" when he emerged from prison and resumed his boxing career—advice Tyson failed to take.)

The day after King's assassination hallucination, I reached Eddie Burns, the press spokesman for the New York City Police Department. He told me, "This is all a hype by Don King. It never happened. Nobody attempted to harm King. King's PR guy is hyping the press. This is a hoax."

On Thursday, May 14—eleven days after Katz's first story—two FBI agents arrived at King's corporate office on East sixty-ninth Street with subpoenas for financial records, computer discs, and the grand jury testimony of several DKP employees. The subpoena was drawn to cover all the insurance claim documents, contracts, bank records, and invoices involving Lloyd's of London that Maffia had targeted.

King retaliated swiftly. He sued Maffia for the unpaid portion of his $25,000 loan to buy his apartment—about $16,000. King also filed a formal complaint with the state Board of Regents, accusing Maffia of professional misconduct and challenging his license as a certified public accountant.

It would take a year before Maffia got a letter exonerating him from all of King's false allegations and affirming that his CPA's license was secure. After he received this letter, Maffia signed an immunity agreement with the U.S. Attorney's office.

Late in 1994, during our last interview, Maffia said to me, "At times I regret what I did, but in the end, I would still do it the same way again. I got nothing out of this. I received no monetary gain. I made some enemies. Don tried to hurt me in different ways. I got some strange phone calls.

"I think Don was shocked by what I did. I think he underestimated me because I'm so quiet. He underestimated my resolve. I always spoke softly and slowly to him, and he might have interpreted that as weakness. He is so bombastic he thinks calmness is weakness. Don's problem is that he stopped listening to other people. He performs, but doesn't communicate. He didn't know me, that I just do things honestly."

The federal investigation went on for two years and two months. John Ryan of the IRS, who started it, retired. Sarah Chapman got married. Mary Jo White was appointed to be the new U.S. attorney.

Maffia's information about an insurance fraud on the Tyson-Stewart fight was supported by all the documentation. But Tyson told two FBI agents who interviewed him in prison that he would not testify against King, that he was afraid of being vulnerable to reprisals in prison for being "a rat."

But the documentation was assembled for the fraud on the Chavez-Brazier fight—contracts, canceled checks, ledger entries, correspondence, and the sworn proof of loss. Moreover, current and past employees of DKP testified in the grand jury about the documents and office conversations about their preparation.

Meanwhile, the methodical prosecutors felt no rush to indict, and King began to stall the investigation. It took months for the FBI to get a court-ordered handwriting sample from King under oath. King's lawyer, Bob Hirth, briefly became a target of the investigation (although he was never charged with any wrong-doing), and he had to hire his own attorney, Steve Kaufman, to represent him. King then hired Peter Fleming as his new lawyer, one of the best, who had won an acquittal for John Mitchell in 1974.

The British executives of Lloyd's and the underwriting syndicate cooperated totally, through their New York attorney, Donald Cayea. The British syndicate turned over every document in their files relevant to King's insurance claims, including faxes, contracts, invoices, wire transfers, correspondence with brokers and claims adjusters.

The feds filled a whole "war room" with more than 100,000 indexed documents. They briefly considered drafting a broad indictment against King, but discarded the notion, remembering the 1985 case had been criticized as too complex. Chapman's narrow, simple objective was a guilty verdict, not a trial that would help expose the whole corrupt system of boxing.

Hauser wanted the government to separately bring a complex civil antitrust suit against King for monopoly. Such a strategy would have brought the case before a judge rather than a jury, with a civil standard of proof that was the "preponderance of the evidence" rather than the higher standard of "beyond a reasonable doubt." It would also have placed the resources of the whole

Department of Justice behind the charge and brought the WBC and WBA sanctioning bodies into the case for their rigged rankings and extortionate sanction fees.

Hauser understood Sarah Chapman's need for one neat, narrow, winnable case after the government's haunting failure against King in the tax trial. But he still would have preferred "two bites at the apple," because he was in awe of King's survival magic, fully aware of his escapes from the first-degree murder conviction, the ABC tournament sandal, the FBI sting, the 1985 tax trial, and the skimming of millions from Mike Tyson.

Finally, on July 14, 1994, King was indicted on nine counts of wire fraud—eight of them committed after Maffia left DKP.

The heart of the government's charge was that King submitted as part of his insurance claim an altered contract between himself and Chavez. This fake contract contained a typed-in rider that indicated that King had paid Chavez $350,000 in nonrefundable training expenses. But this rider was not part of the contract Chavez had actually signed.

The indictment charged that during the summer of 1992, after the insurance claim had been paid to King, King concealed from Chavez that there had been an insurance recovery of training expenses. In essence, King was double-dipping from both Lloyd's and Chavez.

The actual wire frauds were faxes between King, Lloyd's, Gagliardi Brothers Brokers, Adams Loss Adjusters, and Hanleigh Management. The final fraud was the wire transfer of $671,000 into King's bank account, in April 1992.

When a reporter called King's office seeking a quotable reaction, King's assistant, Al Braverman, who had been part of the ABC tournament fraud eighteen years earlier, took the call.

"I think it's a complete crock put down by a bitter accountant who got fired for fucking up," Braverman said.

The day the indictment was announced King was inaccessible to reporters because he was busy in Phoenix, Arizona, stealing another fighter. He was somehow convincing Michael Carbajal, the 1988 Olympic silver medalist at 108 pounds, to sign with him.

King was promising Carbajal a series of million-dollar fights and a signing bonus to come with him and abandon Bob Arum, who had promoted all his fights and thought of Carbajal so much a member of his family that he didn't have a written contract with him.

A few months later, however, Carbajal would lose his first title fight under King to Humberto "Chiquita" Gonzales, the 108-pound champion of the WBC and the IBF.

The wire-fraud indictment of King did seem a little bit of a letdown, a technical way to level a giant who has led a life of Shakespearean proportions.

The federal government had investigated him for twenty-six months and all they indicted him for was nine incriminating faxes. To those who followed the broad sweep of King's life, to those who saw him as a character out of a novel by Dreiser, or compared him to Citizen Kane, it seemed so *undramatic* after so dramatic a life.

It felt a little disappointing for King to get caught, just like any other aging businessman, committing felonies by facsimile.

Here was a man who killed two men, reinvented himself in prison, and rose to become friends with presidents and a flag-waving Vegas patriot.

Here was one of the most famous, and most interesting, people in America, who had promoted some of the greatest fights in history—Ali-Foreman, Douglas-Tyson, Holmes-Norton, and the Homeric Ali-Frazier III.

Here was a brilliant showman who outnegotiated corporate titans like Steve Ross, Donald Trump, Steve Wynn, Roone Arledge, Sonny Werblin, and Frank Biondi.

Here was an international confidence man so clever he fleeced the treasuries of whole countries like Zaire and the Philippines.

Here was a very rich man who had such a remorseless memory that he could betray so many friends who loved him—Lloyd Price, Connie Harper, Muhammad Ali, Don Elbaum, Michael Dokes.

Here was a deal-maker so greedy that he diverted and skimmed millions from Tyson, Holmes, and Witherspoon—and got away with it.

And he is indicted for cheating the world's largest insurance syndicate, not a fighter.

It did seem a little like getting Al Capone for taxes after he had arranged dozens of underworld executions.

A few hours after the indictment was announced, Joe Maffia and Tom Hauser shared a beer at Hauser's apartment. There was no gloating, just a search for emotional closure on a joint adventure.

Maffia was a little puzzled by the limited scope of the indictment, but when he read it over, he was also pleased that he would play only a subordinate role at the coming trial.

"After I read it, I felt relief," Maffia said. "I realized most of the paperwork on the Chavez claim was done after I left the office. Other employees handled the paperwork. They would be the main witnesses, not me. Don got the money in April 1992, six months after I left the office.

"It was a relief to know the paperwork would speak for itself at the trial. Other employees would have to testify. No one would be able to say I did it, I signed the letters, I sent the faxes. No one could say I made them do it."

As Maffia sipped his beer, Hauser was answering the phone and giving interviews to reporters who were calling for reaction and comment.

Maffia heard Hauser tell one of the reporters, "Joe is the real hero. Everybody *talks* about Don King, but Joe *did* something about Don King."

This was an essential distinction.

"Boxing is the only jungle where the lions are afraid of the rats" was a line I used on the PBS documentary on King that Charles Stuart and I wrote and produced in 1991.

Lions were afraid of Don King. Larry Holmes and Saoul Mamby, two champions, were afraid to tell the whole truth about King to the federal grand jury in 1982. Mike Tyson wouldn't testify against King in the Lloyd's of London investigation.

But Joe Maffia, the accountant who spoke softly, did the right thing. He did not relish doing it, and he was not without a measure of fear.

But as Cus D'Amato often told his pupils, "The hero and the coward both feel exactly the same emotion of fear. The only difference is that the hero learns how to control his fear. And then he does whatever he has to do."

Index

I n d e x

Index

Index

I n d e x